CW01197538

CÁDIZ

HELEN CRISP AND JULES STEWART

Cádiz

The Story of Europe's Oldest City

HURST & COMPANY, LONDON

First published in the United Kingdom in 2024 by
C. Hurst & Co. (Publishers) Ltd.,
New Wing, Somerset House, Strand, London WC2R 1LA

Copyright © Helen Crisp and Jules Stewart, 2024

All rights reserved.

The right of Helen Crisp and Jules Stewart to be
identified as the authors of this publication is asserted
by them in accordance with the Copyright, Designs and
Patents Act, 1988.

Foreword © Ana Romero Galán, 2024.

Distributed in the United States, Canada and Latin America by Oxford University Press, 198 Madison Avenue, New York, NY 10016, United States of America.

A Cataloguing-in-Publication data record for this book is available from the British Library.

ISBN: 9781911723615

Printed and bound in Great Britain by Bell & Bain Ltd, Glasgow

www.hurstpublishers.com

To
Oliver and Helen

CONTENTS

List of Illustrations		ix
Foreword by Ana Romero Galán		xiii
1.	In the Beginning	1
2.	In Roman Hands	19
3.	Moors on the Coast!	41
4.	The King of Spain's Beard	63
5.	1812 and All That	91
6.	In the Eye of the Storm	119
7.	Cádiz at War	147
8.	Cádiz is Risen	171
Listings Section		195
Acknowledgements		229
Notes		231
Bibliography		241
Index		245

LIST OF ILLUSTRATIONS

1. Early map of the Cádiz area from the Norman B. Leventhal Map & Education Center at the Boston Public Library. Credit: piemags / DCM / Alamy Stock Photo.
2. Pillars of Hercules statue at Ceuta. Credit: Chris Hellier / Alamy Stock Photo.
3. Phoenician male and female sarcophagi in the Museo de Cádiz. Credit: Album / Alamy Stock Photo.
4. Remains of the Phoenician dry dock under the Old Town. Credit: Simon Roth.
5. Terracotta figure of the goddess Astarte worshipped by the Phoenicians. Credit: WHPics / Alamy Stock Photo.
6. Exquisite Phoenician jewellery excavated from burial site in Cádiz. Credit: Album / Alamy Stock Photo.
7. Cádiz falls to the Romans under Scipio Africanus. Credit: World History Archive / Alamy Stock Photo.
8. First century bust of Julius Caesar. Credit: PhotoStock-Israel / Alamy Stock Photo.
9. Cádiz Roman theatre seating and part of the stage. Credit: Simon Roth.
10. Cádiz Roman theatre, the tunnel to the auditorium. Credit: Simon Roth.

LIST OF ILLUSTRATIONS

11. A replica of the *Santa Maria*, Christopher Columbus's flagship, sails the Atlantic. Credit: Niday Picture Library / Alamy Stock Photo.
12. Sir Francis Drake, line engraving by J. Fougeron. Credit: Wellcome Collection, public domain.
13. Painting of the English ships and the Spanish Armada in battle August 1588, probably design for a tapestry. Credit: incamerastock / Alamy Stock Photo.
14. Capture of Cádiz, 1596, in the Anglo-Spanish war, by James Grant. Credit: history_docu_photo / Alamy Stock Photo.
15. Castillo de San Sebastián, built as part of the seventeenth-century fortifications of Cádiz. Credit: Helen Crisp.
16. Baluarte de la Candelaria, seventeenth-century fortification to protect the harbour entrance. Credit: Simon Roth.
17. The Casa de las Cinco Torres, Plaza de España, Cádiz. Credit: Simon Roth.
18. Catedral de la Santa Cruz de Cádiz, built 1722–1835. Credit: Simon Roth.
19. Casa del Almirante, dating from the late seventeenth century, built as the town palace of the Admiral of the Fleet of the Indies. Credit: Helen Crisp.
20. The Tavira Tower, highest of the merchants' watch towers. Credit: Simon Roth.
21. Church of Santiago, Plaza de la Catedral. Credit: Helen Crisp.
22. Merchant's watchtower viewed from Plaza San Francisco. Credit: Simon Roth.
23. Church of Nuestra Señora de la Palma, barrio de la Viña. Credit: Simon Roth.
24. The Battle of Trafalgar, 1805. Credit: Nigel Reed QEDImages/ Alamy Stock Photo.
25. The declaration of the 1812 constitution, commemorative painting from 1912. Credit: Heritage Image Partnership Ltd / Alamy Stock Photo.

LIST OF ILLUSTRATIONS

26. Oratorio San Felipe Neri where the 1812 Cortes met. Credit: Simon Roth.
27. Oval interior of Oratorio San Felipe Neri, showing the balconies where the public could observe the proceedings of the Cortes. Credit: Simon Roth.
28. The Battle of Trocadero, 1823. Credit: imageBROKER.com GmbH & Co. KG / Alamy Stock Photo.
29. Portrait of Lord Byron (1788–1824). Credit: British Library via flickr, no known copyright restrictions.
30. Ornate streetlamp in Calle Ancha celebrating the Cádiz maritime tradition. Credit: Simon Roth.
31. Enemy canon repurposed to protect the building corner from passing traffic, Plaza San Augustín. Credit: Simon Roth.
32. Murals by Goya in the Oratorio Santa Cueva, Cádiz. Credit: Simon Roth.
33. The Cádiz city arms in stained glass at the town hall. Credit: Simon Roth.
34. Mudéjar-style courtyard of the Casino Gaditano, founded as a gentlemen's club in the nineteenth century. Credit: Simon Roth.
35. Statue of nineteenth-century politician Emilio Castelar in the Plaza de la Candelaria, Cádiz. Credit: Simon Reddy / Alamy Stock Photo.
36. Portrait of Isabel II, 1859, by Dionisio Fierros Álvarez. Jl FilpoC via Wikimedia Commons, CC BY 4.0.
37. Ornate nineteenth-century door knocker at Calle José del Toro, 13, Cádiz. Credit: Simon Roth.
38. Gran Teatro Falla. Credit: Helen Crisp.
39. 'Merry hours with the pretty senoritas of Cadiz'. Image from a nineteenth-century stereograph souvenir. Credit: Library of Congress, no known restrictions on publication.
40. One of the impressive old trees of the Alameda Apodaca. Credit: Simon Roth.

LIST OF ILLUSTRATIONS

41. Balneario de la Palma Spa. Credit: Helen Crisp.
42. Devastation following the 1947 munitions explosion in Cádiz. Credit: Album Archivo ABC / Alamy Stock Photo.
43. The interior of the Café Royalty restored to its 1912 splendour. Credit: Helen Crisp.
44. Street in the barrio de la Viña. Credit: Simon Roth.
45. Mercado Central de Abastos, Cádiz. Credit: Simon Roth.
46. Cruise ship moored in the Puerto Comercial, Cádiz. Credit: Simon Roth.
47. View of the modern port of Cádiz. Credit: Simon Roth.
48. One of the many singing groups in the Cádiz Carnival. Credit: Emilio J. Rodríguez Posada via Wikimedia Commons, CC BY-SA 2.0.
49. Holy Week procession, brotherhood of the Virgen de la Palma, Cádiz. Credit: Jose Lucas / Alamy Stock Photo.
50. Café Las Nieves, one of the oldest cafes in Cádiz. Credit: Simon Roth.
51. Flamenco performance at Peña Flamenca la Perla de Cádiz. Credit: Lucas Vallecillos / Alamy Stock Photo.
52. Calle Compañía, Cádiz. Credit: Simon Roth.
53. Ancient streets of Arcos de la Frontera. Credit: Hajotthu via Wikimedia Commons, CC BY 3.0.
54. Ubrique, unique leatherworking town in Cádiz province. Credit: Xemenendura via Wikimedia Commons, CC BY 3.0.
55. Flamenco dancers outside a bar in Jerez de la Frontera. Credit: Peter Ekin-Wood / Alamy Stock Photo.
56. Buying *turrón* at La Dulcería de la Rondeña, Calle Sagasta, Cádiz. Credit: Helen Crisp.
57. Chequered courtyard of the Hotel Boutique Convento, Cádiz. Credit: Helen Crisp.
58. Punta Candelaria. Credit: Simon Roth.
59. Cádiz seafront at Avenido Campo Sur, looking towards the cathedral. Credit: Simon Roth.

FOREWORD

For us, the people of Cádiz, it all began on a hilltop. Yes, for us and for almost the rest of the Western world, given that three thousand years ago, in this remote corner on the southern tip of Spain, the Phoenicians founded their first city on the European continent. We are indeed fortunate. We Gaditanos, as the people of Cádiz are called, are blessed by our geographical location and – as one of the most famous Gaditano writers, Ramón Solís, once said, our climatology – that fabulous Levante wind. We are snugly ensconced between two seas, the Atlantic and the Mediterranean, and two continents, Europe and Africa. Levante is cyclical, so we never know why or when we will feel the gust of a wind so powerful that it sweeps away all traces of humidity and likewise not a few sorrows of the soul. These were the two gifts of fate that motivated the voyages of the people of Tyre, today's Lebanon, to our shores, the Bay of Cádiz, which is in reality an enormous nest of water, land and salt filled with storks. It is specifically here, at the Cerro del Castillo, the true gateway to the city of Cádiz, that I have chosen to write these words.

It is on this hillock outside the town of Chiclana de la Frontera near Cádiz that we hear the heartbeat of the mythical isles of Gadeira, this cocktail of islands, isles, river, waterspouts and marshland, ebbing and flowing to the rhythm of the Atlantic. I would often listen to it as a child and today I am seeing it through my adult eyes: our ancestors, the finest mariners of the ancient world, sailed across these waters on their celebrated vessels famed for the *hipoi*, or seahorse, attached to the bow, when they were hit by colossal Levante winds blowing through the Strait of Gibraltar. It would most certainly have been as furious a squall as that which tears through this very spot today. This is where we find the last Phoenician vestiges discovered in Spain, known as Nueva Gadeira in honour of this magical land in which all is liquid and constantly changing. Terrified by the roaring winds, the traders from the East sought shelter at this place and from the hilltop they cast their gaze on the greatest treasure imaginable: a universe of blue, shadowy grey and white, over which reigned the city of Cádiz.

From this hilltop in Chiclana, squeezing your eyelids closely together to keep out the sand that flies with the east wind from the Sahara, you could almost imagine the monumental silhouette of Archelaus, son of Phoenix, grandson of Agenor, king of Tyre.

We can imagine watching him set in place the first stone of the altar in the Melkart Temple, as a gesture of thanks to the gods for having arrived safely at what we today call the Sancti Petri Castle, a short distance along the coast, south of Cádiz. This is the quintessential watchtower that every summer fills us with awe when observing the legendary sunsets once witnessed by Julius Caesar. The Phoenicians found so great a store of magic in this land brimming with silver that they wished to reciprocate in gratitude: from the inner sanctums of their *hipois* they brought us an alphabet, chickpeas and purple dye, along with an open spirit of curiosity. Many years afterward, we perhaps blended this open spirit with political liberalism to become what we are today, indomitable Gaditanos.

FOREWORD

And so, perched on this lookout point of stone, glass and legend, I can dream of what we are and whence we came. The catalyst of this intellectual endeavour is Jules Stewart, at once a gringo writer, Madrileño and Londoner, who popped up in my life via email in the autumn of 2023, at the very moment this hilltop spot was opened. There are no coincidences in this misty sea of Cádiz. This is called *fatum*, or fate, which in this case came from the hand of Paul Preston, one of the greatest living British Hispanists. Professor Preston requested me to lend Stewart a hand and that was that. This was especially the case when the author boldly announced his intention to emulate, in part, the work of the nineteenth-century erudite Adolfo de Castro to write a history of Cádiz, and in part its province, 'from the earliest days.' That was that. We met in the venerable Royalty, the last Romantic-age café in Andalucía. It was there that I discovered that he was not alone in confronting this colossal task: he was accompanied by Helen Crisp, his established co-author.

Emulating Francisco de Quevedo's poem, this man stuck to a moustache who I met for the first time in the Plaza de la Candelaria was also the author of *Madrid: The History*, a splendid chronicle of the Spanish capital which I had read some ten years ago. This book, the first of a trilogy later to be penned in collaboration with Helen Crisp, presented Madrid to the Anglo–Saxon world before it became the bustling and international city that it is today. This first narrative of Madrid was my introduction to the Stewart–Crisp style, a delightful read brimming with historical detail and an undisguised love of Spain. This can be explained by Stewart's origins as a Hemingwayesque character from Brooklyn Heights who in 1962 first set foot in our country, which he was reluctant to leave. Today he is a regular traveller between London and Pamplona, but in the past he spent many years in Madrid, where he had a family and earned his living as a reporter for Reuters. His Madrid would today be unrecognisable: he took

FOREWORD

up lodgings on the banks of the Manzanares, a foul little river that bears no resemblance to today's marvellous Madrid Río Park where people enjoy strolling about among herons, ducks and the scent of rosemary.

Half a century after this earliest atavistic visit to Spain, I observed Stewart reflected in the mirrors of Café Royalty, with the same expression of curiosity he must have felt on his original contact with the country. This was his first exploratory visit to Cádiz, and this is where he explained his plans and requirements. Like in an Indiana Jones film, the writer couple left the Royalty equipped with the good advice of two authorities: the archaeologist Paloma Bueno, the lady of Cerro del Castillo, and my dear Uncle Domingo, the intrepid Colonel Galán de Ahumada, quite possibly the finest navigator I have known, as much a lover of the history as the sea. The contacts multiplied until a good number of sources wove a web of visits to Cádiz and research in the National Library of Madrid and the British Library in London. The investigative efforts of this energetic duo gave rise to this book, which we hope will soon be translated into Spanish so that many Spanish readers will be able to enjoy it.

After the Royalty, our next get together was in Madrid's Círculo de Bellas Artes café, another illustrious landmark located between the Gran Vía and Paseo de Recoletos, a memorable terrain similar to the Gadeiras that I share with the authors. By this time Stewart had blocked out the structure of the book. He is a person with a focus on artistic detail, a fact I could attest to when I received the Christmas card – of course a photo of Café Royalty – with an image of his typewriter stamped on the envelope. The same can be said of my birthday mini pastry, in a box that could never be binned. With the same attention to detail he puts in his life, Stewart writes of the 126 watchtowers still standing in Cádiz. We like to think that they help us 'see

FOREWORD

them coming', as we Gaditanos are deemed to be 'very long', in the double sense of the expression: intuitive and sarcastic. The British know a thing or two about the latter.

So it was with that exquisite attention to detail, Crisp and Stewart gave birth to this book on Gades, Qadis, Cádiz or Cadi, as we say in our distinctive vernacular, swallowing the last letter. The pages are a gallery of our ancestors and those who are not our forebears but who left us their legacy: Archelaus, Hamilcar, Hannibal, Hasdrubal, Scipio Africanus, Lucius Cornelius Balbus, Julius Caesar, Tariq bin Zayid, Fernando III, Alfonso X the Wise, Isabella the Catholic, Christopher Columbus and Fernando VII. These names reverberate with history and adventure and some, like the 'Felon King', with wickedness. The authors do not omit an account of the half dozen times that Perfidious Albion took it upon itself to attack Cádiz, starting in 1587 when Francis Drake – 'sir' to you and 'pirate' to us – entered the scene.

Three centuries after the English incursions came the French. That was when everything changed. In August 1809, while Napoleon's troops were advancing across Spain, Sir Richard Wellesley, Ambassador of Britain and Ireland and brother of Arthur Wellesley, the 1st Duke of Wellington, arrived in Spain, with his army having just defeated the French in the Battle of Talavera de la Reina. The people of Cádiz were so overjoyed to greet this diplomat and ally against the hated French that they unhitched the horses from his carriage and dragged it to his residence in the Callejón del Tinte. The outpouring of Anglophilia that engulfed Cádiz thanks to the Wellesley brothers endures to this day: we the Gaditanos love to dress up as British and we are fond of tweed, silk handkerchiefs and anything of hunting green colour.

The British ambassador took up residence in Cádiz in the nineteenth century because, as was the case in Phoenician times, geography is the essence of our city, in reality a city-ship built

FOREWORD

on the bay. If 3,000 years ago in the past the masters of the sea brought us the alphabet, two centuries ago enlightened individuals gave us liberty, which is intimately connected with freedom of expression. Crisp and Stewart devote one of my favourite chapters to these valiant men: Gaspar Melchor de Jovellanos, Agustín Argüelles, Diego Muñoz-Torrero, Francisco de Paula Martínez de la Rosa and so many more heroes who joined forces in one of my best-loved places in Cádiz, the San Felipe Neri Oratory. It lies a few minutes' walk from my birthplace, the now-vanished Hospital de Mora, in the heart of the historic centre. The Oratory, an austere baroque temple, was the scene of one of the greatest attempts to modernise Spain. This is where the 1812 Magna Carta was signed, our beloved Pepa, which for the first time in the country's history proclaimed the sovereignty of the Spanish nation. Crisp and Stewart bring this to the fore in abundant detail.

There is a well-known song composed during the French invasion which goes like this: 'With the bombs launched by the blowhards, the women of Cádiz fashion ringlets. The upright women of this land are prepared for war from birth.' Indeed, we men and women of Cádiz were able to defeat the French, but in spite of the warnings in the *Duende de los Cafés* newspaper, we were unprepared for perfidious King Fernando VII and his betrayal of the Constitution. The patriot Rafael del Riego attempted to stop him but it was already too late. This is part of the sad history of Spain sung by Gil de Biedma, one that we Gaditanos prefer to ignore, to focus instead on the positive aspects described by Crisp and Stewart in this book: the garum fish sauce and anchovy entrails which was the Romans' caviar. Tuna, sea bream, oysters, clams, seafood in general. Likewise, the sherry of Jerez praised by Shakespeare in eight of his works, the women that Lord Byron found so enchanting and who in Roman days used castanets (Juvenal's *puellae gaditanae*) and the

FOREWORD

dances already known in the days of Trajan. We Gaditanos are all of this: Phoenicians, Romans, Arabs, Jews, Berbers, Latin Americans, Andalusians, Spaniards and Europeans.

Crisp and Stewart have done it again. First, with their wonderful history of Madrid and now with this book. This tireless couple has revealed our secret world, concealed from foreign eyes for 3,000 years, along with our infinite capacity to live life to the fullest. I wonder if Melkart-Hercules and all the past and future gods can protect my land from the magic spell cast on this nation's capital with the publication of the authors' first book on Spain: the constant wanderings through the streets of Madrid by millions in search of eternal happiness. In Cádiz they might have it easier, as expressed in 1858 by the immortal Adolfo de Castro: 'Cádiz became the homeland of Spain more than a mere sanctuary, a sturdy and safe refuge where love of freedom stood strong despite the challenges, where life seemed eternal and pain was unknown, no sad words were heard and there was no fear of evil.'

Cerro del Castillo, Chiclana de la Frontera (Cádiz),
22 March 2024

Ana Romero Galán is a celebrated Spanish journalist and author, co-founder of the national daily *El Mundo* and former correspondent in London and New York, where she obtained her master's degree in journalism from Columbia University.

1

IN THE BEGINNING

The Old Testament speaks of Jonah, who was sent by Yahweh, the God of the Israelites, to the city of Nineveh to rebuke its people for their wickedness. But the Hebrew prophet was determined not to set foot in Nineveh, for he did not wish to confront these people, who were among Israel's greatest enemies. To avoid having to fulfil his mission and to escape the Lord's wrath, Jonah fled on a ship bound for 'Tarshish'. In retribution for this act of defiance, the Lord unleashed a great storm to devastate the ship. The crew placed the blame for this tempest on Jonah. He was cast into the raging sea, after which the waters returned to calm. Jonah was swallowed by a great whale, in whose belly he lingered in despair, praying to God for forgiveness. The prophet feared all was lost, but after three days and nights the sea monster disgorged him onto the shores of Tarshish, the destination of his voyage, whence he embarked on a momentous overland journey eastward to accomplish his divine mission and counsel the citizens of Nineveh to repent or be destroyed in forty days.

Where, or for that matter, what was Tarshish is shrouded in obscurity. The prophecies of Isaiah, Jeremiah and most comprehensive of all, Ezekiel, are said to have linked Tarshish to a distant land located at the western edge of the known world, today known as Spain. The country was a source of silver, iron, tin and lead, much prized by the Phoenician traders who were to embark on their epic voyages to this realm. Untapped metal lodes were a powerful attraction, especially silver, for which there seemed to be an inexhaustible demand in the ancient Middle East. Silver was used by the Assyrians as a standard for many commercial transactions, including credit and loans, which lay at the heart of their economy.

The name Tarshish is cited in the Old Testament, in the Book of Genesis, but not as a settlement. Most confusingly, it is said to be the name of one of the sons of Noah, the builder of the Ark. It is also acknowledged by several ancient historians to be the eponym of an unidentified country far distant from Palestine. That said, most contemporary scholars would fix the location of Tarshish on the Iberian Peninsula itself, linking it to the Phoenician colony of Tartessos, which lay to the north of Cádiz at the source of the Guadalquivir River. The people of Tartessos occupied the provinces of Huelva, Sevilla and Cádiz between 900 and 500 BCE. Several millennia after this biblical saga was written, the identity of Tarshish remains a puzzling and often contradictory enigma.

The nineteenth-century British Egyptologist, Sir Peter le Page Renouf, believed the name Tarshish merely signified a shoreline and, as the word occurs frequently in connection with Tyre, he believed it to be a great Phoenician port sited on the southern coast of Lebanon. Other scholars, such as Thomas Kelly Cheyne, argued that Tarshish and Tiras, both quoted in Genesis, are in fact different names for a single nation. Cheyne held that it might have been related to the Tyrrhenians, who were mariners unrelated to the Greeks and for the most part pirates, or the ancient Etruscan people of what is today Italy.

IN THE BEGINNING

Isaac Abarbanel, a fifteenth century Jewish-Portuguese scholar and statesman described Tarshish as the city known in antiquity as Carthage, today recognised as Tunis.

While it may seem more than a trifle far-fetched, some nineteenth-century commentators went so far as to claim that Tarshish was in fact a name for Britain. This idea stemmed from the fact that the merchants of Tarshish were traders in metals, especially tin, which was mined in Cornwall. Other theorists place Tarshish in Mozambique, or even southern India or northern Sri Lanka. Several academics contend that Tarshish could have been located in Malta as Tarxien is a town in Malta, the site of places of worship dating from approximately 3150 BCE. The pronunciation of Tarshish in Maltese is similar to Hebrew, which these erudites declare in defence of their hypothesis, while all megalithic sanctuaries from the neolithic period of Malta are assigned to the island's Tarxien era.

Homer identified Tarshish as the port of Gadir, the Phoenician name signifying 'compound' or 'stronghold', which the Greek poet says was founded eighty years after the legendary Trojan War. This would place its origin in the second half of 1200 BCE. The Greek mathematician and geographer Eratosthenes spoke of the ten-year conflict being waged between 1194 and 1184 BCE, which corresponds roughly to archaeological evidence of a catastrophic burning of Troy.

Like Homer, Rufus Festus Avienius, the Latin writer of the fourth century CE, firmly believed that Tarshish was the ancestor of Cádiz. The same theory is espoused by Father Mapple in Herman Melville's novel *Moby Dick*, published in 1851. Mapple is a former whaler who became a preacher in the new Bedford Whaleman's Chapel of Massachusetts. Ishmael, the novel's narrator, hears and records Mapple's sermon on the subject of Jonah and how he was swallowed by a whale but did not turn against God:

With this sin of disobedience in him, Jonah still further flouts at God, by seeking to flee from Him. He thinks that a ship made by men, will carry him into countries where God does not reign but only the Captains of this earth. He skulks about the wharves of Joppa and seeks a ship that's bound for Tarshish. There lurks, perhaps, a hitherto unheeded meaning here. By all accounts Tarshish could have been no other city than the modern Cádiz. That's the opinion of learned men. And where is Cádiz, shipmates? Cádiz is in Spain; as far by water, from Joppa, as Jonah could possibly have sailed in those ancient days, when the Atlantic was an almost unknown sea. Because Joppa, the modern Jaffa, shipmates, is on the most easterly coast of the Mediterranean, the Syrian, and Tarshish, or Cádiz, more than two thousand miles to the westward from that, just outside the Strait of Gibraltar.[1]

Thus, Tarshish was to become the Phoenician colony of Gadir – known as Gades by the Romans, Qādis under more than five centuries of Moorish rule and finally Cádiz – located on the River Tartessos, the modern Guadalquivir, once a waterway navigable from as far as Córdoba, 160 miles to the north in the Andalusian heartland.

The founding of Gadir

One can imagine the astonishment and, indeed, the acute sense of alarm the Late Bronze Age peoples living around the coastal area that would later become Gadir must have felt – bearded men and long-haired women, attired in ankle-length woollen skirts or kilts and tunics – at their first sighting of the approaching Phoenician flotilla. The *gauloi*, or trading vessels that bore a giant rectangular sail and rounded hull, were escorted by the terrifying warships, with eyes fitted on the bow to frighten enemies, as well as horses' heads to honour the sea god Yamm and used for ramming an opponent's craft.[2] Why had these mariners embarked on a 3,500 mile expedition into the unknown, throwing into

IN THE BEGINNING

disarray the native inhabitants' long-established traditional life of foraging and fishing? Who were these voyagers of such fierce demeanour, who came ashore brandishing swords, spears and shields?

As for the second question, the seafarers who landed on these Atlantic mudflats were of Semitic ancestry, bearing the dark complexion and pronounced facial features common to natives of the Levant, the coastal regions of what are today the nations of Syria, Lebanon and northern Israel. Can the origins of these enigmatic souls we have come to call the Phoenicians be verified with any degree of accuracy? Were their roots to be found, as some historians have alleged, in Erythraea? If this were the case, could this semi-mythical place be located on a map? Erythraea, as best we know, was an ancient Greek island in the Aegean Sea, abutting the western tip of Turkey. It was one of Greece's twelve Ionian trading colonies, founded sometime before 1000 BCE. What has been called the Erythraean Sea is itself another geographical riddle, anciently applied to the Indian Ocean, later to the Arabian Gulf and finally to the Red Sea.

Sometime before 2000 BCE, a Middle Eastern people, speaking a Semitic language, ventured westward and occupied the coast of the uncharted reaches of the Mediterranean. Certainly by 1250 BCE these explorers, who have come to be known as the Phoenicians, were well-established as navigators and traders of the known Mediterranean world, enjoying the commerce that had once been in the hands of the Minoans of Crete. The Phoenicians were organised in city states, the greatest of which were Tyre and Sidon, both located in present-day Lebanon.

Their language and religious cults bore a similarity to those of other Semitic people, and in this respect, apart from the development of their seafaring culture, they could be considered close cousins of the Canaanites of northern Palestine. The Phoenicians lived for some time under the influence of the

Egyptians, but with the weakening of Egyptian power, their seamen came to independently dominate the Mediterranean. They set sail to the edges of the known world, and there is some evidence they may have even navigated along the western coast of Africa and possibly as far as the East Indies.

The Phoenicians held a monopoly on trading in the great cedars of Lebanon, they manufactured glassware and metal articles, and they coloured cloth with the famous Tyrian dyes obtained from shellfish. They were also skilled architects, a fact to keep in mind when seeking traces of the Phoenician presence in Gadir. 'Though never a great military power, Phoenicia grew strong as a trading partner to mightier empires and virtually controlled Mediterranean commerce by 1000 BCE,' says Spanish historian Mark Williams. 'Expansion was chiefly triggered by the need to find raw materials, mainly metals, for the manufacture of luxury goods for the neighbouring (and often threatening) Assyrians and Babylonians.'[3]

The native people of Gadir knew of the vast silver mines that lay in their territory. It was tales of these riches that had lured the Phoenicians to sail to their farthest-flung destination at the gateway to the Atlantic. Their purpose in coming was to use Gadir as a base for controlling the traffic of silver and other precious metals mined in the region. In this sense, the colonisation was a signal moment in history, a precursor, to be precise, of the epic of the Spanish conquistadors who made their fortune by connecting the 'Old World' and 'New World' through their lust for gold and silver.

Choosing sites for colonial settlement followed a consistent pattern. Despite changes in Spanish coastal geography over the past three thousand years, these Phoenician preferences are still identifiable. The essential combination included a sheltered anchorage for their ships, fresh water, sufficient arable land for subsistence farming and a hillock for the colony itself. Gadir

IN THE BEGINNING

fulfilled all these requisites, though it must be noted that the city's geography at the time presented challenges for aspiring colonisers.

The Phoenicians were clearly a determined lot to have dropped anchor at what in the remote past was no more than an inhospitable tract of land, whose surface area shrank from 30 feet to around 6 feet at high tide. The Cádiz of today is of course less an island than an artificial peninsula, thanks to the strip of land built on the marshy isthmus to allow a railway line and motor road linked to the Isla de León mainland. In antiquity, the region lacked a stable source of drinking water, which added to the topographical problems of maintaining a productive settlement.

Apart from the main island itself, Cádiz was encircled by numerous islets that made up an archipelago, visible to mariners from the Guadalete River. Strong Atlantic gusts from North Africa were another hindrance to anchoring in the bay. It was almost impossible to find shelter from the violent winds that swept the flatlands. Historian Mark Williams states,

> By 1500 BCE the cultural centre of gravity was shifting to the valley of the Guadalquivir River. Here agriculture thrived and the nearby Sierra Morena mountains held major deposits of copper and silver. These metals became the linchpins of the fabulous lost civilisation of Tartessos, the most intriguing riddle in ancient Iberian history.[4]

Non Plus Ultra

So far, no archaeological finds have conclusively verified 1100 BCE as the precise date of the first Phoenician presence in Cádiz. To the frustration of archaeologists and scholars, this is a city in which documented history and legend intertwine. This historical muddle is embodied in the city's coat of arms, which bears the figure of Hercules clad in a lion's fur flanked by two lions he grasps by the manes, with a column on opposite sides of the crest; engraved on the border is the Latin inscription: *Dominatorqve Hercvles Fvndator Gadivum*, 'Heracles, Founder and Ruler of Cádiz'. Known as Hercules Gaditanus, he was a Romanised version of Melkart, the tutelary god of the Phoenician city state of Tyre and protector of Cádiz from its earliest days. For the ancients, the world was considered a land mass surrounded by an ocean swarming with monsters, hence a motto was inscribed on the columns warning those tempted to venture into these waters: *Non Plus Ultra* (Go No Further).[5] This realm of fantasy has always represented a conundrum for anyone seeking to pin down with a degree of accuracy the first appearance of Phoenician traders on the shores of Cádiz.

Greek mythology has it that Africa and Europe were once connected by an isthmus. By using his superhuman powers, personified in the two lions on the shield, Hercules split the continent in two, opening up the Strait of Gibraltar, some 50 miles south-east of Cádiz. One column rises in Abyla, the Punic name for Jebel Musa in Morocco. The pillar on the northern side of the divide stands in Spain. Gadir was the farthest limit of the Western world known to the Greeks and the tribes of the Levant. According to myth, Eurystheus, king of Tiryns (a Peloponnesian hill fort said to be the birthplace of Hercules) had ordered the hero to travel to the island of Erythia, thought to refer to today's Cádiz. There, as the tenth of his fabled Twelve Labours, Hercules was tasked with capturing the cattle of the fearful monster Geryon. To commemorate the extensive journey and the successful completion of his labour, Hercules took it upon himself to perform his mountain-crushing feat, and by doing so, opened a sea channel to the unknown Atlantic.

It is hardly surprising to find the history of Cádiz immersed in a quagmire of conflicting hypotheses. What is never questioned is that Gadir was always the most important of the Punic cities in

IN THE BEGINNING

the Western Mediterranean. 'The Phoenician settlement lies deep below the Roman and modern cities and they are all surrounded by the gigantic 16th century fortifications that dominate the city today,' says historian Richard J. Harrison. 'Gadir was originally sited upon a small islet separated from the main island by a narrow channel, which was filled in and built over completely in Roman times, when the city expanded rapidly.'[6] Until recently, limited excavations revealed little more than that the ancient nucleus was on this islet, the sole area of habitation, while its cemetery lay away from it on the northern shore of the main island. Sanctuaries probably occupied the ends of the two reefs of the westernmost edge of the islet and island, although these have been heavily eroded and quarried for building stone.

The Phoenicians left behind almost no written records of their ventures beyond the Strait of Gibraltar, despite having invented a writing system that became the root of Western alphabets. Originally referring to themselves as Canaanites, relatively little is known of the Phoenicians. The name itself is of Greek derivation and was adopted from the word *phoinix*, loosely translated as 'red people'. This is possibly an allusion to the colour purple-red, which in turn may refer to the Phoenicians' production of a famed purple dye, extracted from the *murex* sea snail, that would tint the cloaks of emperors for centuries.

The Temple of Herakles-Melkart

Archaeologists have been debating for years the location, or indeed the very existence, of a Phoenician temple within the boundaries of modern Cádiz. It stands to reason that there was such a sanctuary as ancient narratives abound of a famous temple in the location. The most noteworthy were put forward by Greek historians Herodotus, Strabo and Arrian, who all made references to the Phoenician temple, writing between 484 and 74 BCE. In fact, the most detailed documentation that survives for any early religious building in the Western Mediterranean concerns the temple built outside Gadir, dedicated to Melkart. This was the principal monument in the west to the Phoenician deity and was famous throughout the ancient world from at least 500 BCE.

The American fine arts professor William Edward Mierse believes the Temple of Hercules Gaditanus, or Herakles-Melkart, was built in the eighth century BCE, outside the confines of the Phoenician settlement of Gadir:

> It was, even during the Roman period, one of the most outstanding sanctuaries in the Western provinces. This holy place was the treasure of Gadir, the most important Phoenician city on the Iberian Peninsula and one of the most significant sites in the far Western Mediterranean. As such, it must have served as the model for other Phoenician temples and for native architectural experiments during the centuries after its establishment.[7]

The first century BCE Greek geographer and philosopher Strabo relates how the Phoenicians, on what he maintains was their third expedition to seek out the Columns of Hercules, founded a settlement he called Gádeira, an ancient Greek name for Cádiz. There they erected a sanctuary on the eastern side of an island and built their settlement itself to the west of this spot. According to Strabo, the temple contained two bronze columns bearing a dedication, together with the list of expenses incurred by the building of the temple itself.

The main reason archaeologists have experienced such difficulty in identifying the temple's location is the shifting geography of Cádiz, influenced by changing watercourses and extensive human intervention over the centuries. Today, anyone strolling along the main streets of Cádiz, admiring the high fashion shops or stopping off for a coffee at one of the city's many smart cafés, two thousand years ago would have been treading water. A remarkable feature of the geomorphological processes at work on the coasts of the Gulf of Cádiz is the estuarial mouths of several large rivers, namely the Guadiana, Piedras, Tinto-Odiel, Guadalete and Guadalquivir. These estuaries all flow between sandy barriers and marshlands that are subject to coastal erosion and deposition, storms, climate change, and embankments and channels built through human activity. Altogether this has affected the site where the city of Cádiz now stands. In the Middle Bronze Age, the present-day peninsula of Cádiz was divided into at least three islands.

A recent discovery by researchers at the University of Seville has revealed an extraordinary archaeological find, thanks to digital terrain modelling, which enables the landscape from thousands of years ago to be traced. This technique has identified a monumental structure in the Bay of Cádiz. Ricardo Belizón, a PhD student at the University of Seville, devised a new hypothesis that traces of the temple were to be found in the Sancti Petri canal, a shallow channel in the Bay of Cádiz, between the towns of Chiclana de la Frontera and San Fernando. The researcher discovered several aberrations in the terrain that revealed the totally anthropized coastline, with a large building (the possible temple), several breakwaters, moorings and an inner harbour. The reason experts have so far failed to uncover the temple is simply because it has been submerged for centuries.

Measuring 1,000 by 500 feet, the same dimensions as the island on which it stood, the rectangular structure lies at a depth of 10 to 33 feet underwater and seems to fit with descriptions in the classics that make reference to the location of the temple and its definition as a great Phoenician monument. According to Greek and Roman chronicles, this complex was accessed through two columns, with a frontispiece that depicted the Labours of Hercules, within which was an eternally burning flame. The sacred area was separated from the mainland by a canal and was accessible to Phoenician, Punic and Roman ships. It was renowned for the large number of relics from the ancient housed in these confines.

The identification of this as the temple's site is supported by the noted archaeologist Richard J. Harrison, who says it was located 11 miles from Gadir, at the far end of a long, thin island which had the city at its northern end and the shrine at the other, connected by a road. 'The site today is known as Sancti Petri, a rocky islet isolated from the main island by two millennia of coastal erosion on the seaward side,' Harrison explained. 'It is formed of a conglomerate rock, rising about three metres above high tide level and still measures 400 by 500 metres, although it was formerly larger…The Classical descriptions of this site agree that there was a large temple, built in the Phoenician style of architecture. It was very old, with huge timber beams in the roof. The rites and sacrificial rituals associated with it were purely Phoenician.'[8]

From the fourth century BCE, the Greeks identified Melkart with their own sacred hero Herakles, and as such he became the subject of a popular cult across the Greek world. Herodotus had affirmed early as the fifth century BCE that Melkart was none other than Herakles himself. When the Greek historian told of his visit to the famous sanctuary of Herakles at Tyre, he was describing the Temple of Melkart. The Twelve Labours of Hercules, which took the hero on travels far and wide, may have been an attempt by the Greeks to account for the presence of Phoenician colonies throughout the Mediterranean. Coastal settlements like Gadir were thought to have been founded, in one way or another, by Hercules/Melkart, a belief no doubt related to the Phoenician practice of building a temple of devotion to Melkart in the colonies they were to establish on their sea voyages.

IN THE BEGINNING

Classical sources recount that many renowned individuals, distinguished by their deeds or nobility, visited the temple. The Roman historian Livy narrates that Hannibal arrived at the island to offer his vows to the gods before embarking on what was to be the second Punic War of 218–201 BCE.[9] It was here, in 69 BCE, that Julius Caesar journeyed to Gadir as a Roman quaestor.[10] That was when, after his visit to the temple, the future Roman conqueror had a prophetic dream that foretold of his dominion over the world. This revelation came after he had wept in front of the bust of Alexander the Great. Caesar was despondent that Alexander, at the same age as Caesar, had created a great empire while he, as a mere Roman quaestor, had not achieved the greatness he so desired.

These historical chronicles often make mention of 'a changing environment, in contact with the sea, subject to the changing tides, in a temple where there must have been port structures and a seafaring environment,' says Milagros Alzaga, head of the Centre for Underwater Archaeology (CAS), who was a participant in Belizón's project.[11]

For more than two centuries, this area has been yielding important archaeological finds, now on display in the Museum of Cádiz, such as large marble and bronze sculptures of Roman emperors and various statuettes from the Phoenician period. The showstoppers are without doubt the two Phoenician sarcophagi, male and female. The male sarcophagus, which dates from around 400 BCE, was discovered in 1887 at an archaeological site called the Necropolis of Punta de la Vaca. The find was considered so significant that it became one of the driving forces behind the creation of the museum. The figure is that of a mature man, with neatly trimmed hair and beard. In his left hand he holds a pomegranate, and in his right, a faded crown of painted flowers. The figure is dressed in a full tunic, with only his naked feet exposed.

CÁDIZ

The early twentieth century Spanish archaeologist Pelayo Quintero Atauri was convinced that a female sarcophagus similar to the male one must exist. He searched throughout the city, excavating various Phoenician and Roman sites, but could not find what he sought. Atauri was intrigued by the elusive 'Lady of Cádiz', the name later given by archaeologists to the sarcophagus, which dates from 480 BCE. Sadly, his quest never came to fruition and he gave up the search in 1939. In 1980, years after Atauri's death, an excavator stumbled upon a large, marble object, which turned out to be the female anthropoid sarcophagus. The supreme irony is that it was unearthed while demolition work was being carried out on Atauri's house in the Calle Parlamento. Like the male sarcophagus, the female's body was contained in a rectangular ashlar coffin. It represents a young woman, one with idealised features, wearing a tight-fitting ankle-length tunic.

Defining the exact spot on which the Phoenicians erected their temple is a subject that has triggered a heated debate among academics and archaeologists. Researchers at University of Seville have teamed up with colleagues from Córdoba to challenge the theory advanced by the University of Seville and the claim that they have located the temple at the bottom of Caño de Sancti Petri. The University of Cádiz side disputes this claim, arguing it could never have been the site of the temple, since its shallow depth would have made the channel unnavigable for ancient vessels aiming to lay anchor at Cádiz.

The Cádiz-Córdoba faction have come up with an alternative hypothesis, namely that the shrine once stood atop the Cerro de los Mártires, a hillock lying a third of a mile inland in the municipality of San Fernando. The team identified a rectangular structure 984 feet long and 492 feet wide, containing remains that could be part of the ancient shrine. They explain that the legendary sanctuary of Hercules Gaditanus, or Melkart in Phoenician times, was a key pilgrimage site.

IN THE BEGINNING

The temple must have begun as a small shrine, probably similar to the Phoenician sanctuary discovered at Kommos on southern Crete. As the colony of Gadir developed, the building may well have been embellished and could have begun to assume an aspect more like that of the Phoenician Temple of Astarte at the Greek city-kingdom of Kition, in Cyprus. Later Arabic sources, which describe the ruined temple, refer to a tower as part of the structure. In its final form, the temple may well have had a raised central unit, symbolising a tripartite holy of holies. It was in these various manifestations that the temple provided models for builders of sanctuaries elsewhere in the western extremities of the Mediterranean.

Mythology aside, recent archaeological digs in and around Cádiz have uncovered remnants of Phoenician artefacts dating from the eleventh and tenth centuries BCE, substantiating the theory that Cádiz was a port of call for Phoenician traders more than three thousand years ago, and their first trading post in the Western Mediterranean. Millstone fragments have been found at Cerro del Castillo in nearby Chiclana, made from Phoenician material between the seventh and sixth centuries BCE. These circular stones, used for grinding wheat and other grains, share the same petrographic texture and geochemical composition as flat archaic querns recovered from the cargo of a seventh century BCE Phoenician shipwreck found near Malta. The millstones from Cádiz point to widespread Phoenician trade in basaltic rock.

Chiclana, which lies some ten miles south of Cádiz, was for the Phoenicians a point of refuge from the biting Atlantic winds. Archaeologist Paloma Bueno Serrano has carried out extensive work in the area, the result of which shows that the Phoenicians sought shelter in this settlement on their journeys to Cádiz. Here they were able to anchor their ships in safe waters. They erected a great wall to protect their vessels from the gale-force winds and they turned Chiclana into a rest stop where, as Bueno Serrano affirms, they erected the Temple of Melkart.

In September 2006, in Chiclana's historical centre, behind the Church of San Juan Bautista, the archaeologist discovered vestiges of ancient Chiclana. 'We carried out twelve digs in a 4,000 square metre area to determine the limits of Chiclana's remotest past,' she says. 'I was astonished to unearth a virtual treasure trove of artefacts. This discovery stands as a before and after of local history. It enabled us to push back the accepted origins of Chiclana by some two thousand years.'[12]

Bueno Serrano explains that her team was able to fix the presence of Chiclana's first inhabitants in the Late Bronze Age, between 1200 and 800 BCE, described by some as the Tartessian Age. 'After the 6th century BCE, the town began to expand beyond the Phoenician walls,' she says.[13]

During its roughly 500 years of Phoenician rule, Gadir had gone from a sparsely inhabited rural area to a major trading city, home to settlements, sanctuaries, defensive walls and a port built in the seventh century. But Phoenician dominance over the Mediterranean was not to last. It may be that their empire had extended itself too far and they had spread themselves too thin. The sixth century saw turbulence at the heart of the Phoenician Empire in Tyre, ultimately leading to the collapse of their control over Iberia. This created a power vacuum in the Western Mediterranean, and two competing empires wanted to fill it.

Rome began its military operations in Iberia against its rivals the Carthaginians in 209 BCE with the capture of Cartago Nova, today the Mediterranean port of Cartagena. The Romans devised a twin offensive for taking the city. An attack by sea would block supplies and reinforcements reaching the defenders. The fleet was to hold the fort until capitulation had been confirmed. The land attack would involve infantry units marching along the banks

IN THE BEGINNING

of the Guadalquivir River to Astapa, in antiquity an Andalusian hilltop town, to join forces with the Gadir rebel faction.

A sombre mood prevailed in Gadir when it became known that Roman legions had begun their advance toward the southern coastal region. The Carthaginian generals Mago and Hasdrubal, both brothers of Hannibal, had displaced the Phoenicians as the dominant force in the city. These two commanders now fled south to the port after the decisive Roman victory over Carthage at the Battle of Ilipa. The citizens of Gadir had heard of the merciless reprisals that the conquering Romans exacted of those who resisted their armies. 'This explains why a group of conspirators made their way to Cartago Nova, where they struck a pact with Scipio Africanus to hand over Gadir, its port and naval vessels, along with the troops and commanding officers stationed in the city,' say historians Fierro Cubiella and Juan Antonio.[14] Mago took command of the Gadir corps and promptly ordered the arrest of the conspirators, who were rounded up and dispatched to Carthage to meet their fate.

Cádiz had yet again become a maritime battleground between different powers vying for control of the city, as it was to be throughout most of its history.

2

IN ROMAN HANDS

With the decline of Phoenician power in the East and the rise of Carthage in the West, Gadir became the focal point of a struggle for control of the Mediterranean. In 573 BCE, Tyre, the heart of the Phoenician Empire, fell to the Babylonian king Nebuchadnezzar after a prolonged siege. This defeat plunged Phoenicia into chaos, eventually leading to the loss of the last of the independent city states of Phoenicia across the Mediterranean and shifting their political and economic control to Carthage – a powerful city in today's Tunisia, which had itself previously been a Phoenician colony. In 500 BCE, Carthage captured Gadir and made it part of its expanding empire.

For nearly four centuries Gadir was part of the Carthaginian territory in southern Spain. Carthage also had dominions along the coast of eastern Spain, as well as their lands along the southern shores of the Mediterranean in modern day Libya and Tunisia. However, the Carthaginians did not control much of the territory beyond the coast. Various independent Iberian tribes inhabited the area directly inland of the Carthaginian coastal strongholds. But Carthage's main rival for control of

Spain was not the loosely organised native peoples, but the Roman Empire, which had seized land in northeastern Spain in 206 BCE. The conflict between Rome and Carthage would come to dominate the last centuries of the first millennium BCE across the Mediterranean.

When tribes from these lands appealed to Rome for support to prevent Carthaginian encroachment on their territories, Rome initially sent a commission to find the truth of what was going on. As the Carthaginians did not cooperate with the commission, it achieved nothing. The fighting continued against the native Iberian tribes, with the Carthaginians under Hannibal making territorial advances towards the Ebro River. The Romans became concerned that the Carthaginian success might encroach on their dominance over northeastern Spain, with the tribes questioning if Rome was the strongest power, and decided to launch two campaigns against Carthage, one to North Africa and the other to Spain. The Romans and Carthaginians had already clashed, fighting for control of the islands of Corsica and Sicily in the first Punic War, (264–241 BCE). This second Punic War from 218–201 BCE saw thousands of men mobilised on both sides and hundreds of ships, along with the famous elephant-mounted troops of Carthage. Troops were moving hundreds of miles across Spain and North Africa to fight on the different fronts. After a series of battles, in 212 BCE the Carthaginians looked poised for victory in Spain but well-led Roman troops pulled off a last-minute rally against them, which Roman historians wrote up in heroic terms. The Romans then fled the field as the Carthaginian attack intensified. However, the Carthaginians failed to follow through and the Romans turned and attacked their poorly guarded camps, slaughtering thousands. The first campaign ended in stalemate.

As feared, Iberian tribes did revolt against Rome after the Roman defeats in battle against the Carthaginians and showed no signs of renewing their loyalty. In 211 BCE Rome started a new campaign with larger forces, determined to end the power of the Carthaginians. After some initial battles the armies retired to their winter quarters, which saw Hannibal lead his men back to Gadir. During the second Punic War between Carthage and Rome, Hannibal well understood the benefits of the city's location and made it his first Spanish base. Carthage plundered the surrounding area for its resources in what was to be a futile attempt to repel Rome.

In the spring of 210 BCE Rome sent large reinforcements to Spain, backed up by a fleet, intending to finish the Carthaginians once and for all. An early victory by the more strategically led Roman forces enabled them to take Cartagena, the main Carthaginian city on the east coast of Spain, through a combined land and seaward attack. After this, the Romans did not need to fight any further battles on the eastern coast of Spain and all their forces converged to take the south.

As they progressed, the Roman commander Publius Cornelius Scipio went out of his way to woo back the local tribes to Rome, returning their hostages held by the Carthaginians. He successfully won back those who had defected, along with those who had initially thrown in their lot with the Carthaginians but now had a sense of the way the tide was turning. For the next couple of years, the arena for the Punic War shifted, as Carthage took the battle to Rome, with naval attacks on Italy, Sicily and Sardinia.

In 207 BCE war flared up again in southern Spain covering much of the territory that is now Andalucía. Battles continued for the next two years with victories gained by both sides. Eventually Rome prevailed, in part due to disarray among the Carthaginian generals, and also their former allies changing sides.

With the end of the second Punic War and the defeat of Hannibal, the Carthaginians sued for peace. Rome was now the supreme force in the Western Mediterranean while the people of Gadir, aware of the fact that their prosperity depended on seafaring and trade, joined forces with the Romans once the Carthaginians had been soundly defeated. In the autumn of 206 BCE Gadir was peacefully handed over to Scipio Africanus's forces, with the signing of a treaty through which Gadir became a 'federated city'.

Civitas foederata

The peaceful submission of Gadir to the Romans meant that far from being taken as a booty of war, the city, now a Roman colony, was granted several favours and dispensations. The city's ruling authorities signed a treaty with their Roman rulers, which guaranteed that their citizens' rights and privileges would be respected in return for military allegiance with Rome. This document contained a clause stating that Gadir was to be treated as an 'allied community' (*civitas foederata*), placing it in the most elevated category of autonomous settlements under Roman rule. Its legal and political system remained intact, and citizens were declared exempt from any tax obligations. The Romans then instituted their province of Baetica, the modern-day Andalucía, split into four districts. Gadir was one of these dominions and was given jurisdiction over a large sphere of Roman colonial areas, including Tangier and several other North African territories.

One binding requisite was that in the event of war, Gadir was to provide troops to fight alongside the Roman legions. Henceforth, Rome's only visible presence in the city was the stationing of a military garrison. For Gadir and its citizenry of mixed Phoenician and Iberian heritage, it was life as usual, the city now freed from its Carthaginian masters.

The Punic Wars marked the starting point of Cádiz's involvement in military engagements that were to become a hallmark of its history. More than any other Spanish city, Cádiz has for centuries been the scene of conflict, be it attacks by enemy fleets or land battles against foreign invaders. This would make sense — as the Romans were well aware — given the city's unique geographic location at the crossroads of two seas as well as two continents, with mutually hostile naval forces vying for control of the ocean trade routes. This martial legacy is reflected in the remarkable assemblage of military installations, historical and contemporary, in Cádiz and the surrounding region, with three army bases, twenty barracks, eight batteries of cannon and five missile launch sites, as well as other facilities operated by today's armed forces.

Apart from its role as a tactical military bastion, Gadir held the same attraction for the Romans as it did for the Phoenicians, namely as a source of much sought-after mineral ore. Chief amongst this were the silver deposits of the Sierra Morena, drawn from the mines around the Río Tinto and Linares in the upper valley of the Guadalquivir River. Far from suffering a decline in its sea trade, the city's commerce under the Romans enjoyed a boom of prosperity thanks to the mining and trading of these valuable minerals. Strabo claims that the natives of Gadir, who were committed by treaty to providing ships and fighting men for the Romans, spent more time at sea than on dry land. Another ancient chronicler, the Greek sophist Philostratus, relates that the sea worshippers of Gadir erected a bronze statue of the general and naval strategist Themistocles, as a symbol of their fervour for maritime commerce and admiration for this leading spirit behind Athenian oceanic power.

The early period of Roman suzerainty brought an influx of traders and manufacturers from surrounding regions. These new arrivals sought to partake in the boom that the city's prominence had driven as the principal port for shipment of goods to Italy and Roman markets elsewhere in the east. In the early days of

Roman rule, Gadir saw its population soar to 50,000 people, nearly half the number of its current inhabitants. Gadir prospered under Roman rule. Its location was beneficial economically, mainly for its production of much sought-after fish sauce, as well as strategically, given its role as a naval base, as Gadir had a long history of shipbuilding.

One of the challenges facing Romans in their newly acquired western colonies were the pirates that had long been a serious menace to sea traffic throughout the Mediterranean. By the first century BCE, what had begun as a nuisance had now become a full-blown plague on shipping, led by Cilician pirates who roamed the entire Mediterranean.[1] In 67 BCE, the Roman General Pompey received orders to eradicate this menace, which was endangering the passage of ships laden with the mineral and other wealth crucial to Rome's commercial interests. As the coastal region of Spain, and especially the Strait of Gibraltar, was a vital sector of the sea routes that were under attack by these brigands, Pompey placed one of his army commanders at Gadir to coordinate the military operations against these buccaneers. After several hard-fought sea engagements, the operation, with vital assistance from vessels and warriors supplied by Gadir, met with success. The pirates were denied the use of their land bases, which greatly reduced and in due course put an end to their plundering of Roman trade.

A close associate of Pompey during his time in Gadir was Lucius Cornelius Balbus, son of a very wealthy merchant family native to Gadir. For his support and help to the Romans, Balbus gained Roman citizenship for himself and his family, and on Pompey's return to Rome in 71 BCE Balbus went with him. There he rapidly assumed considerable influence, in part due to his enormous wealth but it is likely that he also had great personal charm and intelligence. He remained a close personal friend of Pompey and also became friends with Julius Caesar.

Caesar appointed him as his chief engineer when Caesar was propraetor (administrative representative for Rome) for Hispania in 61 BCE and when Caesar was proconsul for Gaul 58 BCE. As friend of both Pompey and Julius Caesar, Balbus was put in a difficult position on the outbreak of the civil war between them. While not openly coming out against Pompey, Balbus appears to have moved behind the scenes to gain support for Caesar.

The Roman civil war that was being waged between arch enemies Julius Caesar and Pompey came to a conclusive end in 48 BCE at the Battle of Pharsalus in central Greece. Caesar had previously struggled without success to reduce his opponent at Dyrrhachium, in what is today Albania. He then marched his legions to Pharsalus to confront his opponent's undisciplined levies, mostly conscripted farmer-soldiers. When Pompey saw that all was lost, he fled to Egypt and was subsequently murdered by Ptolemy, his former ally, who feared offending Caesar by offering shelter to his defeated enemy.

Since Gadir had thrown its support behind Caesar, following Balbus' lead, once the civil conflict ended Caesar granted the city municipal status and Latinised its name to Gades. This was later reaffirmed by Augustus, the founder of the Roman Empire, who bestowed on the colony the title *Augusta Urbs Julia Gaditana* ('The August City of Julia of Gades'). It was during his reign that Gades came to have five hundred *equites*, or Roman nobles, out of a population of fifty thousand, more than any other city in the Spanish possession. The *equites* constituted the second of the property-based classes of ancient Rome, ranking below the senatorial class.

After Caesar's assassination in 44 BCE, Balbus continued to have influence in Rome, securing the favour of Octavian as he became Emperor Augustus. Balbus was the first naturalised Roman citizen to become consul. Once the empire had been established Gades entered a period of splendour such as it had never known. As the city's consul, Lucius Balbus oversaw the construction of Gades Nova, a new port district that flourished during the imperial period through trade in minerals, dried fish, fish sauce, wool and what were reputed to be the best wines in Spain. Spain's sherry wineries are today found in the nearby town of Jerez de la Frontera. This wine has always been treasured far and wide, not escaping the praise of William Shakespeare, who praises its virtues in eight of his plays.

One of the city's principal commercial exports, if not its prime economic staple, was seafood, as much prized throughout the Mediterranean in Roman times as it is today. Even in pre-Roman times the Iberians salted their catches of tuna, mackerel and sturgeon in the waters off Gades. The Phoenicians were reputed to have constructed fish-salting installations to conserve seafood. Salt fish from Gades was already known at Athens by the fifth century BCE. Even more profitable was the fish sauce made from the viscera and blood of fish that had been salted together with whole small fish, such as anchovies.

Varieties native to the Atlantic, such as tuna, were a natural profitable export to foreign markets. Tuna was the prize catch, a migratory species which could grow to 5 feet in length and weigh up to 600 pounds. Strabo refers to many plump, fat tuna in the waters of Gades. Fish were also caught in rivers but the requirements to salt them for travel gave the monopoly to coastal regions, Gades foremost amongst its neighbouring Spanish colonies. From the Atlantic coast came oysters and mussels of great size, conger eels, lampreys and other edible species. The dory, caught at Gades, was one of the choicest of fish in foreign markets.

Trade was encouraged by the relative security of travel and transportation of goods within the empire and the use of empire-wide coinage. There was some barter but as time went on most transactions became monetary. The number of Roman shipwrecks discovered in the Western Mediterranean gives some idea of the volume of trade with Spain, as does the curious Monte Testaccio in Rome, which is essentially a rubbish heap consisting of an estimated fifty million pottery amphorae used to ship olive oil from Spain. Even today the mound is around 115 feet high and covers almost 247 acres.

During the heyday of its prosperity under the Roman Empire, the population of Gades would have enjoyed all the amenities of being a regional imperial centre, along with the security of the rule of Roman law, imposed by the proconsul and the Roman troops garrisoned in the city acting as an imperial police force. The legionaries would mete out swift justice to anyone who was suspected of disobeying the law or being disrespectful to Rome or the emperor. To prevent local revolts and conspiracies from brewing, legions generally included a mix of soldiers from all over the empire, with legionaries posted far from their country of origin. Thus, the soldiers stationed in Gades could have included Gauls from France, Africans (from the area of modern-day Libya and Tunisia), eastern Europeans, soldiers from across Italy and even troops from far-off Britain.

'Voluptuous Gades'

Although archaeological remains have not yet been found, the size and status of Gades mean that the city would have incorporated all the major civic structures of a Roman city. These would include a forum, or public square, which usually had a temple to Jupiter on the north side, with a basilica along another side where the local magistrates and empire officials would carry out their public work, with a market taking up the centre of the forum. Cities of the empire had a certain uniformity in their development and architectural style, so it is safe to assume that there would have been a multitude of shops and workshops in such a large city, including potters, bakers, shoemakers, cloth merchants and metal workshops, as well as taverns and inns. The usual layout would be two main streets, the *cardo* running from north to south and the *decumanus* from east to west, with the forum at the intersection, although the roads may have been somewhat constrained by Gades' island location. The shops would front onto these main streets under a colonnaded walkway, with their workshops behind.

Given its location, it is likely that the wealthy merchants and empire officials of Gades would have had their villas and farms outside the city in the countryside beyond the coastal marshes. It was typical that the wealthy local families would vie with each other to pay for city amenities to benefit the community, such as drinking fountains, road paving, temples, theatres or even building the city walls. The emperors were keen to encourage this as a display of loyalty. Other ways to raise the revenue for such building projects were through the charges levied from those taking up positions such as priesthoods, magistrates and other local offices.

Bathhouses were an essential part of civic infrastructure and were often paid for through these fees. We can be assured that a city the size of Gades would have had several bathhouses, supplied by the aqueduct, with associated public latrines serving the densely packed apartments where most of the population lived. Bath complexes were among the first structures built once any city was newly occupied, or a garrison established. The bath complex typically comprised changing rooms, the hot bath (the caldarium), a cold plunge pool (the frigidarium) and a warm swimming pool (the tepidarium), although in smaller baths the tepidarium was often a comfortably heated room in which to relax. Time at the bath was central to the rhythm of Roman life, with different times set aside for men and women to attend the baths, usually women in the middle of the day and early afternoon, with men attending late afternoon or evening, after the working day. One segment of the population not admitted to the baths were slaves, along with children, as the baths were an adult-only location. In addition to the actual baths, many complexes also included exercise rooms for weight training and wrestling, indoor ball courts and space for massage and other treatments.

It follows that this age of prosperity stimulated a penchant for leisure and entertainment. These pursuits were vibrantly reflected in the celebrated dancing girls of Gades. This was a well-known attraction, a spectacle that prompted the Roman humourist Martial to describe the city as 'Voluptuous Gades'. The Roman satirical poet Juvenal was more explicit when he referred to the dancers as *mancipia*, or 'privileged slaves'. Juvenal described the ladies as being skilled at executing 'wanton gestures', accompanied by bronze castanets like those used in various traditional musical forms in Morocco today, while swaying to the native melodies of Gades. A distinguishing feature of the Cádiz style is that it was always more erotic than the restrained versions associated with Sevilla and Granada. According to classical accounts, troupes of these slave girls were hired out to provide stage entertainment for the general populace, as well as special favours for the elite. That the Cádiz style of dancing bears some parallels with the flamenco of present-day Andalucía has been remarked on by many commentators. Rather than an unbroken cultural inheritance from the days of Phoenician settlement, it is more likely to have been introduced into the region by the Arabic invasion of the eighth century or migrant gypsies in the fifteenth century.

The dancers' fame went before them: their talents were sought after in other parts of the empire and not restricted to the audiences of Gades. Once again Juvenal, who must surely have been a devoted fan of the girls, speaks of the *puellae gaditanae* (ladies of Gades) performing in Rome at the time of the emperor Trajan in the first century CE.

In Gades itself, the dancing girls would have had many venues to strut their musical talents. No doubt parties, most probably bacchanals dedicated to the Roman god of wine Bacchus, were arranged in the stately homes of the city's patrician community. The ordinary citizenry, on the other hand, would have required a venue of considerable size to accommodate an entertainment-hungry populace, such as a municipal theatre. In the first century BCE, work was underway to address this demand on a truly grandiose scale.

The Roman theatre

In 1980, a fire broke out at Talleres Vigorito, a Cádiz foundry that had stood for nearly two hundred years facing the sea between the Cathedral of Santa Cruz and Calle Obispo Félix Soto. The blaze was so devastating that after an official inspection, the building was declared beyond repair and would need to be demolished. The first people to set foot on the newly opened grounds were a group of schoolchildren playing on the site. 'My son and his friends were burrowing about in the small shafts that began to appear on the vacant spot under the warehouse,' says Antonia Ruiz, whose flat faced the grounds. 'The neighbours feared that their children might fall into what looked like tunnel openings, so we notified the town hall.'[2] As the excavator began knocking down walls, the workers discovered a site as remarkable as it was unexpected and called in the city hall building inspectors to investigate. They in turn brought this to the attention of a team of archaeologists who, to the astonishment of all, were able to identify beneath the ruins a relic of something built more than two thousand years ago: nothing less than the oldest Roman theatre in Spain. Researchers were able to determine the theatre had been constructed around 70 BCE, during the reign of the emperor Vespasian. At that time, the Romans had decided to expand Gades by creating a new neighbourhood, Neapolis, now known as Santa María and El Pópulo, where they would erect a theatre worthy of this favoured city.

The theatre was so massive it would have required razing a sizeable portion of what is today Cádiz's heritage neighbourhood of El Pópulo to excavate it in its entirety. The edifice featured a 400-foot diameter *cavea*, or enclosure, with seating for 10,000 spectators. It was one of the few Roman edifices of ancient Hispania mentioned by classical authors, including Cicero and Strabo. What has been preserved for public viewing are parts of the rows of seats that can be accessed through a passage, or vomitory. In keeping with this type of Roman construction, the first row is inclined forward. The lower gallery, or what would today be called the stalls, are fashioned of rough locally quarried stone known as *lapis Gaditanus*. This was a common feature of many buildings still seen in Cádiz. Light reaches this covered lower gallery through skylights placed above the spot where the orchestra sat. At the time of writing, the stage itself is undergoing restoration work.

The exact date of the theatre's inauguration is unknown, though it was during the city's period of greatest prosperity. In all likelihood, the patrician Balbus family would have been the driving force behind its construction. Cicero verifies this assumption in his writings, and moreover, he tells a rather chilling tale of Balbus, who had one of his own plays staged at the theatre but was so dismayed by what he regarded as a poor performance by the lead actor that he had him put to death.

The public flocked to the Roman theatre to watch a wide variety of stage shows, from Greek drama and Etruscan dances to pantomimes and short comedies. Women were seated in a special section that could shelter their eyes from scenes that might be considered offensive to feminine sensibilities.

The great theatre of Gades stood as a reflection of the Romans' deep-rooted bind with their colony. Likewise, it symbolised the conviction that this outpost at the westernmost edge of the known world formed an integral and permanent part of the empire. A citizen of Gades was recognised as a subject, holding identical rights to those of a Roman. This social equality was even displayed in the realm of the theatre. Natives of Gades who for whatever reason happened to find themselves in the imperial capital were granted special privileges, in recognition of the city's support for its Roman overlords. One of these was an inscription, found on rows eleven and twelve of the Flavian Amphitheatre, better known as the Roman Colosseum, which reads: 'Reserved for People of Gades'.[3]

The theatre prevailed for nearly three hundred years as a symbol of the great wealth Gades had enjoyed in the classical period. It was abandoned at the end of the third century CE and soon became the target of looters. Nearly a thousand years were to pass before Alfonso X the Wise of Castile ordered a fortress to be built on its ruins. By that time, the theatre had been largely reduced to ruins and remained buried, its existence recorded only in the writings of Cicero and others. Archaeological excavation work has succeeded in recovering part of the theatre, but the most important area of the complex awaits completion: the stage and the entrance are yet to be revealed.

The vast theatre is the most impressive but by far not the only remnant discovered to date of Rome's presence in Gades.

Aqueducts and roads

In 2018, Hurricane Leslie battered Spain, bringing the heaviest rainfall on record to parts of the country. Cádiz did not escape the devastation caused by this storm, which resulted in flooding to parts of the city. Playa de Cortadura is a long strip of fine-sand beach that extends along one of the margins of the road that connects Cádiz with San Fernando. Local residents who came out to inspect the damage caused by the Atlantic storm that had ravaged the city's sea front were startled to discover the ruins of a first century CE Roman aqueduct. The site lies roughly parallel to today's Plaza de Asdrúbal, a square itself recently built on top of an empty plot of land that had been abandoned after the demolition of the old Cádiz bullring.

A group of astonished locals began busily digging away in search of buried treasure, before they were warned off and the site was taken over by the Association for the Investigation and Dissemination of Cádiz Heritage.[4]

Found alongside the aqueduct were fragments of a stone roadway that dates from the sixteenth or seventeenth century. So far, experts have identified the remains of two walls 31 inches thick and more than 6 feet in height that once formed the boundaries of the pathway. The aqueduct was used until 1755, when it was destroyed by a tidal wave triggered by the great Lisbon earthquake, whose shockwaves left more than a thousand dead in Cádiz. Not 6 feet from this thoroughfare, archaeologists have identified up to seven fragments of what is believed to have been part of the aqueduct. Researchers believe there could also be an older Roman road right underneath its seventeenth-century counterpart or running parallel to it under the sea.

Two of these fragments are still joined together with the original mortar, which is very rare to find. It has now been determined that the aqueduct stretched for some 50 miles north to transport water to the city from Tempul, one of the natural springs of San José del Valle in the upper reaches of Cádiz province. The spring runs for several miles, which made this a key source of water for Cádiz as well as the nearby town of

Jerez de la Frontera. Historians believe the Cádiz patrician Balbus ordered the construction of the aqueduct to supply water to the Neapolis.

The Cádiz aqueduct is held to be one of the greatest achievements of Roman water engineering in Spain. The channel had long sections of rounded stone archways, a typical feature of the Roman construction style of the period. Some sectors ran underground to ensure the water flowed at the proper pressure when it reached the large basins next to Puertas de Tierra, a bastion built around remnants of the old defensive wall at the entrance to Cádiz. Large stone blocks with a lead pipe passing through them were positioned at the end of this section. The aqueduct, along with the theatre, are a testimony of the importance Rome accorded Gades, but neither one pinpoints with exactitude the location of the Roman settlement. Centuries of urban development that followed the withdrawal of Rome from Hispania has complicated the task of locating and identifying the original foundations.

'It is possible that it adjoined the canal, in the present-day district of El Pópulo (where the theatre was found) or Santa María, which would situation it near the Puertas de Tierra, the gateway to the old town,' says historian Manuel Bustos Rodríguez.[5] It is precisely this spot, by the San Roque fortification, where water deposits that supplied the city were found.[6] Water ran through outlying *caños*, or rivulets, to the rest of Gades. These *caños* were also used for carrying goods on small double-bow dinghies called *candrays*. What is known is that the epicentre of Roman activity was the port area which, as Strabo relates, was commissioned by Balbus. This initiative may have responded to the need to shift the main trading port further from the town centre, with the silting up of the urban canal. The port became the seat of trade for a variety of agricultural and fishing products, as well as the anchorage for the powerful Roman fleet.

As imposing as it undeniably was, the aqueduct is not the only expression of Rome's resolve to make Gades, along with the rest of Hispania, a permanent possession. Roman control of Iberia was founded upon a comprehensive network of roads. They generally followed the course of major rivers, like the Ebro, Tagus and Duero. This approach to road building in Hispania allowed the Romans to break up hostile tribal confederations.

The road known as the *Camino de la Plata*, or 'Silver Route', which was started in the second century BCE, became one of these major passageways across the peninsula. Its name was misleading, for it was not a trade route for silver or other precious metals. The *camino* was used by Roman troops to contain the Lusitanians, and in particular the forces of the rebel Roman general Sertorius in the region that today comprises large segments of Portugal. Under the emperor Augustus, who ruled in the first century BCE, it was extended to become a major trunk road linking Astorga in the north to Mérida in the south. The original Roman road that connected Mérida to Astorga was later extended to cross the entire Iberian Peninsula. Between the first century CE and second century CE, emperors Tiberius, Trajan and Hadrian had the road extended almost in a straight line to Gades.

Although an extraordinary testimonial to Roman road building skills, the *Camino de la Plata* must take a backseat to the Via Augusta, which joined Spain with Gaul and Italy. Rome's intended long-term commitment to Gades was enshrined in the road built during the reign of the emperor Augustus. Of all the roads constructed by the Romans in ancient Hispania, the Via Augusta stands out as the longest and busiest. The road's predecessor, the Via Herculea, stretched from the Pyrenees range to Cartago Nova, today the city of Cartagena on the Mediterranean coast. It branched off into an extension that ran the full distance to Gades. Most of the construction work made use of previous roadways from the days of the Roman Republic, and upon completion, it stood as a key communications and trade link between cities, as well as the major Mediterranean ports. It was an enduring piece of engineering that was still in use as late as the tenth century CE, during the Muslim occupation in Spain.

As the core axis of the road network in Hispania, the engineering work of this 930-mile-long highway, with a width of 20 feet that allowed for carriages to pass in opposite directions, defied every challenge of geography that lay in its path. The road's main purpose was to link Spain to the capital of the empire. With Gades as the starting point, it followed an inland course, running along valleys that lay parallel to the Mediterranean coast, then winding its way gradually to the uplands, it ascended across the Pyrenees to traverse France and terminate in Italy. From Gades to Rome, it served as a stone-paved roadway allowing for chariots and Roman troops to protect the empire's territories against hostile intruders, as well as a trade route for transporting foodstuffs, metals and other commercial goods from Spain.

Given that the Roman occupation of Gades lasted more than 500 years, it stands to reason that the physical legacy of their presence would stretch beyond a theatre and aqueduct. There is speculation that somewhere under the streets of Cádiz lies the ruins of an amphitheatre, which would have constituted a far larger edifice than the theatre that was discovered in 1980.[7]

The first person to signal its presence was Juan Bautista Suárez de Salazar. The early sixteenth century historian referred in one of his books to 'colossal gladiators' locked in mortal combat in 'an arena of fourteen tiers', which would have made it the largest amphitheatre outside Rome.[8]

Contemporary scholars believe traces of the amphitheatre may have been visible four centuries ago, when Suárez de Salazar published his claim. The building boom of that period could have buried all traces of the structure, which may have stood near the Santa María district, in today's city centre. There have also been literary references to a Roman circus in Gades, where the populace would have been treated to fights between wild beasts and similar spectacles in the ring. Like the amphitheatre, there is not yet any conclusive archaeological proof to uphold these theories.

Classical writings, as well as references dating from the later Moorish occupation of Cádiz, speak of a great lighthouse, raised in the first century BCE, at the time of the civil war between Caesar and Pompey. It is said the lighthouse arose at La Caleta, by the rocky outcrops where the San Sebastián and Santa Catalina castles stand. As with the amphitheatre, there is a persuasive argument in favour of both structures having once been a feature of Roman Gades. The answer awaits further archaeological research.

'Here lies the city of Gadir'

With the exception of the theatre and aqueduct, Cádiz offers few visible artefacts that can attest to more than half a millennium of Roman presence in the city. The visitor will find a Roman columbarium in Calle del General Ricardos, in the city centre. Designed to hold cremation urns, this underground enclosure covered with a white coating of marble powder contains many different types of Roman tombs. A Roman fish-salting factory was found in 1995 in the historical district of Cádiz, on a plot of land once occupied by the Teatro de Andalucía. This workshop was a crucial element of the seafood export trade. Records show that the factory was in operation until the early fourth century CE. It was built around a large courtyard, with a tank set in the ground. The plant's preserved remains consist of a set of basins lined with hydraulic cement and a lower central area for cleaning.

Apart from that, the Roman dominion of Cádiz has left a pale shadow over the city after centuries of urbanisation, a succession of natural disasters and the inevitable erosion of time.

By the early fifth century CE, Roman control of its Spanish colonies was in a terminal state of decline, though in the East the Byzantine Empire survived for nearly another millennium until the loss of Constantinople in 1453. What was left of the empire in the West was severely shaken in 410, when Visigoths, a wandering nation of Germanic people, sacked Rome. The Vandals, another and more barbarous German tribe, pillaged the once mighty imperial capital and two decades later deposed Romulus Augustulus, the last emperor.

One after another, the Spanish provinces fell to the Visigoth warriors who raided Roman territories to establish their own kingdoms in Spain. The Visigoth defeat of Roman power in Baetica, one of three Roman provinces in Hispania, brought with it the destruction of Gades. Little trace of that period in the city's history remains visible. The fortunes of Gades followed Rome's downward drift.

A verse by the Latin poet Rufus Festus Avienius speaks sadly of the state of decay he witnessed on a visit to Gades:

> Here lies the city of Gadir, once called Tartessus, a great and opulent city in ancient days, now poor, now abandoned, now a field of ruins. We saw nothing of worth here, with the exception of the solemnity of Hercules.[9]

The steady withdrawal of the former empire from cities no longer under its hegemony brought a commensurate decline in trading activity. This inevitably had an impact on Gades, one of Rome's most intense trading metropolises. Many oligarchs of commerce moved to their rural estates, where they felt more secure. Gades faded into obscurity, no longer a mercantile centre of gravity. Sea commerce waned as early as the second century when raiders from the former Roman province of Mauretania Tingitana made Mediterranean sea lanes too hazardous for commercial shipping. The decline of Gades was exacerbated in the fourth century by a series of earthquakes that left much of the city and its coastline in ruin.

In 522 CE, the city was overrun by the Byzantines, a mix of different ethnicities, most of whom spoke Greek and practised Eastern Coptic Orthodoxy. Thus it was that in the space of less than 150 years, Gades had passed from the hands of the Romans to the Vandals, then the Byzantines and finally the Visigoths, who were to hold the city for less than a century. The collapse of Rome's northern and eastern frontiers and the assumption of power by various Germanic tribes ruptured Hispania's connection with its own cultural past. Among the tribes that dismantled and then resettled what had once been the Roman Empire, the Visigoths played a notorious role. This tribe, infamous for the sack of Rome in 410 CE, eventually ended as the overlords of the former province of Hispania.

It was at this time, in the early eighth century, that another army of invaders, the most formidable Gades would ever know, was preparing its onslaught across the Strait of Gibraltar.

3

MOORS ON THE COAST!

The year 711 CE is deeply ingrained in the Spanish psyche, for that was the fateful date on which an army of Arabs and Berbers[1] unified under the aegis of the Islamic Umayyad Caliphate and crossed the Strait of Gibraltar to land on the Iberian Peninsula. They were soon in control of almost the entire Iberian Peninsula, where they were to remain for nearly eight centuries. In terms of lightning speed and ferocity, the eighth century Muslim invasion of the Iberian Peninsula was a lesson in the military tactic of surprise.

The unwary Visigoths were in the midst of Easter celebrations when the Umayyad Caliphate host, estimated at up to 9,000 cavalrymen under the Berber commander Tariq ibn Ziyad, disembarked on the coast near the Rock of Gibraltar, which at the time was known by its Greek name 'Calpe'. The triumphant invaders renamed the spot after their leader as the Mountain of Tariq – Jabal Tariq – which has become corrupted over time to Gibraltar. They quick-marched to an undefined place by the Guadalete River in Cádiz province, there to engage King Rodrigo in a battle that was to seal the fate of the Visigoths in Spain.

CÁDIZ

Despite outnumbering the enemy, according to contemporary sources, the Visigoth defenders suffered a crushing defeat on that day. The Muslim army launched a series of hit-and-run cavalry attacks, while the defending lines manoeuvred en masse. A Visigoth cavalry wing that had grasped the hopelessness of their situation secretly pledged to stand aside. This gave the enemy their decisive opening. In the final hours of battle, the Christian army was routed and Rodrigo, along with a cohort of his nobles, lay dead on the ground.

Thus began centuries of Muslim hegemony over Hispania. The Islamic hordes swept across the Iberian Peninsula with speed and tenacity unmatched by the raiders who had preceded them, including the Vandals. Within three years, Cádiz and all its surrounding territories had been subjugated to Muslim rule. The Moors left an abundant stock of records detailing the advance of their armies across the Iberian Peninsula. The documents that have been preserved concerning Cádiz speak of a place reduced to ruins, in which the Muslims built a mosque and held what was left of the town as a military base of operations.

With the departure of the Romans, the invasion of Germanic tribes and finally the conquest by the Moors, more than 1,600 years of grandeur and opulence had come to an end. The once-powerful westernmost seaport of the Phoenicians and Romans was to languish, depopulated and in decline, for more than five centuries. According to historian Manuel Bustos Rodríguez,

> Arab sources are in agreement that Cádiz in the 8th century was in a state of decay. In those days, the city was probably nothing more than a shelter for farmhands and fishermen. Some 20th century authors take a less severe view, but for the Arab writers of the era, Cádiz was an accumulation of remains from the Roman occupation. They were, however, impressed by some of the ancient monuments, above all, the aqueduct. There are also references to the Sancti Petri Castle, near the

MOORS ON THE COAST!

Hercules sanctuary, the lighthouse crowned by a humanlike figure and the water reservoirs.[2]

The potentates from North Africa became known as the Moors, a word derived from the Latin word *Maurus*, used to describe Berbers and other people from the ancient Roman province of Mauretania in the Maghreb. The word is still used today in the traditional expression, *¿Hay Moros en la costa?* or, 'Any Moors on the coast?' It is a way of asking if there is visible danger in sight, or in the negative, *No hay Moros en la costa*, 'The coast is clear.'

The conquest of Al-Andalus

There is ample evidence to confirm the swiftness with which the Moors carried out their conquest. In fewer than eight years, the North African invaders had taken possession of the entire Iberian Peninsula, save for a few strips of territory tenaciously held by the Basques and Asturians. Marching northward from Cádiz and its province, in quick succession Tariq's troops went on to capture Écija, Córdoba, Sevilla and the rest of Andalucía, which became known as the kingdom of Al-Andalus.[3]

Just why Tariq embarked on his bellicose exploit is a question that lies in the realm of speculation. In all likelihood, the Berber leader was not the first to launch a strike against the Christian kingdom across the water. Arab chronicles speak of the Umayyad governor Musa ibn Nusayr having crossed the Fretum Gaditanum, the Gulf of Cádiz, a few years prior to the main invasion. The attempted incursion was repelled, but this did not dampen the Moors' appetite for territorial expansion to what they perceived to be a land of abundance. It is entirely probable that word had reached North Africa as early as Roman times of merchant ships full of foodstuffs and valuable minerals sailing from the port of Cádiz. This would have instilled a strong incentive in the inhabitants of the parched desert to take possession of these abundant lands that lay a mere day's sailing across the water.

Hypotheses abound, some bordering on the realm of fancy. Several historians have laid the blame for the invasion at the feet of King Rodrigo himself. The tale goes that the Visigoth monarch was spying on palace ladies one afternoon, all of whom were draped to varying degrees in luxurious Indian silks, bathing in a garden pond in his capital city of Toledo. Rodrigo was stunned by the beauty of Florinda, the most striking of the group, whom he took and seduced in the bushes. Florinda's father, the powerful nobleman Count Julian, was at the time serving as governor of Ceuta, the Spanish enclave on the African side of the Strait. The Count flew into a rage when he learned of Rodrigo's deed. He vowed to take his revenge by approaching the Moors with a plan to invade Spain and overthrow the Visigoths.[4]

As far-fetched as this theory may seem it is linked, at least symbolically, to a historical reality. In the early eighth century, when the invasion took place, Spain's Visigoth kingdom was torn asunder by internal strife between Rodrigo and several of his formidable nobles, many of whom were seeking to expand their powers. The Visigoths made up a very small percentage of the population, estimated at one to two per cent; they were constantly on their guard trying to control the rebellious indigenous population, while also in constant territorial battles with each other. The country was suffering from widespread political instability. In short, Hispania was easy pickings for a well-organised enemy force from abroad, one that needed little prodding to embark on this momentous foray.

Having taken control of large amounts of Spanish territory the Moors almost immediately embarked on internal conflict among themselves, rooted in the tribal divisions of the armies that made up the Moorish forces, most notably those between Arabs and Berbers. While the Berbers from Morocco made up much of the

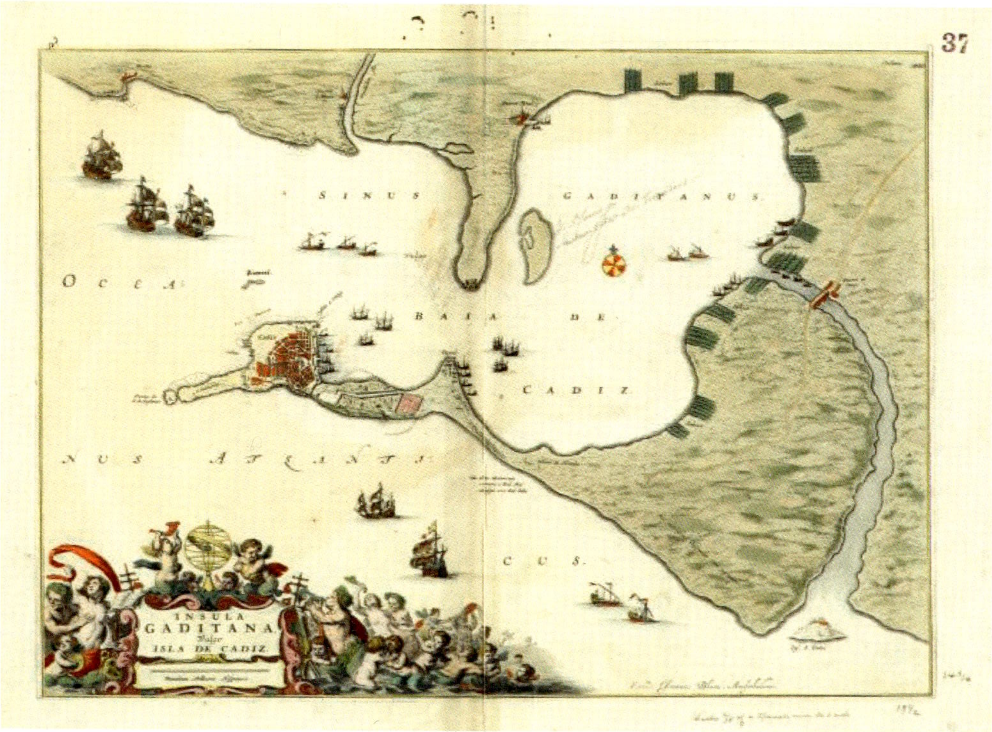

Fig. 1: Early map of the Cádiz area from Norman B. Leventhal Map & Education Center at the Boston Public Library.

Fig. 2: Pillars of Hercules statue at Ceuta.

Fig. 3: Phoenician male and female sarcophagi in the Museo de Cádiz.

Fig. 4: Remains of the Phoenician dry dock under the Old Town.

Fig. 5: Terracotta figure of the goddess Astarte worshippe by the Phoenicians.

Fig. 6: Exquisite Phoenician jewellery excavated from burial site in Cádiz.

Fig. 7: Cádiz falls to the Romans under Scipio Africanus.

Fig. 8: First century bust of Julius Caesar.

Fig. 9: Cádiz Roman theatre seating and part of the stage.

Fig. 10: Cádiz Roman theatre, the tunnel to the auditorium.

Fig. 11: A replica of the *Santa Maria*, Christopher Columbus's flagship, sails the Atlantic.

Fig. 12: Sir Francis Drake, line engraving by J. Fougeron.

Fig. 13: Painting of the English ships and the Spanish Armada in battle August 1588, probably design for a tapestry.

Fig. 14: Capture of Cádiz, 1596, in the Anglo-Spanish war.

fighting force, they were recent converts to Islam and felt they were looked down on by the Arabs. There were many disputes about distribution of land and other booty, leading to ongoing fights between factions. The colony could have come to an early end, had not events at the centre of the Islamic Empire in faraway Damascus taken a turn that led to a new leader arriving in Al-Andalus. The ruling clan of the caliphate, the Umayyads, were overthrown by the Abbasid dynasty in the 740s, who moved the capital of the empire to Baghdad and vowed to destroy all members of the former ruling family. One grandson of the Umayyad Caliph escaped, Abd al-Rahman, who found refuge with Berber relatives on his mother's side. After several years in disguise, he seized the opportunity of the internal conflicts in Moorish Spain to use his royal heritage to become proclaimed as emir of the province. Abd al-Rahman made Córdoba his capital and unified Al-Andalus under his strong rule. While the rest of the caliphate came under the Abbasids, Umayyad rule of the territories in Spain meant that Al-Andalus was no longer within the Islamic Empire; as power moved eastwards, Spain, at the western edge of the Islamic world, seemed a backwater of little consequence to the Abbasid rulers. The dynasty founded by Abd al-Rahman continued until the eleventh century.

While the Moors were tightening their grip on Cádiz and its surrounding territories, 600 miles to the north an event took place that was to unleash the longest war in history. In 718, the Visigoth nobleman Don Pelayo (Pelagius in English) raised his sword on a hilltop in Asturias, the northern kingdom he had founded in that same year. Pelayo proclaimed the start of the Reconquista, the crusade that in 1492 ended with the defeat of the last Moorish stronghold in Granada. Pelayo wasted no time in embarking on his campaign against the Umayyad Caliphate. Within weeks, he had routed the Moors at the Battle of Covadonga in the Picos de Europa, the first major victory for the Christian army.

'The highest culture in the West'

The Muslims bypassed Cádiz to focus their attention on bigger trophies, specifically Córdoba and Sevilla, two cities that became icons of the grandeur of Islamic culture. There was some building in Cádiz during its 551 years of Muslim settlement. The main mosque for the city was built on the site where the Church of Santa Cruz now stands, the city walls were rebuilt with three massive gates with guard towers, and a castle defended the harbour. Unloved but not entirely ignored, on several occasions Cádiz came to play a role that for centuries past, as well as for those to come, formed an integral part of its existence: that of a setting for naval operations against raiders from the north and in the local wars between different Islamic powers. Cádiz may have ranked as an outpost of no great cultural or architectural worth, yet accounts survive that attest to the city's port having performed an important task as a safe haven for Moorish warships.

In 772, Abd al-Rahman I, the emir who built the colossal mosque of Córdoba, designated Cádiz the nerve centre of the Muslim fleet. Later, in the ninth century, the port played an active part in the defence of Lower Andalucía against Viking raiders. In 844, the Normans were able to storm ashore to sack Medina Sidonia, an affluent hilltop municipality 20 miles east of Cádiz. They were repelled by a contingent of fifteen Córdoban warships that were stationed in the Bay of Cádiz.

Colonisation is almost never a happy experience for those whose land is taken over by a foreign power. In the case of the Muslim occupation of Cádiz and the rest of Al-Andalus, the occupation could not in all fairness be dismissed as a simple case of oppression. There was no attempt to abolish people's customs, language or, at least in the early stages, their faith. Non-Muslims were restricted from carrying arms or riding horses and were expected to avoid certain colours in their clothing, green in particular, as being associated with the Prophet. In the early period of the Umayyad Spain the social and cultural relations between Muslims and Jews were relatively comfortable, with Jews in particular able to attain high social positions as doctors and functionaries within the court. There were strict rules about marriage and inheritance: a non-Muslim could not inherit from a Muslim and no Muslim woman could marry a non-Muslim, but a Muslim man could marry a Jewish or Christian woman. Christians and Jews paid a special poll tax and were allowed to practise their religion, until the twelfth century when restrictions were imposed by the newly arrived Almohad tribes. Many Spaniards took the logical road to escape persecution by converting to Islam, yet so unpopular had been the Visigoth regime that after its collapse, Christians and Jews alike were quick to collaborate without offering great resistance to their new rulers.

'In Andalucía the Muslims...set about creating, or recreating, the highest culture in the West, the only high culture in Europe at the time and one that rivalled those of Constantinople, Damascus and Baghdad,' says cultural historian Allen Josephs. 'In all Al Andalus, which extended its influence as far as Toledo, Zaragoza and Valencia, there were no "Dark Ages" and Córdoba, the new Muslim capital, became one of the most splendid and enlightened cities in the world.'[5]

By the tenth century CE, the Muslim caliphate of Córdoba had risen to become the cultural centre of Al-Andalus as well as the most populated city in Europe. Its famed library contained Arabic, Latin and Hebrew translations of ancient Greek texts, and its mosque, a UNESCO World Heritage Site, is considered one of the world's greatest examples of Muslim religious architecture.

Many customs originated from the Islamic courts of Damascus and Baghdad and therefore became the way that the nobility of Al-Andalus organised their palaces, and in turn many of these conventions spread to the European courts. These included a return to personal hygiene not seen since the Romans, with an emphasis on bathing and short hair that was kept clean with regular trips to the bathhouse. In culinary matters, there were many changes of custom and the types of food served. The idea of serving banquets in courses, rather than all of the dishes being brought out at once, along with the use of a tablecloth to provide a clean setting for the food, were adopted. Different foods were introduced and became an established part of the local diet, including asparagus, artichokes, rice, spinach and aubergines, all of which were grown with sophisticated irrigation systems. Fruit trees were planted, including apricots and the citrus fruit for which Andalucía is famous; oranges, lemons and grapefruit were all introduced to Spain during the Moorish period. Sweets became more common as sugar cane started to be grown, leading to many local recipes for sweetmeats made from sugar, nuts and eggs, which have been overtaken as special symbols of Christian festivals.

The people of Cádiz certainly do not harbour any ill will towards their former Muslim rulers. Every year since the sixteenth century, the city has been celebrating its Moorish heritage in the Fiesta de Moros y Cristianos held in the nearby hill town of Benamahoma, where mock battles between Christian and Moorish armies are recreated in a spirit of fun.

Almoravids and Almohads

It can truly be said that few cities throughout their history have known so many days of glory and moments of destitution as has Cádiz. Four centuries on from the Moors landing on Spanish soil, Cádiz continued to linger as a possession largely neglected by the Muslim overlords of Al-Andalus. It was not until the twelfth century that the city began to emerge from its state of prostration, to reclaim a position of relevance in the events that were to shape the destiny of Spain. The Moors at that time regarded the Strait of Gibraltar as an increasingly strategic component of their political thinking and with it, the city of Cádiz.

Cádiz historian Manuel Bustos Rodríguez speaks of the hordes of Berbers known as Almoravids who crossed from North Africa to the Peninsula to confront the Christian armies of the Reconquista in the eleventh century. The Almoravids were the new power from Morocco, made up of tribes from the far south of the country. They had swept in with a creed of asceticism and religious purity, training their youth in monasteries known as *murabits*, which combined teaching in faith and fighting skills. These warrior monks were called Al-Murabitun, which became Latinised as 'Almoravid.'

'In 1135, King Alfonso VII deployed his men to Jerez (twenty miles north of Cádiz) and successfully battled his way as far as Algeciras,' Bustos Rodríguez says. 'Coinciding with the presence of these Muslim reinforcements and the fall of the Umayyad Caliphate of Córdoba in 1031, Cádiz once again stepped onto centre stage in a protagonist role, most importantly in 1145 when the Almoravids were replaced by the Almohad Muslims.'[6] It is likely that the first Almohad landings on Spanish soil were at Cádiz, whose port offered a greater margin of security than those around the more turbulent area of the Strait of Gibraltar.

The Moors left chronicles that speak of life under the Almoravid rulers as a time of peace in Cádiz. Having occupied almost all of Al-Andalus, by the end of the twelfth century their power started to decline, with the steady Christian reconquest of territory under Islamic occupation and the spread of internal dissention among Moorish factions. This was exploited by Almohad tribes, a new Berber dynasty from North Africa, whose power progressively increased across the Peninsula. By 1150, the Almohads had taken Morocco as well as Sevilla, Córdoba, Badajoz, and Almería in the Iberian Peninsula. The Almohads made Sevilla their capital in Al-Andalus, while retaining Marrakesh as their centre of power in North Africa.

It is also probable that their military success was facilitated by the intercession of Yusuf ibn Tashfin, who led the Almoravids in the takeover of al Andalus and established naval bases in Cádiz. These new invaders took it upon themselves to destroy the statue that stood atop the Temple of Hercules, having heard that it contained precious metal, which turned out to be copper. Once subjugated to Almohad domination, Cádiz took on the strategical role as a place to anchor and assemble the fleets for the Moorish maritime forces.

La Reconquista

The Muslims had placed Cádiz within the *cora*, or administrative district, of Medina Sidonia, their favoured regional township in Lower Andalucía after Córdoba and Sevilla. In 1248, Sevilla was taken by King Fernando III, 'the Saint', an event that spelt inevitable doom for the caliphate. As Fernando marched south, Puerto de Santa María, Jerez, Medina Sidonia and Arcos, amongst others, fell in quick succession to the Christian monarch.

It was not until 1262 that Fernando's son, King Alfonso 'the Wise' of Castile and León, effectively drove the last of the Muslims from their bastion in Qādis, now baptised with its Christian name of Cádiz. Alfonso's capture of Cádiz is depicted in triumphal Victorian style by the nineteenth-century Spanish artist and sculptor Matías Moreno, whose painting is on display in the cathedral. Now the entire region surrounding the Guadalquivir, which flows into the Gulf of Cádiz, was under Christian control. Holding the river basin was a tactical necessity, since this was the only means of effectively frustrating a Muslim attempt to retake any part of the Peninsula via the largest navigable waterway in Spain. Cádiz, despite its weakened state, was still seen as a key factor in military tactics. The city enabled the Christian army to impede any enemy land or sea action between the different river outlets on a critical 15-mile stretch from Tarifa to Algeciras along the coast.

One of Alfonso's first acts after taking Cádiz was to place a large cross on a rise overlooking the bay, an embodiment of Christian supremacy over the waters that separated the Iberian Peninsula from Africa. Following the tradition of the Reconquista in other cities captured from the Moors, the monarch had a church, the Iglesia de Santa Cruz, built on the remains of the mosque, which he lost no time in demolishing. Alfonso then relocated the Roman Catholic Diócesis de Asidonia-Jerez from Jerez de la Frontera to Cádiz, as an acknowledgement that the city now stood as the spiritual capital of Cádiz province. The last Muslims were expelled from Cádiz in 1264 after a bloody and failed attempted uprising against the Spanish. More building works followed to ensure the security of the city.

'Alfonso X reinforced the wall of the city, using what was left standing from the Almoravid period, some remains from the Roman period and incorporating a number of Arab buildings,' says historian Manuel Bustos Rodríguez. 'The wall spanned the length from the old Hospital of San Juan de Dios and its square, through the Calle Pelota to the old cathedral. Gates or arches opened at each turning of the wall. They were known as the Blancos, the land entry to the city, Pópulo on the seafront...and Rosa, on the western coast. The remains of three arches have been left standing, while most of the wall has vanished, in spite of some discoveries in recent years. The Medieval city formed a perfect quadrangle.'7

No sooner had the king seized command of Cádiz, than he launched a campaign to repopulate the city. He ordered his aide, Gillen de Berja, to bring in families from Asturias and other points north. It is said that this may account for the unusually large number of light-complexioned, blue-eyed people in the city. Many of these people flocked to Cádiz on the promise of work to be had in the docks, which the king promised to build in the port. So it was that before long, Cádiz became the seat of Spain's royal shipyards. The first group of northern immigrants settled in the Pópulo district, where one can still find contemporary monuments such as the Blanco and Rosa archways. The Arco de la Rosa is one of the entrances to the old town, named after the small chapel, dedicated to the Virgen de la Rosa that was built above the arch. It is likely that the name of 'de la Rosa' referred to a family with this surname, who lived in a house next to the arch. Originally, passing through the arch required a dog-leg move, necessary because a now-vanished tower stood in front of the arch. Above the arch, which was enlarged to allow carriages to pass, a machicolation defends the entrance and from this boiling oil could be poured onto invaders.

The Arco de los Blanco was another entryway to the central Pópulo district. Adjacent to the wide vault that makes up the passageway, the Blanco family, from whom the door takes its current name, built a chapel in the seventeenth century dedicated to the Virgen de Los Remedios. This chapel has since disappeared. The arch houses an alabaster image of Nuestra Señora de los Remedios, a sculpture of Italian origin from the mid-sixteenth century. This arch was the one that suffered the most from abandonment over the years and it was so close to collapse in 1602 that it had to be extensively repaired. In 1949, it was designated an Asset of Cultural Interest by Spain's Ministry of Culture.

Two years after the liberation of Cádiz, the battlefront shifted to the region around the Strait of Gibraltar. In 1275, the Banu Marin, or Marinid tribes, from northern Morocco, known to the Spanish as the Benimerines, crossed the Strait with a battle squadron. The attempted invasion, under the forceful leadership of Abu Yaqub Yusuf, who had vanquished the decaying Almohad Empire in Morocco, was swiftly repelled. Alfonso was wary of the Benimerines, but he convinced himself that once word of his victory got back to North Africa none of the tribes were likely to attempt an assault in force. His suspicion was confirmed when the Spanish monarch struck a deal with Muhammad II, the former Muslim ruler of Granada, who agreed to end support for the hostile tribes in exchange for a cash payment.

The rising birthrate registered after Cádiz was captured from the Moors did not in itself explain the increase in population from the mid-thirteenth century onwards. The wave of immigration that slowly gathered pace after Alfonso's victory brought a continual influx of migrants from across Spain and other European countries. The magnet that induced them to uproot and move to what was for many a distant new home was the lure of cashing in on a flourishing economy. 'In Cádiz and its bay area, it was relatively easy to find employment, or even pick up the crumbs that dropped from the tables of the rich or take advantage of support offered by charitable institutions,' according to Manuel Bustos Rodríguez.[8]

Some had undertaken the journey to Cádiz against their will. Slaves from Africa were supplied by European traffickers. They were brought in en masse and were to account for an appreciable segment of the city's future economic growth.

Once Cádiz had been incorporated into Christian Spain, women from other regions, most of them not too far from Cádiz, generally found work as domestic servants or were employed in taverns and inns. There were a few exceptional instances of women who exceeded what were deemed, at the time, the conventional limits of female endeavours. Bustos Rodríguez makes mention of the thrice-widowed María de Aranda Mateos, whose husbands had all owned print shops. In each case, Aranda Mateos took over and single-handedly ran the businesses of her deceased spouses. A different case was that of Rosario Cepeda, whose intellectual prowess caused something of a stir when at the age of twelve, she translated a work by the Greek poet Anacreon into Spanish, as well as one of Aesop's fables. In recognition of her extraordinary abilities, the Cádiz town hall appointed her an honorary alderman.

In 1492 King Fernando of Aragón and Queen Isabel la Católica conquered Granada, an event that brought the dethronement of Boabdil, the last ruler of the emirate, and marked the end of Muslim rule in Spain. In January of that year, Boabdil handed over the keys of the Alhambra to the Spanish monarchs, symbolising the formal transfer of power to Christian sovereignty. It is said that Boabdil wept bitter tears when he symbolically surrendered the keys to the Alhambra palace to the monarchs whom Pope Alexander VI granted the title of Catholic Monarchs. On the day of Granada's fall, Aixa, Boabdil's outraged mother, recriminated her son with the words, 'You weep like a woman for what you failed to hold like a man.'

The New World

Historical fact or anecdotal hype, this episode nonetheless marked the end of the Reconquista and opened the gates to what was to become the Spanish Empire. For Cádiz, it brought the city back into prominence as the country's major trading port. Eight months after the fall of Granada, Christopher Columbus

MOORS ON THE COAST!

set sail with a fleet of three caravels, the Niña, Pinta and Santa María, on his historic voyage of discovery to the New World. The port chosen for his first Atlantic crossing was Palos de la Frontera, roughly 50 nautical miles northwest of Cádiz.

It would almost certainly have caused shock in Cádiz that the Genoese explorer had chosen this lesser port as the point of departure for his momentous journey. Palos was a town with a naval industry that was slowly dying for lack of trade, and it was desperately looking for new opportunities. It had thrived for decades on commerce with Africa, particularly the region of Guinea. However, after the signing of the Treaty of Alcáçovas in 1479, which divided the Atlantic Ocean and overseas territories into two zones of influence, Portugal had won the exclusive right to trade with Guinea, while Spain continued to trade with North Africa. Spain was therefore looking to find new routes for trade by sailing west across the Atlantic, beyond the sphere of influence assigned to Portugal. Another factor that helps explain Columbus's choice of Palos de la Frontera over Cádiz is that Palos also happened to be the hometown of the wealthy and influential shipowners Alonso and Vicente Pinzón. They had provided the caravels granted by the Crown for this voyage, in which both brothers also took part.

In October that year, two months after departing from Spain, Columbus and the crews under his command arrived at the islands now known as the Bahamas and Hispaniola, becoming the first Europeans to set foot in the Caribbean. Believing he had reached East Asia, Columbus dubbed the indigenous peoples he encountered there *indios* (Indians), kidnapping several to present to King Fernando and Queen Isabel on his return to Spain.

The following year Columbus chose Cádiz as his base to assemble the fleet for the second voyage to the New World. The explorer saw it as a cosmopolitan and open city, one better suited than Palos for the next leg of his search for a sea route to the

Orient. This was to be a massive undertaking with which the port of Palos could not have coped. At this point there was a sizeable colony of Genoese living in Cádiz, at the time a key destination for migration and trade for compatriots of Columbus, who made up about ten per cent of the population. They supported Columbus financially as he prepared for the voyage and also provided some of the crew members, upon whom he felt he could rely.

Columbus weighed anchor in September 1493 with a fleet of seventeen ships and 1,500 crew. After a stopover in the Canary Islands, the flotilla reached the island of Dominica in November. They carried on to La Española in the Antilles, and after a series of setbacks and near disasters, Columbus loaded up twelve ships with all the local goods available and sent these back to Spain while he set out to explore other islands. The first contingent of caravels arrived in the port of Cádiz bearing a cargo of gold, spices and exotic birds, as well as another group of native captives. However, this cargo fell far short of what was hoped for from this hugely expensive voyage.

Having failed to find a navigable route to China, Columbus returned to Cádiz in March 1496, bearing tales of copper mines that had been opened, as well as an abundance of precious gems and exotic plants. It was enough to whet the Catholic Monarchs' appetite for untold riches in the New World, so they cautiously made a third investment in another voyage to be led by Columbus.

Six ships left Sanlúcar de Barrameda in May 1498, three filled with explorers and three with provisions for the settlement on the recently colonised Caribbean island of Hispaniola. It was clear now that on this third voyage, Columbus was expected to find great prizes and to establish the flag of Spain firmly in the New World, an enterprise in which Cádiz was to play a lead role. The choice of Sanlúcar was by all accounts fortuitous and by no means a rebuff of Cádiz 30 miles to the south on the Atlantic coastline. Twenty-one years later, in 1519, Ferdinand Magellan would also hoist sail from Sanlúcar de Barrameda on the first circumnavigation of the globe. Both ports can be mentioned in the same breath, and in fact, it was in Cádiz where Columbus laid anchor on his return to Spain in October 1500. The name of Cádiz left its mark early on in the New World. 'Nueva Cádiz' was the name bestowed on the first city settlement founded in South America, on the shores of Cubagua Island, part of today's Venezuela, which Columbus sighted in 1498.

The Catholic Monarchs were quick to recognise the value of Cádiz as a hub for trade with the Old as well as the New World. As early as 1493, Fernando and Isabel issued a royal decree emphasising the importance of Spain's trading relations with North Africa. The Crown granted Cádiz a concession on the flow of merchandise from Morocco and other parts of the African continent. These routes needed to be secured for Spanish vessels, and to this end, in 1497 Spain launched a naval foray under the Cádiz commandant Pedro de Estopiñán to conquer the city of Melilla, a crucial enclave on the northern coast of Morocco. Melilla, along with Ceuta, remain the two Moroccan towns still held by Spain.

Columbus put to sea from Cádiz on his fourth voyage, leading a fleet of four caravels, in May 1502. He returned more than two years later, broken in body and spirit. His harsh treatment of his own men led to near mutiny among the crews, and the indigenous peoples encountered had been savagely treated in a forerunner of what was to come with the next waves of exploration from Europe. The explorer had failed to find a passage to the Far East. This expedition also proved to be the least profitable and most dangerous of his voyages, having come back bearing little in riches for the monarchs, with the loss of many members of the crew and three of the four ships. Columbus died almost four years to the day later, in May 1506.

CÁDIZ

Christopher Columbus did not live to witness the enormous impact his voyages were to have on the history of both the Western and Eastern hemispheres. His journeys laid the groundwork for Spain's conquest of the New World and the creation of the largest empire the world had ever known. One of the chief beneficiaries of Columbus's adventures was Cádiz, more precisely the bay and its nearby ports. From around 1493, Cádiz held a virtual monopoly on the exchange of goods with what were to become the Spanish colonies of the New World. In that year, the Catholic Monarchs enshrined this privilege in law in a royal decree, which also addressed commerce with North Africa: 'It shall be that from time immemorial to today, all vessels delivering or unloading cargo from the Berbers, shall do so from the port of Cádiz and no other place.' This royal favouritism set in motion a boom such as the city had never known. During the reign of Alfonso X, who ruled from 1252 to 1284, Cádiz's inhabitants numbered no more than 750 souls. By the mid-sixteenth century, or what can be termed the beginning of the city's modern era, this had expanded to more than four thousand ordinary citizens plus an unregistered number of noblemen and their families. Cádiz was growing in population and prosperity as it became the acknowledged main link to trade with the American colonies.

A merchant city

The city's relevance to the rest of Spain was to be found not so much in an expanded population as in its new-found role as a great commercial and financial centre. During the sixteenth century, Cádiz was to witness an influx of merchants and bankers from places as far afield as the Basque Country and Genoa, entrepreneurs who were well aware of the opportunities that awaited across the Atlantic.

MOORS ON THE COAST!

In the time of the Moors, the Guadalquivir River was navigable for more than 160 miles, from the Atlantic Bay north of Cádiz to Sevilla and beyond to Córdoba. Successive centuries saw an escalation of erosion and land-disturbing human activities along the riverbank, primarily in the form of agriculture and construction. By the sixteenth century, Guadalquivir's silting up had become ever more severe, and this process started to disrupt navigation on the river. Owing to the gradual but steady accumulation of silt in its lower reaches, the Guadalquivir was now only able to provide river passage up to Sevilla, whose port, until the sixteenth century, had been the most important in Europe in terms of trade volume. This placed Sevilla in a position of great economic strength, to the point that by 1540 it outranked Antwerp as Europe's financial centre. However, shortly after achieving this prominence as a port, the condition of the river forced Sevilla to forfeit its monopoly on trade with the New World.

In 1503, Sevilla was the first city in Spain to be designated the seat of a Casa de Contratación, or House of Commerce. It was created by Felipe I, king of Spain and emperor of the Holy Roman Empire. Its function was to act as a central trading house and procurement agency for the New World, North Africa and the Canary Islands. This body regulated shipping between both points, and its principal function was to keep a registry of all the goods shipped across the Atlantic and act as arbiter in commercial disputes. The choice of Sevilla as the seat of the Casa de Contratación in 1503 was not an arbitrary decision. Cádiz at that time still ranked as little more than a small, underdeveloped island city. Its port, like most harbours, suffered the disadvantage of lying on the coast, rendering it open to the sea and therefore exposed to hostile navies. In 1530, the authorities of Cádiz received warning of an impending attack by Hayreddin Barbarossa, the notorious Greek pirate and hero of the Ottoman Empire known as Redbeard. Barbarossa was aware of the city's weak coastal defences, especially at a time when the Spanish fleet was anchored in Italy for the coronation of King Carlos I. It was only quick action by the Genoese admiral Andrea Doria, who at the time was in Cádiz assembling provisions, that drove off the corsair and saved the city from being sacked. The port's vulnerability is manifest in the city having to see off no fewer than four major invasions in the space of two hundred years. Ships entering the port of Sevilla, on the other hand, could sail safely up the Guadalquivir River, until its silting up in the mid-1500s, to a protected bay, moreover one with better land communications with the rest of Spain.

With the Guadalquivir River becoming impassable and the consequent slow decline of Sevilla, Cádiz was destined to take over as Spain's primary port of trade with the South American continent, known as the Indias. In 1717, King Felipe V confirmed this historical reality by transferring the Casa de Contratación to Cádiz, which held the title for more than seventy years, until the institution was abolished in 1790. In that year, King Carlos IV replaced it with an all-powerful magistrate to preside over matters of navigation and commerce with the Indias. Meanwhile, the city was to embark on an epoch of frenetic activity that transformed Cádiz into an urban centre of cultural and economic splendour. This was to be the age of grand baroque palaces and the construction of a plethora of the city's distinctive watchtowers.

Despite the massive expansion of Spain's trade with South America, it would be wrong to underestimate the importance of commercial links between Cádiz and North Africa, above all with Morocco. The *corregidor*, or chief magistrate of Cádiz, stated in 1532 that if the trade route between Cádiz and North Africa were to disappear, the city would lose more than two-thirds of its income from duties levied on cargo.

MOORS ON THE COAST!

The flow of trade with Africa had been a reality from the earliest days of the Christian conquest of the Bay of Cádiz and its surrounding ports. In the sixteenth to eighteenth centuries, this relationship became institutionalised, albeit not exclusively restricted to commercial traffic. Spanish privateers would habitually set out from Cádiz on raids across the Strait in search of whatever plunder they could lay their hands on, from gold to slaves.

It was inevitable that word of Cádiz's thriving mercantile activity would spread to other parts of Europe. Spain dominated these routes until the sixteenth century. That was when the English and French decided to grab a share of the treasures from North African markets. Covetous French merchants moved in with a vengeance, transporting mostly North African skins and leather products from Morocco to Marseilles, Rouen and Saint-Malo. Rivalry for Spanish shippers ratcheted up when English shipping companies dispatched fleets to Morocco and other North African destinations. The sixteenth century was to witness English ships making their way to the Bay of Cádiz in a spirit quite different to that of commercial competition. It was a foretaste of things to come. The French harboured similar designs on Cádiz when in the early nineteenth century, a squadron of their ships sailed into the bay. The city was about to put to the test its fame for seeing off attacks from hostile nations on land and water.

4

THE KING OF SPAIN'S BEARD

A unique sight greets the visitor to Cádiz, whether they come by land or sea. It is a spectacle not to be found elsewhere in Spain or, for that matter, in any coastal city of Europe. In the distance, a display of 126 watchtowers can be seen on rooftops across the city's old quarter. With the exception of Torre Tavira, which is open to the public, all the rest belong to private homeowners. These towers, which originally numbered 160, are scattered between the northern and eastern sectors of the historic district.

The watchtowers were once an essential feature atop the dwellings of the city's leading merchants who traded with the Americas, the West Indies and the Philippines. These structures began to dominate the skyline during Cádiz's golden age of the seventeenth and eighteenth centuries, when the city dominated the merchant shipping lanes between mainland Spain and the New World colonies that turned Cádiz into the hub of Atlantic trade. Cargoes of cotton, gold, tropical wood, spices, silk, sugar and tobacco were pouring into the city. The watchtowers were erected to provide a lookout point for merchants to get the first view of their own ships returning to port, as well as looking out for those of competitors among the thousands of ships from across the Atlantic and the Strait of Gibraltar, laden with goods of every description. From the tops of these towers, shipping merchants could use telescopes to spot their vessels while they were still out at sea and coming in to drop anchor in the port. Each tower flew a distinctive pennant of the shipowner, so that the ship's captain could identify the owner's tower. The tower and ship could then communicate with each other using their own individual signal system. The watchtowers in fact served a twofold purpose. In addition to being an observation point, they were also used as a secluded space for business meetings. Most of these towers were built westward facing on top of the grand houses of the mercantile aristocracy, many of which were situated at the entry to the canal leading to the harbour.

The towers were for the most part one- to two-storey rectangular turrets with wood-panelled interior walls. A noted exception is the watchtower in Calle José del Toro, the only one in the city with an octagonal configuration. It is known locally as La Bella Escondida, or the Hidden Beauty, because it cannot be seen from street level. No more watchtowers were built after 1792 when the municipal authorities, doubting their future usefulness, banned any new constructions.

Privateers and Protestants

Had the watchtowers existed a century before the years of the trade boom, they could have detected the advance of a less-welcome sight on its approach to the Bay of Cádiz. From an early date, the civil and military authorities were aware of the need to protect the port against potential enemies covetous of the valuable cargoes being unloaded on an almost daily basis. In 1554, Giovanni Battista Calvi, an Italian military engineer in the service of the Spanish monarchy, was brought to Cádiz to appraise the readiness of its defences. After an initial assessment, Calvi returned three years later and concluded that the bulwarks, escarpments and gun embrasures would have to be reinforced if the city was to successfully see off attacks by sea, which were already posing a menace. The year before Calvi carried out his first study, more than twenty North African galleons had set out from the Moroccan coast to launch an attack on Cádiz. It was sheer good fortune that a storm forced the flotilla to return home empty handed.

At that time the throne was occupied by Felipe II, a monarch who dreamt of exploiting the Spanish Empire to the fullest. The king's father was the Holy Roman Emperor Charles V and king of Spain Carlos I. Felipe came to the throne in a state of inadequacy, desirous of matching the deeds of grandeur that had been achieved by his illustrious father in his forty-year reign. Carlos I had sent the Conquistadors to the New World on a mission of conquest. In little more than two decades, vast territories from Mexico to Bolivia had fallen to Hernán Cortés, Francisco Pizarro and other adventurers.

Felipe saw the colonies as an instrument to enrich the royal coffers and enhance his own standing as the king who made Spain the wealthiest and most powerful nation state in Europe. Cádiz was his chosen vehicle for channelling treasure from the New World colonies into Spain. In 1558, more than 150 years before the Casa de Contratación was officially transferred to Cádiz, while goods were still being forwarded up the Guadalquivir River to Sevilla, Felipe issued a decree authorising ships from the American colonies to unload leathergoods and sugar in Cádiz. Three years later, this royal edict was expanded to include high value items such as gold, silver and pearls.

Meanwhile, tension had been mounting with England in the latter years of Felipe's reign. This was primarily an issue of religious confrontation between rival Catholic and Protestant countries. In 1570, Pope Pius V excommunicated Elizabeth I of England. For his part, fourteen years later Felipe II secretly signed the Treaty of Joinville with the Catholic League, whose purpose was to combat the spread of Lutheranism. Felipe was also incensed by an almost relentless series of attacks by English pirates on Spanish galleons carrying stores of riches on their way home from the West Indies. So infuriated was the Spanish king that he could perceive of no other option than to crush the country that was defying his command of the crucial trade routes between Spain and its colonies. Felipe II summoned his military commanders to the El Escorial Monastery in the hills north of Madrid to plan the invasion of England by a fleet of warships to be known as the Invincible Armada.

The decision to invade England came in 1587, after the execution of Mary Queen of Scots, Spain's Catholic ally, on the orders of her cousin Elizabeth I. This was the final straw for Felipe II in the religious tensions between the two countries. The king had now unequivocally resolved to topple the reign of Elizabeth I and reinstate Catholicism. The conquest of England would also bring to an end attacks by privateers – armed ships that were privately owned but commissioned by the English Crown to attack the ships and colonies of Spain in the Americas during any period of declared hostilities between England and Spain.

Francis Drake and the Invincible Armada

The collective memory of the name 'Drake' and what took place in the port more than 500 years ago never fails to enliven a conversation among the people of Cádiz. 'Her majesty [Elizabeth I], being informed of a mighty preparation by sea begun in Spain for the invasion of England, by good advice of her great and prudent council, thought it expedient to prevent the same.'

THE KING OF SPAIN'S BEARD

Thus relates the sixteenth century writer Richard Hakluyt of the English queen's scheme to send Admiral Sir Francis Drake to destroy the Armada, which was at that moment being put together in Cádiz in preparation for the strike against England. According to Cádiz historian Juan Antonio Fierro Cubiella,

> The Spanish Ambassador to France, Bernardino de Mendoza, conveyed word to Madrid in 1587 of a squadron of English warships anchored off the Isle of Wight. He sent a follow-up report on 12 April, alerting the Spanish authorities that the ships had set sail from Plymouth. But his warnings were not given the attention they merited.[1]

Drake was a talented navigator and a court favourite with Elizabeth I. He had accumulated considerable private riches from privateering on the Spanish Main (those colonies on the mainland of America with a coastline on the Caribbean Sea or the Gulf of Mexico) and used much of the wealth he gained to further finance Elizabeth's conflicts with Felipe II. On one of his early raids, he intercepted a mule train taking silver and gold through Panama, ready to be loaded onto the Spanish ships. The haul was too much for Drake's small galleon, so he abandoned the silver and carried off a fortune in gold. These exploits led to Drake being regarded as a hero adventurer in England and a pirate in Spain. Having viewed the Pacific Ocean for the first time from a vantage point in Panama, Drake led the first English expedition to circumnavigate the globe over a three-year period from December 1577 to 1580. He sailed across the Pacific Ocean, which to that point had been exclusively controlled by Spain, and plundered ships and colonies as he went. He and his men landed on the west coast of North America, in what is now California, claiming the territory for England as New Albion. On his return to England, Queen Elizabeth awarded him a knighthood. This inaugurated a protracted era of Drake being involved in conflict with Spain as he had returned from the Indies with vast quantities of gold and silver looted from Spanish ships. As tensions escalated between the two countries, a state of war was declared in 1585, the Anglo-Spanish War, which continued until 1604. Drake was the obvious candidate to deal with the Spanish Armada as Spain fitted out its warships in Cádiz in preparation for the invasion of England.

Elizabeth I was determined at all costs to sabotage any of Felipe II's attempts to invade England. The queen provided Drake with four Royal Navy warships, an array of twenty smaller armed vessels and a contingent of three thousand men. This war party, tasked with scrutinising Spain's military preparations, intercepting the enemy's supplies and, if possible, attacking the Armada while still in port, was financed by a group of London merchants who would pocket a share of the booty in proportion to their investment. The queen, as commander-in-chief of the Royal Navy, was to receive fifty per cent of the takings.

A week after Drake sailed from Plymouth in April 1587, Elizabeth felt the need for a change of strategy and conveyed a counterorder to Drake to call off any hostilities against Spanish ships or ports. This never reached Drake's hands, as the ship bearing the message was hit by gale-force winds and forced to return home. It is possible that Elizabeth did not fully intend the message to reach Drake but was providing herself with some political cover of plausible deniability. On his voyage around Spain's northern coast, Drake encountered two Dutch ships off Galicia, whose officers confirmed that the Spanish Armada was indeed anchored in the Bay of Cádiz. The Spanish fleet was made up of roughly 150 ships and 18,000 men. It was at the time the largest flotilla ever seen in Europe. Felipe's ships were making final preparations to weigh anchor and put out to sea. Destination: England.

Armed with the inside information from the Dutch officers, Drake and his crews hurried south to Cádiz, determined to keep the element of surprise on their side. No sooner had the enemy been spotted lurking at the entrance to the port, Cádiz's chief civilian official Juan de Vega transmitted an urgent appeal for help to Alonso Pérez de Guzmán, the Duke of Medina Sidonia, who was in command of the Armada. Guzmán made haste to Cádiz that same night, determined to repel the English onslaught. He sent whatever ships were already outfitted for battle to engage Drake's fleet, but these were forced to retreat in the face of superior firepower. The port's artillery batteries began shelling the invaders, but again, they were able to inflict only relatively little damage on the heavily armoured Royal Navy galleons.

Drake entered the Bay of Cádiz on the evening of 19 April 1587. He lost no time in letting loose a cannonade on the Spanish ships and the city's shore defences. An exchange of fire ensued throughout the night without a let-up, and the barrage continued for the next twenty-four hours. The outcome was almost a foregone conclusion. The English ships were longer, lower and faster than their Spanish rivals. The decks fore and aft had been lowered to give greater stability and this meant more guns could be carried to fire lethal broadsides. Drake's ships were also more manoeuvrable than the heavy Spanish vessels.

The English squadron began to withdraw at dawn, leaving in its wake approximately twenty or more sunken and out-of-commission Spanish galleons. The Bay of Cádiz had been turned into a graveyard of Spanish ships, an achievement that inspired Drake to pompously proclaim, 'I have singed the beard of the King of Spain!'

Drake's mission could at best be defined as a delaying action. The Armada had been dealt a serious, albeit not fatal, blow. It would be necessary to push back the planned invasion of England by little more than a year, though given the final outcome of the venture, Felipe II could well have saved himself the trouble and expense of rebuilding his taskforce. Once the Invincible

Armada had reached enemy territory in July 1588, they faced a heavy attack from defending English ships which then effectively blocked the Channel, cutting off the Armada's escape route back into the Atlantic and south to Spain. The Spanish ships were forced to sail north around Scotland and then the west coast of Ireland, where they encountered heavy storms. Through the English attacks and the havoc of the storms, of the 150 vessels that set out, only sixty-five returned. The following year, Felipe dispatched another smaller fleet of about a hundred ships. This too ran into stormy weather off Cornwall and was forced back to Spain by ferocious winds.

The capture of Cádiz

It is true that Spain was still the greatest power in Europe in the late sixteenth century, yet the naval defeats against England had aroused a deep ignominy. More so when the English took the decision, two years before Felipe II's death in 1598, to exploit the enemy's perceived weakness and send out an invasion that would once again see English warships descend on Cádiz.

Drake's destruction of Armada vessels that Felipe II had deemed to be invincible, along with the final disaster of his fleet at sea, sent the king into a deep depression that lasted seven years. Then in 1595, when Felipe was approaching his seventieth birthday, he came to the realisation that to salvage his reputation in history, he would need to achieve victory in the intermittent and undeclared Anglo-Spanish War.[2] To this end, the king devised a plan to assemble a second grand armada for a strike at England. Unbeknownst to the people of Cádiz, their city was to once again become a battleground for the two great seafaring powers of Europe.

The English had already agreed to a military coalition with the Dutch, who were eager to join forces with an ally who would support the revolt to free themselves from Spanish dominion. The Netherlands was under the rule of the Spanish branch of the Habsburg dynasty from 1556 to 1714. By June 1596, an English-Dutch force of more than a hundred warships, under the command of Admiral Charles Howard, 1st Earl of Nottingham, and General Robert de Devereux, 2nd Earl of Essex, was ready to embark on its mission. The fleet was joined by another twenty ships from the United Provinces, led by Admiral John de Duyvenvoorde, which were put under English orders.

The allies had initially set out for Lisbon intending to sink the Spanish Armada that was being fitted out in the Portuguese shipyards. This was to be a direct assault on Felipe II since Portugal, from 1580 to 1640, belonged to the Spanish Crown. A radical change in strategy came once word reached Howard that the Spanish galleons from the Indies had arrived and were anchored at Cádiz. Lisbon could wait, for here was a prize too tempting to ignore. It was an opportunity to capture great quantities of treasure bound for the Spanish Crown. It also presented an opportunity to sack and destroy Cádiz itself, thus wiping off the map Spain's principal trade link with the New World colonies.

The alarm went up in Cádiz on 30 June 1596, when a taskforce of between 157 and 160 English-Dutch ships were sighted approaching the bay. There at first reigned a state of confusion and disbelief. The people of Cádiz awoke to a horizon of sails some 3 miles out to sea. Guided more by wishful thinking than the obvious reality, many believed this to be the gathering of clouds of an approaching storm. In that sense, they were closer to the truth, though this was to be a tempest unlike anything the city had ever witnessed. That morning, General Devereux sent several units out in longboats to attempt a landing on the Caleta de Santa Catalina beach. Fortune was on the side of the defenders that day. The raiding party was taken by surprise when they met with a shoreline too hostile to dock safely. The soldiers were forced to beat a hasty retreat to their ships.

Cádiz had marshalled a defence force of seven companies of infantry, three of which were local units and the rest composed of fighters raised from the Basque Country, along with foreigners resident in the city. Several neighbouring towns brought in infantry and cavalry reinforcements to engage in what was shaping up as a battle to decide the city's survival. Historian Juan Antonio Fierro Cubiella states:

> The Spanish sea defence consisted of four Armada galleons, which were fortuitously passing through the bay en-route to Lisbon, where they were to form part of the second Armada. They were joined by three frigates and eighteen galeras, which were normally deployed as coastal defence vessels.[3]

Devereux himself now led a landing party of thirty skiffs carrying one thousand men armed with muskets, arquebuses and pikes. They made their way toward the Castle of San Lorenzo on the Puntal bulwark at the tip of the bay. Early in the assault, cannons on Devereux's ships had put the fortification out of action. They met with no resistance when Devereux alighted from his boat to raise the English standard on the still-smoking rocky promontory.

Cádiz had been able to muster only five hundred foot soldiers and another three hundred cavalrymen to confront the invaders. Most of the defenders were raw recruits lacking in battle experience and without a strong chief commander to guide them. Resistance was hopeless: the defenders fell back, leaving the city open to inevitable pillage. On the night of 1 July, Howard gave the order to commence the sacking of Cádiz.

The population of Cádiz at this period was around 6,000 and that day saw the start of the exodus of many citizens, the poorest on foot, while women, clergy and nobility escaped by sea. What was left of the Spanish defence force set fire to the galleons of the Indies fleet to save it from falling into enemy hands. The blaze lasted three days before the last of the ships had sunk beneath the waves.

Howard liberated the upper classes of a sizeable quantity of booty, mostly silver and gold jewellery, paintings and Oriental carpets. The foot soldiers made off with whatever they could loot. Some members of the city's nobility who had locked themselves in stately homes, surrendered the following day and were obliged to pay an exorbitant ransom in exchange for their freedom. At four o'clock that afternoon, those who had been taken prisoner were freed. These included priests, nuns and several aristocrats disguised as clergymen. The English then crossed the isthmus to sack the hunting lodges and wineries on the Isla de León.

Ineffectual resistance carried on for almost a fortnight. The sporadic hostilities were given scant attention by invaders, who busied themselves organising victory festivities. Two weeks after the landing, the English went about confiscating church bells and holy images that had survived, loading them on the ships preparing to depart.

On 16 July, leaving behind the remains of the cathedral and several convents that had been reduced to ashes, Howard's fleet weighed anchor and sailed from the Bay of Cádiz. The city authorities had refused to pay a 120,000-ducat ransom, a sizeable fortune equivalent to around £14 million today. This unleashed a wave of destruction, and several hostages were taken and sent off to English prisons, where they lingered until an undisclosed ransom was finally paid in 1603. As Fierro Cubiella points out, 'The devastation was such that it marked a before and after in the history of Cádiz. The losses were colossal and included manuscripts, property, stately homes and more. This episode cast doubt on the security of the Spanish Empire in general.'[4] The destruction was immense; very few buildings in today's Old

Town date from before 1600. Along with the cathedral and major churches, at least 120 homes were totally destroyed and hundreds more seriously damaged by fire.

Rebuilding the city

'The 1596 attack and sacking of Cádiz marked a milestone in the city's history and, in particular, its urban morphology,' says historian Manuel Bustos Rodríguez. 'Following on from this tragic episode, a considerable number of inhabitants abandoned the city, parts of which had vanished in the flames, while almost all historical buildings had suffered major damage. A survey revealed that a quarter of all homes had been torched, along with some notable monuments, like the cathedral, of which only the pillars remained intact.'[5]

The municipal authorities were in despair, to the point that a debate arose on whether to rebuild what was left of the city on its original site or move it to another location offering greater security from attack. There was a proposal to abandon Cádiz and move what remained of its population to Matagorda or Puerto de Santa María. In the end, this idea was abandoned in favour of fortifying the city's defences against any future attack. Felipe II and, after the monarch's death in 1598, his heir Felipe III granted Cádiz an exemption from paying taxes to the Crown to help the city rebuild its shattered infrastructure and defences and encourage the return of the many emigrants who had fled during and after the English-Dutch invasion. Felipe III further assisted the city by assigning his top military engineer, Cristóbal de Rojas, the task of refortifying Cádiz. Rojas carried out an inspection of the walls and other fortifications, which he declared defective but in reasonably sound condition, and thus could undergo repair work rather than having to build anew. In 1598 repair work had begun on Santa Catalina Castle, a crucial piece in the defence of La Caleta, the exposed beach abutting the harbour. The island of San Sebastián, opposite La Caleta, was endowed with a watchtower that also served as a lighthouse to guide friendly traffic into port. In 1602, work got underway on the cathedral. This was followed by the reconstruction of the Santa María Convent and the Church of San Francisco, both emblematic structures that today adorn the city's landscape. The rebuilding work continued as the palaces of the nobility, monasteries, convents and merchants' townhouses, along with tenements for the poor, were rebuilt from the ruins or newly constructed. It took many years to restore Cádiz to a recognisable semblance of its former status, an ambitious project that lasted throughout most of the seventeenth century.

The English plundering and bombardment of Cádiz had caused such a sense of outrage in Spain that it eventually inspired the pen of the sixteenth century novelist Miguel de Cervantes. The author of *Don Quixote* wrote a book of novellas called *The Exemplary Novels*, one of which was 'The Spanish English Lady'. It tells the story of the tribulations of Isabel, a seven-year-old girl from Cádiz who is kidnapped in 1596 by an English naval commander named Clotald and taken to London to live with his family. The popularity of this tale has transcended to the present day, as evidenced in the popular 2015 Spanish TV documentary based on the abduction of Isabel.

The All Saints' Day attack

Cádiz would not have to wait long to put its newly constructed fortifications to the test. Little over a quarter of a century after the terrible bombardment and sacking of Cádiz by the English and Dutch, the enemy was back in force. The beginning of the seventeenth century found Cádiz in a state of alarm over the threat of a reprise from English combat vessels, exacerbated by concerns over the city's readiness to see off a second assault. Meanwhile, Spain and the rebellious Dutch Provinces had signed a twelve-year peace treaty in 1609. This agreement was summarily consigned to the dustbin shortly after its expiry date, igniting a renewal of hostilities between the belligerent powers.

The Dutch once again found a willing ally in England, as rapacious as ever to lay its hands on the flow of mercantile trade with the New World. The Duke of Buckingham, a minister strongly in favour of war with Spain and France, appointed Sir Edward Cecil commander of the expedition that counted one hundred warships, albeit mainly merchant vessels that had been conscripted and converted for combat. As the war party was soon to find out, Cecil was a battle-hardened soldier but with scant experience in maritime warfare. The English-Dutch fleet set sail from Plymouth Sound in October 1625 with Cádiz in its sights. It was a logical target, for this was where the New World convoy was docked, with only fourteen galleons and a handful of small open galleys to defend the harbour.

The bombardment commenced in the early hours of 1 November, while people were preparing to attend All Saints' Day Mass in the cathedral that had been rebuilt after its destruction in the 1596 invasion. This time the Spanish had the foresight to position their ships out of range of the enemy's cannons. In fact, it mattered little since Cecil's taskforce had been battered and delayed by Atlantic storms on the voyage. By the time they managed to reach the Bay of Cádiz, the Spanish treasure fleet had long since set sail for the West Indies, following a calmer southerly route.

Cecil initially had better luck with his land assault. His men put ashore at El Puntal fort, where they met with stiff resistance from the defenders. After a touch-and-go clash, with no clear outcome in sight, the English-Dutch formation managed to capture the fort that stood guard over the harbour. It was a pyrrhic victory, for El Puntal did not form a strategic part of the city's defence system.

Having gained a foothold, Cecil sent some ten thousand fighters ashore. This was another tactical error, which saved the city. The soldiers were split into two columns, the main contingent led by Cecil himself. He marched 1,500 men across Puente Zuazo, the bridge that crosses the Caño de Sancti Petri waterway to the San Fernando mainland and the scene of several major battles, past and future. The second column made straight for the urban centre. Valuable lessons had been learned from Howard's invasion and ruthless sacking of the city. Cádiz had constructed a robust defence network of walls and gun emplacements, from which the Spanish were able to repel the attacking forces. After taking heavy losses, Cecil and his men were left with no choice but to beat a hasty retreat to their ships.

Unlike the 1596 invasion, this bid to capture the Spanish fleet turned into a total fiasco. El Puntal fort had been temporarily taken, and the English and Dutch had set ablaze various fisheries, farmhouses and wineries on the Isla de León, by all accounts polishing off every bottle in sight, to the fury of senior officers. Yet the Spanish fleet escaped intact, while Cecil lost a large quantity of ships and troops. Cádiz's successful resistance was in no small measure achieved thanks to the skilful strategy of the city's governor general, Fernando Girón de Salcedo y Briviesca, a person with ample military experience, having served as head of the army and member of the Supreme War Council. After seeing off the English-Dutch expedition, Girón de Salcedo was immortalised by Francisco de Zurbarán in a portrait appropriately titled *The Defence of Cádiz Against the English*, on display in Madrid's Prado Museum.

CÁDIZ

Battle for the Caribbean

Cecil's failed 1625 invasion was a single episode in a broader conflict that came to be known as the Thirty Years War of 1618–48. This first great European conflict was in essence a political confrontation fought mainly between Protestant and Catholic factions. The ultimate victory went to the French and their Belgian and Scandinavian allies. Spain, which had formed an alliance with Germany and Austria, came out the clear loser and was forced to recognise the independence of the Low Countries. Worse still, the Spanish Empire for a time seemed to teeter on collapse. Madrid was losing its grip on Portugal, which finally gained independence in 1668. Spain emerged from the war in a severely weakened military and economic position, having lost its hegemony in Europe.

Despite the broader European hostilities, Cádiz itself had not been subject to direct enemy attack for thirty years, since Cecil's failed 1625 assault. But the weakening of Spanish power encouraged the English to think again about targeting the city that was the gateway to the wealth of the Spanish colonies. With their gaze ever fixed on Spain's lucrative South American trade, the English wasted little time in exploiting their long-standing enemy's vulnerability. In August 1654, the Lord Protector Oliver Cromwell hatched a plan to invade the Spanish colony of Santo Domingo in the Caribbean. Cromwell's idea was to use the port as a launch pad for the conquest of other Spanish possessions in the region. Spain's ambassador in London, Alonso de Cárdenas, got word of this scheme and alerted Madrid to the imminent danger to its Caribbean possession. King Felipe IV cavalierly brushed aside the threat, convinced that England would not make a move without first issuing a formal declaration of war. How wrong his judgement would prove to be.

THE KING OF SPAIN'S BEARD

The English squadron that sailed from Portsmouth was made up of thirty-four galleons and transport vessels, carrying thirteen thousand sailors and troops under Admiral William Penn, with General Robert Venables in command of the fighting force. The mission was to be an outstanding failure, beaten back by a lack of proper armaments and a scarcity of provisions, in particular clean drinking water. The siege of Santo Domingo (Hispaniola) was a week-long battle fought in April 1655. A force of 2,400 Spanish troops led by Governor Don Bernardino Meneses y Bracamonte successfully resisted the attack. After a handful of skirmishes, the English weighed anchor on 14 May and beat a hasty retreat home.

That same month, an emboldened Felipe IV sent Cromwell a memo stating that by royal decree, the English were prohibited from carrying on any commercial activities in the West Indies. Cromwell was not impressed by this diktat: two months later the English raided the islands of Hispaniola and Jamaica. The English remained as desirous as ever of the silver and gold bullion the enemy was sending home to Spain from its South American colonies. The English failed in their attempt to take Hispaniola, after which they invaded and occupied Jamaica and in doing so, started a five-year conflict with Spain in the West Indies, one that was replicated in Europe. Shortly after this brazen strike, Oliver Cromwell formally declared war on Spain in 1655 while forging an alliance with France, a coalition that in the coming years would cause Cádiz considerable anguish.

While Cromwell's Caribbean adventure was underway, a second prong of attack was aimed directly at Spain. Twenty-three warships with Admiral Robert Blake and Vice-Admiral Richard Stayner in charge spent the winter months moored off the coast of Andalucía, lying in wait for the Spanish West Indies fleet's return to Cádiz. There they lay until April 1655 when Blake ordered his squadron to make for the city and blockade the bay. The captains of the Spanish galleons had been forewarned of the threat awaiting in Cádiz and took the decision to wait out the winter docked in the Caribbean. Frustrated by the enemy's delayed arrival, in September Blake sailed to Lisbon to stock up on provisions.

On the evening of 8 September, the Spanish treasure ships were finally spotted some 12 miles off the coast. As the convoy drew near to the Bay of Cádiz, Stayner ordered his sixty-four cannons to open fire on a galleon commanded by Vice-Admiral Juan de Hoyos. The vessel was captured, with its cargo of 45 tons of silver and 1,400 chests of highly prized indigo dye and sugar. The only Spanish vessel to escape the carnage was a twenty-six-cannon galleon, which Admiral Marcos del Puerto, its captain, was able to bring safely into Cádiz port. The capture of these cargoes struck a devastating blow to Spain's already debilitated economy, which lost treasure valued at close to £100 million in current monetary value.

With the temporary disruption of trade between Cádiz and the Spanish colonies and their pockets filled with booty, the English raiders had accomplished their purpose. Blake and Stayner were able to set sail for home, holds packed with precious metals and other valuable goods. On this occasion, Cádiz was spared the ordeal of bombardment and was now free to turn its attention to desperately needed urban renewal, which would be funded by profits from the still lucrative flow of goods from the Indies.

The reconstruction of Cádiz ignited a spirit of renewed confidence among its citizenry. The seventeenth century witnessed a spectacular growth in demographics: from a population of 7,000 in 1600 to 41,000 by the end of the century. In 1647, an outbreak of bubonic plague brought in from North Africa checked this growth, but fortunately for the people of Cádiz, it had a less devastating effect on their city than in other parts of Andalucía. In Sevilla, the epidemic carried off nearly half the city's population. Another spate of plague swept across southern Spain in 1679. This time, in Cádiz people chained themselves together to pray to the saints for salvation. This, the pious would afterwards proclaim, explained the plague's rapid and relatively mild passage through the city.

The War of the Spanish Succession

Two centuries of Habsburg inbreeding came home to roost in 1700 when the incapacitated Spanish monarch Carlos II succumbed to an agonising death, tormented by physical and mental afflictions, an event that touched off an international conflict over rival claims to the throne of Spain. The Bourbons, one of the most powerful dynasties in Europe, were descended from a younger son of King Louis IX of France and had become rulers of France in 1589. Always keen to extend their hegemony in Europe they had been sharpening their knives ever since it became apparent that the king, who could scarcely stand erect or utter an intelligible word, was incapable of producing an heir. It was clear that rival claims to the Spanish Crown would soon become the *casus belli* for a general European conflagration in what became the War of the Spanish Succession, fought between 1701 and 1714.

The European battlefields stretched from Italy and Flanders, but the fighting also extended to Spain's colonial possessions in the Indies. It was inevitable that Cádiz would be dragged into the theatre of war. In late August 1702, an English-Dutch war party once again made its appearance off the coast of Cádiz. Admiral Sir George Rooke was in charge of a massive allied force of 207 ships and 14,000 armed men. The port's capture was crucial to Rooke's strategy. Not only would this help to sever Spain's links with the Indies, but it would also provide the allies with a base from which the English-Dutch fleets could control the Western

Mediterranean Sea. What Rooke did not take into account was the city's strongly fortified defences put in place after previous raids and sackings. The two main forts of El Puntal and Matagorda blocked any hope of landing troops on the beaches. Failing to make an inroad in the assault on Cádiz itself, Rooke turned his guns on nearby Rota, El Puerto de Santa María and Puerto Real. He reasoned that once these towns had been taken, Cádiz would be left without food or supplies and be forced to surrender.

Francisco Castillo Fajardo, 2nd Marquis of Villadarias, who was in charge of Cádiz's defence, could muster in the field five or six hundred horsemen and a corps of several thousand militia. To further bolster his position, Villadarias secured the harbour by drawing a strong boom and sinking two large hulks across its entrance. The English-Dutch raid was doomed to failure. Twenty-five landing craft were destroyed by a Spanish battery. In a furious few hours of fighting, Rooke's troops, having moved a battery near the stronghold, were within firing range of the enemy vessels lying in wait behind the boom. The Franco-Spanish ships were now an easy target for the galleys outside the harbour, poised to strike.

Villadarias, with fewer than five hundred men under his command, held off the invaders for almost a month. Matagorda Fort, which was one of Rooke's prime objectives, held out tenaciously. After several days of shelling, Rooke made clear to his officers that even if Matagorda was taken, the other stronghold guarding the Puntales entrance would make it impossible for the fleet to navigate the narrow passage. Facing the prospect of high losses and almost certain failure, in late September the decision was taken to re-embark the troops and set sail. The attempt to seize Cádiz had ended in abject failure.

During the eighteenth century there was a huge increase in maritime trade with the Americas, and Cádiz was poised to reap the benefits. Felipe V formally transferred the Contract House of the West Indies Board to Cádiz in 1717, meaning that the city was the main European port for the Americas trade. Trade routes led from Cádiz to Havana in Cuba, Puerto Rico, and Rio de la Plata in Argentina, creating the city's 'golden age'. As well as being the centre for trade, Cádiz in the eighteenth century remained the launch city for voyages of exploration, as it had been in the time of Columbus. One of the most ambitious was the Malaspina expedition (1789–1794), led by the Spanish naval officer Alessandro Malaspina, with José de Bustamante y Guerra as second in command. The expedition was commissioned by the Spanish government to carry out a scientific survey of the geography, flora and fauna of the Spanish colonies. It had the enthusiastic support of King Carlos III, who was deeply interested in botany, science and technology, but tragically he did not live to see the results as he died four months before the expedition was ready to sail. Two frigates, *Descubierta* (discovery) and *Atrevida* (daring) were specially built in the shipyards of San Fernando on the southern side of the harbour, and the expedition set sail from Cádiz on 30 July 1789. After a short stop in the Canary Islands, the ships sailed across the Atlantic and then down the coast of Argentina. They rounded Cape Horn and then sailed all the way up the western coast of South and North America, then across the Pacific Ocean to the Philippines, China, Australia and New Zealand before returning to Spain in a voyage that took five years in all. Leading Spanish scientists of the day were in the expedition company, making detailed observations of the land, as well as astronomical observations and collecting hundreds of animal and plant samples as they went, and artists recorded the places and peoples encountered on the voyage. The expedition surpassed the specimens collected by Captain Cook on his voyages in the same era, but sadly very little was shared or published from the expedition. On his return to Spain in 1794, Malaspina joined a conspiracy to overthrow the government and was jailed. The expedition's reports and specimens were put away and were not rediscovered and disseminated until a hundred years later, at the end of the nineteenth century.

Merchants and explorers from all over the Iberian Peninsula and the rest of Europe established themselves in the city, creating a vibrant cosmopolitan culture. Cádiz was considered one of the most important and advanced cities in Spain. It was known as the 'Global Emporium', where people and goods hailing from all four corners of the world crossed paths on their way to new destinations, with thirteen maritime insurance companies, eighty shipping lines and over 600 merchant houses.

The merchants built themselves fine three- and four-storey houses in the major streets and squares of the Old Town, with their watchtowers looking out to sea, which defined the urban landscape. Many of these survive and give the city its air of elegance. The architecture of the merchant houses was designed to suit the commercial purpose, as well as to provide spacious, well-appointed quarters for the wealthy merchants and their families. On the ground floor there was typically a large patio, surrounded by storage space for the merchant's imported wares and an office for the clerks employed to check goods in and out. On the first floor, high-ceilinged rooms with large windows and balconies onto the street would provide space for the merchant's main business rooms and reception areas for guests. The family rooms would also be on this level in a three-storey house, although these would be one floor up in a grander, four storey house. The top floor, with lower ceilings and much smaller rooms, provided the quarters for the domestic servants and warehouse clerks, and above these there was usually a large roof terrace in which the watchtower would sit. These watchtowers, so vital for spotting invading armies off the coast, could do little to prepare the population of this battle-hardened city for the next threat heading its way.

THE KING OF SPAIN'S BEARD

The morning of 1 November 1755 marked 130 years to the day since Edward Cecil's English-Dutch invasion force had landed ten thousand soldiers in Cádiz. Now the city's streets echoed with the cries of terrified people, rushing about in a panic to find shelter from the buildings crumbling about them. Lisbon had been struck by an earthquake, now estimated as having a magnitude of between 8.5 and 9.0. The natural disaster in the Portuguese capital produced a tsunami that swept across the entire Atlantic coast of the Iberian Peninsula.

Cádiz, nearly 400 miles to the southeast, was hit by waves up to 50 feet high. The city walls saved most of the urban area from mass destruction, apart from some of the low-lying neighbourhoods whose streets were submerged under the water. The coastal barrio de la Viña, roughly equidistant between the Santa Catalina Castle and the cathedral, took the worst of it. A celebrated tale dear to the hearts of many people is that of two priests, Bernardo de Cádiz and Francisco Macías, who rushed into the streets bearing the crucifix from the altar of the Church of Nuestra Señora de la Palma. Father Macías raised the cross to the sky and cried out in the face of the oncoming floodwaters, 'This far and no more, Holy Mother of God!' At that moment there occurred a miracle, when Our Lady of La Palma abruptly halted the oncoming whitecaps, thus avoiding what would have turned into an enormous tragedy. A memorial to the two clergymen is today on display in the church.[6] Whether by chance or divine intervention, the historical records state that the flooding did indeed come to a standstill precisely when it reached the far edge of the barrio de la Viña.

In an attempt to save lives, the city authorities issued an emergency order to halt any persons attempting to flee to the mainland along the isthmus. The gates were locked shut, a step that by all accounts prevented mass drownings of the hordes who otherwise would have perished in the surging tide. Word soon spread that the isthmus that connects the city centre to the Isla de León had been cut off. The loss of this escape route from the bay area triggered a state of chaos that saw hundreds rushing to force their way past the soldiers sent to stand guard at the gates. Several people drowned in their attempt to flee, while those who remained lit torches to find their way through the darkened streets. That night, Cádiz was hit by more huge surges caused by the aftershocks of the Lisbon quake. Given the devastation this natural disaster had wreaked and Cádiz's proximity to the epicentre, the final death toll was surprisingly low: an estimated two hundred people perished in Cádiz, less than sixteen per cent of those who died throughout the rest of Spain.

The Battle of Trafalgar

Spain and France signed the Treaty of San Ildefonso in 1796, a pact that aimed to challenge the mounting power of Britain and its incursion on Spain's monopoly of colonial trade. This opened hostilities between the two allies and the court of George III that in 1797 sparked a sea battle off Portugal's Cape of San Vicente, culminating in a resounding defeat of the Spanish Navy. Five years after this setback, Spain's newly reinstated Secretary of State Manuel Godoy failed in his attempt to entice Russia, Sweden and Portugal to join the anti-British coalition. Instead, he threw his support behind Napoleon Bonaparte's scheme to invade England. The Franco-Spanish tactic was to trick the British fleet with a simulated attack on the British Antilles.[7] They believed this ruse would divert the enemy ships from the English coast, leaving it undefended. London did not fall for the ploy. The bulk of the Royal Navy remained anchored close to home. On its return to Europe, the French and Spanish fleet then took the decision to sail to Cádiz.

THE KING OF SPAIN'S BEARD

Cape Trafalgar lies only 30 nautical miles south of Cádiz. It was at this rocky headland that Napoleon's dream of conquering Britain was to unravel. Cádiz enjoyed a brief period of peace from the 1797 clash with the British navy until 1803. The city's economy began a gradual recovery from the costly disruption of its colonial trade, while thought was given to further urban development and continuing work on the New Cathedral, which although commenced in 1722 had halted for lack of funds.

The city barely had time to heave a sigh of relief when news arrived that the British had captured four Spanish frigates on their way from the Indies to Cádiz. Escorted to Plymouth, the ships' cargo was confiscated by their captors. Spain responded by declaring a state of war and in short order, British warships set out to block the port of Cádiz. On 7 October, a fleet of forty ships of the line and frigates under the joint command of Pierre-Charles Villeneuve and Federico Gravina (who later died in Cádiz from wounds sustained in battle) set out to engage Admiral Horatio Nelson's fleet, anchored near the Cádiz coast. They were acting on orders from Napoleon, who had recently crowned himself emperor. It was an unwise decision on Napoleon's part, for the French and Spanish found it almost impossible to navigate the sea in the face of a raging storm. It was then that Nelson proclaimed his famous war cry, 'England expects that every man will do his duty', and so it was.

'Like the proverbial lamb, Spain went willingly to the slaughter as France's ally,' says historian Mark Williams. 'The executioner was none other than Lord Nelson, who himself was killed in the engagement. The British fleet met a French-Spanish navy off Cape Trafalgar on 21 October 1805, in one of history's most decisive battles.'[8]

The Franco-Spanish fleet was decimated by the loss of twenty-two ships, with nearly seven thousand men killed and wounded and a similar number taken prisoner by the British.

Trafalgar ranks as one of those decisive military engagements, like the Battle of the Somme and Battle of Stalingrad, that engendered an outpouring of literary narratives. In Spain, the most popular accounts take the form of historical fiction. The late-nineteenth century novelist of the realism school, Benito Pérez Galdós, published a series of forty-six *Episodios Nacionales*, stories covering events in Spain from 1805 to 1880. *Trafalgar*, published in 1873, was the first of this series of episodes. The narrative is written from the first-person perspective of a young man, Gabriel, who is taken into service by an elderly ship's captain and his wife. They head to Cádiz in October 1805 to lend their experience in the inevitable clash with Nelson and they take Gabriel with them. During the battle, Gabriel and his masters are on board *Santísima Trinidad*, the largest vessel at Trafalgar, a four-deck behemoth with 140 guns.

To mark the Trafalgar bicentennial, in 2005 Spain's most widely read historical novelist, Arturo Pérez-Reverte, published an account of the battle from the viewpoint of a Spanish sailor, a peasant dragged from a tavern to confront the British navy, with no training, scared rigid, yet acutely aware of the craven inadequacy of his commanders. *Cabo Trafalgar* is written in a corrosive below-decks Spanish argot that exudes the tragedy Spain suffered on the day that signalled a turning point in European power relations.

No one in Cádiz would have dared to imagine that in less than three years after the Trafalgar debacle, the victorious British fleet standing at the port would be welcomed as a blessing in disguise. In March 1808, the alliance with France executed a cartwheel when Napoleon invaded Spain. With supreme chicanery, the French emperor had manipulated the Treaty of Fontainebleau between both powers, by which France was granted free rein to annex Portugal. It was an excuse for Napoleon to deploy his army in Spanish territory. The Peninsular War had begun, a seven-year struggle to oust the French from Spain and Portugal. Three days after the invasion, King Fernando VII dispatched his military aide, the Count of Teba, to Cádiz to persuade the city to join the general uprising against the French emperor's invasion force.

5

1812 AND ALL THAT

One spring morning in 1561 King Felipe II of Spain, with several thousand court attendants and troops travelling in company, climbed into his royal carriage in Toledo to embark on a historic journey north to Madrid. The dour Habsburg monarch, though he never issued an official proclamation, had often expressed a desire to turn his back on the grandeur of Spain's imperial city of Toledo. But how odd that he should wish to move his capital to what had erstwhile been a small Moorish fortress perched on the uplands of the vast Castilian plateau.

The motive for Felipe's decision left people scratching their heads in bewilderment. The monarch did not feel compelled to address the speculation regarding his momentous decision. There were those who reasoned that Felipe was anxious to distance himself from the omnipresence of the Church and the nobility. Others pointed to the fact that Madrid offered an abundance of water, which was falling into short supply for Toledo's expanding population. Still others were convinced that Felipe wished to reside closer to his beloved sanctuary, the El Escorial Monastery, which he was having built in the hills a half-day carriage ride from Madrid. Be that as it may, Madrid now bore the uninterrupted title of capital of the Spanish Empire from that day forward – with two exceptions.

In 1601, the court was once again on the move. Felipe II's heir to the throne, Felipe III, was persuaded by the all-powerful Duke of Lerma to set up his capital to the northern Castilian city of Valladolid. Lerma, a cunning property speculator, had purchased and renovated numerous residences in Valladolid with the aim of attracting the king to the newly smartened and gentrified city. Once his task had been accomplished, the duke began acquiring properties in Madrid's now depressed real estate market. The wily Lerma later sold these holdings at enormous profit when Felipe was persuaded that Madrid, after all, was a more prestigious and practical location for his kingdom.

Two centuries later, after the War of the Spanish Succession ended with Spain's loss of several European territories, Felipe V was installed on the throne. The new monarch was determined to centralise his kingdom into one sovereign unit and also ensure that the country's American possessions remained in Spanish hands. It made geographic as well as commercial sense to relocate the main state bodies in charge of transatlantic commerce from Sevilla, which lay 75 miles inland from the port of Cádiz. Cádiz's star had been in the ascendant since the early eighteenth century. The Casa de Contratación de las Indias had been moved from Sevilla to Cádiz in 1717, as had the Real Consulado de Indias (Royal Consulate of the Indies), which had been founded in 1543 by the Habsburg Emperor Charles V to safeguard Spain's monopoly on transatlantic trade. It was therefore not by coincidence that Cádiz should be recognised as the de facto seat of government during the Napoleonic invasion.

1812 AND ALL THAT

The Peninsular War begins

These were some of the most turbulent years in Spain's history. Between 1808 and 1814, the country was engulfed in internal political and military turmoil as well as conflicts with foreign powers. In this stormy period, a group of progressive politicians, intellectuals and military commanders fought to bring about a unified nation under Spanish leadership. These patriots unfurled the banner of freedom of the press and universal suffrage (for males), along with a radical programme of social and economic reform based on egalitarian beliefs. These principles were set forth in 1810 by an assembly of representatives from across Spain and the American colonies, who gathered in Cádiz.

It was thanks to a series of misdeeds and mishaps by future King Fernando VII that Cádiz became the protagonist of Spain's struggle to throw off the shackles of French occupation. In 1807, as crown prince, Fernando had attempted a coup d'état against his father, King Carlos IV. Having been kept out of government, Fernando sought assistance from Napoleon, who at that time was concocting his own designs on Spain. The crown prince was arrested and later acquitted. Nevertheless, the stain remained etched in people's memories, especially the liberal elements in society whose trepidations were to be borne out by later events. Carlos IV had appointed as his first minister Manuel Godoy, a scheming 24-year-old cavalry officer, who lost no time in taking as his mistress no lesser a personage than the monarch's wife María Luisa. Godoy's ambitions stretched beyond Spain's borders, in this case to neighbouring Portugal. He persuaded Carlos to grant French Emperor Napoleon's army safe passage through Spain, with the objective of invading Portugal and splitting the country into three sectors, one of which would be administered by Godoy himself. Napoleon was outraged by Portugal's refusal to honour his decree prohibiting commercial exchange with Britain throughout continental Europe after the emperor's disastrous 1806 attempt to invade England.

Godoy and the king had failed to foresee Napoleon's true intentions in sending his army across the Pyrenees in 1808. Once Portugal had fallen to the emperor's army, to the vexation of the Spanish, French troops continued to pour across the Pyrenees. Burgos, Pamplona, Barcelona and other strategic cities fell to the invaders.

By March of that year Napoleon's troops had taken Madrid, and the emperor was waging a war to bring the rest of Spain under French occupation. The outcome for Godoy could not have been more ignominious. The disgraced politician spent two days in hiding, rolled up in a blanket to shield himself from an outraged citizenry. Carlos did the 'decent thing' by abdicating in favour of his son, now King Fernando VII, albeit Carlos, along with many Spaniards, would come to regret his decision.

On 19 March, Fernando journeyed from the royal residence of Aranjuez, 35 miles south of Madrid, to the capital to attend what he assumed would be the coronation ceremony. Instead, upon his arrival, he discovered a city that only the day before had fallen into French Army hands. Napoleon refused to recognise Fernando's claim to the crown, which instead was bestowed on the head of the emperor's brother Joseph. Fernando, his father and mother, and Godoy were whisked off to Bayonne, where Carlos made over to the emperor all his royal rights in exchange for a handsome pension. Fernando was likewise divested of his royal title and granted a somewhat less splendid annuity. Fernando was sent into gilded exile at the splendid Château de Valençay in the Loire Valley, the residence of the d'Estampes and Talleyrand-Périgord families.

The only official effort to rescue Fernando VII from his French captivity took place in January 1810. The mission was undertaken by Admiral Sir George Cockburn at the behest of the British government, which had recognised Fernando as the legitimate heir to the throne of Spain. Cockburn put out to sea with a small squadron to Quiberon Bay off the south coast of Britanny, planning to bring about the king's escape. Possibly because of bitter memories of the Spanish defeat at Trafalgar, or perhaps because life at Château de Valençay was not such a hardship, to Cockburn's surprise and dismay, Fernando refused to have anything to do with his British liberator. Cockburn returned to Spanish waters, where in 1812 he hoisted his flag in the HMS *Marlborough* as the commander of a flotilla of warships off the coast of Cádiz.

Despite his mission having ended in failure, albeit through no fault of his own, Cockburn returned to Cádiz in a gladdened state of mind. The admiral, like many of his military colleagues, was a great admirer of the city, for him 'the cleanest' he had ever seen. In his first contact with Cádiz, in the summer of 1810, with politicians engaged in heated debate over Spain's future and an equally spirited bombardment in progress by the French, Cockburn's observations speak of a people determined to carry on with their daily lives, reminiscent of the defiant spirit shown of Londoners during the Blitz, in this 'most singular town.'[1]

'Cádiz is certainly well worth seeing,' he remarks. 'The houses are constructed for the climate. Fire places are not necessary. In many houses the windows are not glazed. Almost every window has an iron railing in front, from the top to the bottom. I presume to prevent people from walking out, as they range with the floor and are always open for air. In the better houses, instead of this they have balconies or verandas, like London's modern houses. There is a porch or double entrance to every gentleman's house, very strong doors and a courtyard inside.'[2]

Like many other English visitors of the time, Cockburn is most impressed by the women he sees in the streets. 'The women of all ranks that I saw were well made and handsome. They dress in black and wear veils till after the evening walk, when they put on white to go to the *terutlias* [social gatherings]. There are several of these assemblies every night, with high play.'[3]

The Second of May uprising

The outward appearance may have resembled something approaching a state of normality, yet no one in Cádiz, or indeed elsewhere in Spain, held any doubts that the task in hand was to drive out the invaders. Napoleon's decision to place his brother on the throne as Joseph I was destined to bring disaster to the French. Defeating the Spanish Army was one thing, but expecting the Spanish people to submit to foreign occupation was quite another matter. This eventually led to a humiliating defeat for the emperor and the hasty evacuation of his armies from Spain. But while Joseph sat on the throne, the Madrid parliament, known then as it is today as the Cortes, was dissolved by the French king, leaving the country without a Spanish administration to speak for the country's legitimate monarch.[4]

It was not long before Joseph's coronation triggered a wave of popular uprisings throughout the country. The crucial event erupted on 2 May 1808, an historic episode immortalised on canvas by Francisco de Goya. That day, some two thousand citizens of Madrid, joined by Spanish troops who had been confined to their barracks, took to the streets in a rising against the French grenadiers and their Mameluke mercenary allies. In the ensuing two months, Spanish patriots began setting up independent military juntas in several provincial capitals, each with its own troops and arsenals. They recognised Fernando as the rightful heir to the throne, a policy embraced by the Supreme Central Junta and its successor, the Regency Council.

The Consejo de Castilla adopted a more accommodating policy toward Joseph I. This central governmental body was composed of royal advisers and policymakers who, for reasons that remain largely obscure, succumbed without much resistance to the French king's rule. The Consejo's capitulation, to all effects, inevitably brought about a break with the regional juntas, which took into their own hands the task of restoring Spanish sovereignty.

While the king, revered by his loyal subjects as El Deseado, the Desired One (later to be labelled El Felón, the Traitor), was spending his days under splendid house arrest in France, he began to dispatch proclamations to his subjects in Spain. The initiative to reassemble the Cortes was embodied in a decree made public three days after the 2 May insurrection in Madrid. In this edict, Fernando instructed the Central Junta to move from the capital to a spot of greater safety, and from there launch a military campaign against Napoleon and oust his brother Joseph I from the throne. The French authorities saw to it that these proclamations were never to reach the hands of the Junta. Pedro Cevallos, one of Fernando's ministers, on his liberation from exile in France, committed the documents to memory and made them known to the Junta as well as the Spanish citizenry.

The Battle of Poza de Santa Isabel

The last naval action involving what survived of the French fleet after the Battle of Trafalgar took place in the Bay of Cádiz in June 1808. This was the Battle of Poza de Santa Isabel, an anchorage close to La Carraca Arsenal. This sea engagement sealed the fate of what remained of the French fleet in Spanish waters, for it was destined never again to sail from the Bay of Cádiz. On 9 June, the Spanish governor of Cádiz, Tomás de Morla y Pacheco, had begun drawing up his battle plan to destroy the French fleet, moored in the Bay of Cádiz, once and for all. The British navy had been blockading the bay for nearly three years following the French defeat at Trafalgar, so Morla knew that all his hopes would ride on securing the backing of Spain's British allies. He therefore sent an envoy to secure the blessing of General Sir John Moore, commander of the British forces in the Iberian Peninsula.

His emissary was a senior Spanish naval officer of Irish lineage, Enrique MacDonell,[5] who not only managed to obtain Moore's consent, but also returned with 400 kilograms of gunpowder to add some muscle to the forthcoming operation. Morla then sent French Vice-Admiral François de Rosily-Mesros a message by optical telegraph, demanding the surrender of his squadron. Rosily had meanwhile received orders from French Navy Minister Denis Decrès to hold fast until the relief column reached the city.

Rosily now found himself virtually at the mercy of the Cádiz garrison's cannons. His only chance of survival, as he saw it, was to go for a holding action. He knew of the taskforce dispatched from Madrid that was marching south toward Andalucía under the command of General Pierre Dupont. Rosily reasoned that if these troops managed to fight their way through to Cádiz, the defending garrison would have to swing its batteries 180 degrees landward to confront the approaching column.

While anxiously awaiting the French Army relief column, Rosily moved his ships to a spot in the bay where he reckoned they could sit safely beyond the range of the Spanish battery. That done, he messaged the commander of the British blockading fleet, Admiral John Child Purvis, offering to effectively render his ships *hors de combat* by having his cannons sent ashore. Purvis summarily rebuffed Rosily's offer. Morla likewise rejected any form of compromise with the French fleet commander. This was too grave an affront to Rosily's honour. When it became evident that the French were going to put up a fight, Morla ordered battery emplacements to be erected on the Isla de León, the island settlement in the Bay of Cádiz that was to become the home of the Cortes, the country's national assembly. The Spanish strategy was to drive a wedge between Rosily's squadron to prevent the French from closing in on La Carraca Arsenal, the northern sector of the Isla de León, or attempting to break the blockade and make good its escape from the Bay of Cádiz. Despite Spanish apprehensions, Rosily did not harbour the slightest intention of fighting his way out, not while he still believed the French relief column was marching toward Cádiz.

By 6 June Morla's battle plan had been finalised and approved by the garrison's military commanders. That day, the Spanish governor sent Rosily a final ultimatum, demanding the surrender of his squadron. As no word was heard from the French side, that same afternoon Morla gave the order for the shore batteries to let loose a fusillade against Rosily's ships. The following morning Spanish vessels in the bay joined the cannonade. There ensued a relentless bombardment that was to carry on until 15 June, when Rosily finally grasped the hopelessness of his situation. He went ashore in a lifeboat to offer his sword to General Juan Ruiz de Apodaca, a citizen of Cádiz. Apodaca graciously returned the sword to Rosily before taking him into custody. The French vice-admiral's capitulation proved to be a wise decision. His foreboding was accurate: the French relief column was not going to arrive in time to rescue his squadron from total destruction. The divisions that were on the march from Madrid under Dupont's command never made it past the village of Bailén in the province of Jaén, more than two hundred miles north of Cádiz.

After a six-day engagement with Spanish forces, French Vice-Admiral François de Rosily-Mesros suffered the humiliation of having to surrender his entire squadron of five ships of the line and a frigate, along with four thousand seamen, to the Spanish. The fleet had been blockaded in the bay by the British for nearly three years since the defeat of Trafalgar.

The battles of Bailén and Ocaña

In mid-July, soldiers of the Spanish Army of Andalucía under Francisco Javier Castaños converged on Dupont's column outside Bailén. Castaños had launched a multi-front offensive against the advancing French troops, causing such confusion in the enemy ranks that the defenders were forced to split their forces. Castaños swiftly moved in to seize the French stronghold at Bailén and drive a wedge between the French divisions. With his army scattered in two wings, Dupont lacked the strength to break through the Spanish line and was forced to negotiate a surrender. Spain's resounding victory at the Battle of Bailén was the first open-field defeat of a Napoleonic army.

The emperor now had no choice but to accept the painful reality that his Spanish invasion was never going to be a walkover. Napoleon had failed to reckon with the Spanish people's determination to wage a ferocious battle to preserve their national independence. In this seven-year conflict, the French Army got its first taste of guerrilla warfare. Indeed, the term 'guerrilla' is the diminutive of the Spanish word *guerra*, meaning *war*. Before the Peninsular War ended in 1814, Spanish guerrillas had tied down more than seventy-five per cent of the French occupying forces, leaving only a small contingent free to confront the conventional British and Portuguese allied army under Arthur Wellesley, the Duke of Wellington.

One unsavoury outcome of the two battles was the fate of the 21,000 French troops taken captive after Poza de Santa Isabel and Bailén. These men languished in the notorious San Carlos prison and on eight pontoons constructed to accommodate prisoners in the Bay of Cádiz. Historian Lourdes Márquez Carmona says:

> Their lives were tragic given the inhumane conditions they were forced to endure. When the situation became untenable the Regency Junta came up with a plan to reduce the number of prisoners. In 1809, the

Spanish sent a thousand detainees to England, another 1,500 to the Canary Islands and 5,300 to the Balearic Islands. Of the latter, 4,500 men were left abandoned on the desert island of La Cabrera where, given the scarcity of goods, some of them resorted to cannibalism.[6]

It was still too early for the Spanish patriots to raise the flag of victory. In November 1809, the Battle of Ocaña, near Toledo, marked the greatest single defeat of Spanish forces in the Peninsular War. The Duke of Wellington saw it coming. In a visit to Cádiz, Wellesley found the Junta planning a string of autumn victories to rehabilitate themselves. In her biography of the Duke of Wellington, Elizabeth Longford states:

> Aghast at such suicidal folly, he tried to dissuade them, but in vain. In November, this Spanish army was utterly broken to pieces at Ocaña. The Central Junta abdicated on 29 January 1810, preparatory to handing over to an elected Cortes.[7]

General Juan Carlos Aréizaga's army of 51,000 men suffered nearly 19,000 casualties in the onslaught of the French cavalry. The Junta General, which was headquartered in Sevilla, packed up and beat a hasty retreat in the face of the advancing French forces. When it transferred to the settlement of San Fernando on Isla de León, Cádiz was the only city in Spain that had successfully held out against French military occupation. There its members took shelter in the relative safety provided by salt marshes and the surrounding bay and the Atlantic.

The Cortes of Cádiz

Following the resounding Spanish military victories in the Bay of Cádiz in 1809 and at Bailén, delegates from various sectors of society assembled in the city to begin a heated discussion on the best vehicle for creating a unified Spanish government.

Politicians, clerics, prominent entrepreneurs and members of the military composed the dominant bloc in the debate that took place to decide on one of three options: convoke a legislative assembly (Cortes), establish a Regency or carry on with the discredited Junta. It was the latter option that initially found the largest number of supporters. In late September 1810, they set up the somewhat pretentiously named Supreme Governing Central Junta of the Kingdom. The moderate faction was less than happy with this arrangement. Then a mere fortnight later, the open-minded politician Gaspar Melchor de Jovellanos came up with a compromise proposal in an attempt to conciliate the rival factions: summon the Cortes to replace the Junta and create a Regency.

On 24 September 1810, the delegates to the Cortes of Cádiz assembled in the Isla de León, which was still under siege by French forces. According to British Hispanist Raymond Carr,

> A military accident stationed the first liberal [the first time the word was used in a political context] parliament in Cádiz, the only town with an open-minded society, a large French colony, a daily performance at the French theatre, a social life devoid of aristocratic prejudice and where the test of status, even for nobles who invested in trade, was wealth.[8]

The nearly three hundred representatives who crowded into the Royal Theatre to attend the inaugural session of the Cortes could never have imagined that the document they were to produce two years later would stand as the model for the classical liberal constitution of Europe in the early nineteenth century. The Constitution of 1812, or La Pepa, as it was nicknamed, was promulgated on 19 March of that year. In the Calendar Day of Saints this is St Joseph's Feast Day. *Pepe* is the Spanish diminutive of José, or Joseph in English, and as the term *constitución* takes the feminine article *la*, the document soon became affectionately known as La Pepa.

1812 AND ALL THAT

The fundamental principle underlying the Cádiz constitution was the concept of national sovereignty. The objective was to limit the despotic powers of the monarchy that had opened the gates to the Napoleonic invasion. At the same time, most of the deputies aimed to strike down the civil abuses and repression that were the norm of the day. This doctrine was inspired and taken forward by a handful of freethinkers who supported a liberal, reformist constitution. Agustín Argüelles was a lawyer and commanding orator who played a key role in drafting the charter. He was, like many of his fellow delegates, a sworn enemy of press censorship, the slave trade and the Inquisition. A towering statue of Argüelles stands in the Madrid neighbourhood that bears his name. It is a tribute to the patriotic statesman, a man of outstanding oratorical skills, who played a key role in drafting the 1812 Constitution. In Cádiz, Argüelles fought vigorously for a far-reaching and unambiguous reform of Spain's antiquated and reactionary social structure. His progressive views would later cost him a spell in prison in Spain's Moroccan enclave of Ceuta. He was later transferred to Mallorca, where he was to spend five years behind bars. On his release, Argüelles continued to fight for liberal change, and rather than face another prison term, he fled to England where he was employed as chief librarian to the Whig politician Henry Richard. Argüelles had befriended Richard, who served as Lord Privy Seal, in 1806 while on a secret diplomatic mission to London for Godoy.

Alongside this charismatic crusader for reform stood the radical priest Diego Muñoz-Torrero, a passionate advocate of separation of state powers. Muñoz-Torrero reached the Isla de León in the summer of 1810, as representative for his home region of Extremadura. He was an extraordinary member of Spain's orthodox clergy in that he wholeheartedly espoused the most forward-looking causes under debate in the Cortes. This avuncular friar rose to become the Rector of the venerable

University of Salamanca, the most august academic title in Spain. Somewhat astonishingly for a clergyman of his time, he was also a staunch supporter of freedom of the press.

In March 1812, he proclaimed his fervent views in an address to the assembly. 'We would be betraying the aspirations of our people and providing arms to the governing forces we have begun to overcome if we failed to declare freedom of the press. Censorship is the last bastion of the tyrannical rule that has instilled fear in us for centuries.'[9]

He was the first speaker to address the inaugural session of the Cortes. In his speech, he put forward a number of far-reaching proposals for restructuring Spain's governmental system and even went so far as to hint at extending the vote and other civil rights to women. So persuasive was the priest's oratory that in December 1810 he was named head of the committee of fifteen deputies that was to draw up the Constitution. Under the merciless hand of absolutism, in 1823 Muñoz-Torrero escaped to Portugal. He was eventually hunted down and died a victim of torture under interrogation, one of the iniquities he had fought to eradicate.

Francisco de Paula Martínez de la Rosa, statesman and dramatist, stood out as a powerful voice of moderation in the liberal faction of the Cortes. He left Granada to escape the advancing French forces and while serving in the Cortes he produced his first stage play, *Lo que puede un empleo* ('What a Job Can Accomplish'), a prose comedy satirising the nobility, that premiered in the Teatro de Cádiz in 1812. He sat as head of the founding fathers of the Constitution, known as the *doceañistas*, those liberals who issued the Magna Carta in *año doce*, or twelfth year, that is, 1812. His overarching ambition was to produce a workable constitution that would be backed by a humbled monarch and the upper middle classes. Martínez de la Rosa became engulfed in politics and in 1834 he was elected prime minister, the first national leader to receive the title of President of the Council of Ministers.

One of the most powerful and stirring figures among the delegates in Cádiz was Gaspar Melchor de Jovellanos, a renowned statesman, author and philosopher. Jovellanos was one of the most illustrious representatives of the Spanish Age of Enlightenment, a writer, poet, statesman and man of letters. He exerted an enormous influence in the Cortes in its efforts to create a framework for reform. Like most of his colleagues who had been forced by the French to abandon their place of birth, Jovellanos was not a native of Cádiz. He hailed from the town of Gijón in the northern coastal region of Asturias, and in the space of three years, he was elected a member of Spain's three most distinguished literary and artistic societies: the Royal Academy of History, the San Fernando Fine Arts Academy and the Royal Spanish Academy.[10]

The fact that none of these prominent deputies was from Cádiz is hardly surprising. Starting in 1810 and in the space of a few months, the city's population doubled, spurred by the influx of some fifty thousand refugees from other parts of Spain under Napoleonic occupation. 'Logically, Cádiz was also the destination for many colonials, be they entrepreneurs, lawyers or members of the military,' says historian Juan Sisinio Pérez Garzón. 'These ranged from the young Ecuadorean José María Lequerica, who performed a noteworthy role in the Cortes, to the Argentinian General Tomás de Iriarte and the Peruvian cavalry officer Dionisio Inca Yupanqui.'[11]

The Cortes held their sessions in San Fernando for five months, until it became apparent that more spacious and dignified chambers would be in order to properly carry out the task in hand. The delegates were also concerned that Isla de León sat a bit too close to the front line of battle. Early in 1811, the assembly moved to the city of Cádiz itself. The deputies chose the Church of San Felipe Neri, an oratory erected in 1679 in Andalusian baroque style and located in the city centre, 4 miles north of Isla de León.

The church underwent a major renovation to adapt the structure to its new function. Chief naval engineer Antonio Prat, who designed the city's defences after the Battle of Trafalgar, was called in to oversee the redesign work. An entrance was opened up at the high altar and flanked by Ionic columns. A canopy was placed above it bearing a portrait of Fernando VII. Semicircular rows of seats and benches were fitted for the deputies, and to the right of the canopy, Prat built a seating area for the diplomatic corps. Another on the other side was installed for stenographers and members of the press, while the upper galleries were reserved for the general public.

La Pepa

The issue of Spain's simmering colonial crisis, reflected in independence movements that had flared up in several countries, was addressed in the Constitution's first article, which emphatically stated, 'The Spanish nation is the joint enterprise of Spaniards of both hemispheres.' The tenets of a justice system based on equality for all was to be extended to citizens of the colonies as well as peninsular Spain. Enshrined in this article was the doctrine of *habeas corpus* and the banning of arbitrary detention, as well as the prohibition of interrogation under torture.

Cádiz became the springboard for Spain's first system of separation of powers in the country's history. Of the Magna Carta's 384 articles, fully 250 dealt with this issue. The state was organised into separate and independent legislative, executive and judiciary branches. The Cortes, with its single chamber of deputies, stood as the nation's legislature. The lawmakers were elected by indirect male vote, that is, those present in Cádiz. Each Spanish colony was invited to send one representative to the Cortes. Egalitarian principles prevailed throughout the constitutional process, to the point that Decree XXXI stated categorically that *criollos, mestizos* and native Americans were given the same status as Spanish citizens if they wished to join government bodies, the Church or serve in the military.

The king was recognised as the chief executive power, though Fernando's role was to be limited almost to that of a republican head of state. In fact, one of the monarch's duties was to sign off all laws decreed by parliament. As for the judiciary, given the widespread legal abuses and despotism that prevailed in Spain at the time, the Cortes imposed strict boundaries and safeguards between the three branches of government.

One of the Constitution's most controversial articles decreed the abolition of Spain's ancient structure of *señoríos*, essentially feudal estates, to be replaced by a system of property rights on a contractual basis. The provinces of Castilla y León, Extremadura and Andalucía were the homeland of vast tracts of Church property. These lands were in theory ceded to farmers or, in some cases, municipalities for communal use. However, the Church exacted a portion of profits earned from farming activities. The Magna Carta effectively did away with enclaves of private jurisdictions then in the hands of the nobility and clergy. As was to be expected, this clause was rejected outright by the great property owners sitting amongst the delegates, several of whom threatened to take their protest to the streets. The prevailing liberal faction of Cádiz reasoned that their age-old system discriminated against small farmers and landowners, since nearly seventy per cent of Spain's agricultural territory was in the hands of a tiny minority of the population. This decree touched off a battle over land rights that remained a bone of contention between reform advocates and the entrenched property-owning hierarchy for more than a century until 1931, when the Second Republic passed the agrarian reform bill.

One of the boldest and most widely celebrated reforms ratified by the framers of the Constitution was the abolition of the Inquisition in every region of Spain. This was driven by the liberal members of the Cortes, largely in response to the Holy Office's condemnation of the backlash against the French, who acted as guardians of Church privileges. The Inquisition, however, remained in force in the Spanish colonies until it was definitively ended by royal decree in 1820, six years before the last of Spain's Latin American possessions had won its independence.[12]

The Constitution's 384 articles were signed into law on 18 March 1812. 'Rain fell on the following day, but this failed to dampen the festive spirit that overwhelmed Cádiz,' says historian Alberto Ramos Santana. 'That day, the deputies and members of the Regency Council swore allegiance to the Constitution, after which they marched in procession to the Iglesia del Carmen to attend a Te Deum.'[13]

When the French troops that were laying siege to Cádiz became aware of what had inspired this outpouring of joy in the streets, they stepped up their bombardments in the hope of stifling the celebratory air, but all in vain because people carried on partying across the city in disregard of the enemy shelling.

Cádiz in the early nineteenth century had thus become the birthplace of the most sweeping programme of social and economic transformation enacted in Spanish history. The Constitution had an impact on all sectors of society, from the monarchy and clergy to land ownership and freedom of speech. Yet there was one blemish that remained untouched and, indeed, was not to be extirpated for more than half a century after the 1812 charter came into effect.

Fig. 15: Castillo de San Sebastián, built as part of the seventeenth-century fortifications of Cádiz.

Fig. 16: Baluarte de la Candelaria, seventeenth-century fortification to protect the harbour entrance.

Fig. 17: The Casa de las Cinco Torres, Plaza de España, Cádiz.

Fig. 18: Catedral de la Santa Cruz de Cádiz, built 1722–1835.

Fig. 19: Casa del Almirante, dating from the late seventeenth century, built as the town palace of the Admiral of the Fleet of the Indies.

Fig. 20: The Tavira Tower, highest of the merchants' watchtowers.

Fig. 21: Church of Santiago, Plaza de la Catedral.

Fig. 22: Merchant's watchtower viewed from Plaza San Francisco.

Fig. 23: Church of Nuestra Señora de la Palma, barrio de la Viña

Fig. 24: The Battle of Trafalgar, 1805.

Fig. 25: The declaration of the 1812 constitution, commemorative painting from 1912.

Fig. 26: Oratorio San Felipe Neri where the 1812 Cortes met.

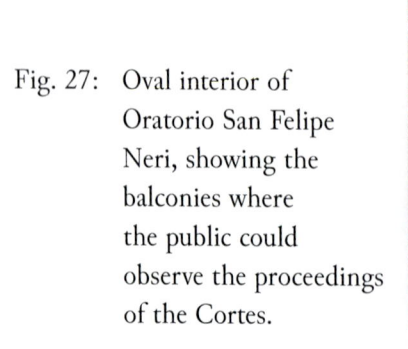

Fig. 27: Oval interior of Oratorio San Felipe Neri, showing the balconies where the public could observe the proceedings of the Cortes.

1812 AND ALL THAT

Callejón de los Negros

It is estimated that in the seventeenth century about ten per cent of Cádiz's population, some three thousand souls, had been in the employ of land barons as agricultural workers or as domestic staff in affluent households. It was not an enviable life but certainly preferable to the servitude imposed on Africans brought in as slaves.

'Estimates of the number of slaves sold at auction in Cádiz between the mid-17th and 18th centuries put the figure at 17,000, though this refers only to the city itself. The total for the entire Bay area is much higher,' says historian José Luis García Serrano. 'Slave vessels from almost everywhere anchored in the Bay of Cádiz with shipments of slaves to sell, like any other product. The majority were domestic slaves, a sumptuous acquisition for the local elite.'[14]

To this must be added the many thousands more for whom Cádiz was a transit point. They were brought in from Africa to be shipped from Spain to the American colonies. There is a narrow street in the city centre called Callejón de los Negros, Alleyway of the Blacks. There are no historical records to substantiate the background to this name, but it is commonly assumed that along this narrow street the newly landed slaves were marched from the dock to the city auction house, there to await passage across the Atlantic, mainly to the Caribbean.

Cádiz had been a prime hub in the Spanish slave trade throughout the seventeenth and eighteenth centuries. The city's role in this market, however, was confined primarily to that of a processing centre. The seizure and delivery of overseas slaves came from elsewhere. In 1788, the London firm of Baker & Dawson, the largest firm of slave brokers in England, sealed a contract with the Spanish Crown to supply three thousand people a year, mostly as agricultural workers in Puerto Rico and on Cuban sugar plantations. The British consolidated their dominance of the market in 1763, after their victory over the French in the Seven Years War. During the remainder of the eighteenth century, the United Kingdom nearly held a monopoly on providing Africans to the American colonies. Between 1760 and 1770, British slave dealers sent nearly half a million people to their Caribbean possessions. British involvement in shipping slaves was made illegal in 1807 but the practice of slavery on plantations in British Caribbean colonies carried on until 1838, unchallenged by all but a handful of determined groups of abolitionists, notably Britain's Society for the Abolition of the Slave Trade, which was founded in 1787.

The contract to supply slaves later fell into the hands of the South Sea Company, which dealt in the wholesale transport of Africans to Jamaica and the Antilles. Following in the footsteps of this commercial enterprise, throughout the eighteenth and into the nineteenth century Spain's Real Compañía de Comercio de La Habana (Royal Trading Company of Havana) acquired slaves from the Caribbean islands, supplied for the most part by British merchants. The merchant Miguel Uriarte, a native of Cádiz, obtained a ten-year contract to dispatch 1,500 people a year to Cuba. Uriarte and his associates set up their own enterprise, Compañía General de Negros (General Company of Blacks), which added the name 'Gaditana' to their masthead to identify its Cádiz origin.

Slave ownership in Cádiz, as distinct from the city's trafficking and auctioning of Africans for shipment overseas, began to decline in the early 1700s, owing to a combination of economic circumstances. Mainly, it was far more lucrative to put these people up for auction than to have to shelter and feed them. By the next century, keeping slaves had all but disappeared from city life. It speaks volumes of the mind-set of the day that while the citizens of Cádiz, including members of the enlightened intelligentsia, were loath to keep slaves as personal property, no such misgivings applied to the ongoing trafficking of Africans to the colonies. These workers continued to represent a key contributor to Spain's economic wealth, primarily as harvesters on plantations that exported huge amounts of sugar to satisfy the Europeans' new-found craze for sweetened coffee, tea and cocoa drinks. This would help explain why the Constitution did not include any provisions in favour of abolishing the Atlantic slave industry.

Despite what some might consider its shortcomings, the Constitution of 1812 represented a historic landmark in the development of European political enlightenment. The Duke of Wellington, on a visit to Cádiz to meet with the Cortes, expressed high praise for this document. 'I wish that some of our reformers would go to Cádiz and see the benefits of a sovereign popular assembly and of a written constitution,' he wrote in a letter to the Chancellor Lord Bathurst.[15]

From the Desired One to the Traitor

By 1813, the game was up for Napoleon and his army of occupation. In July of the previous year, Wellington had scored a resounding victory over Marshal Auguste de Marmont at Arapiles, a few miles south of Salamanca. In June of the following year, a Spanish, British and Portuguese coalition definitively broke the enemy forces under King Joseph Bonaparte and Marshal Jean-Baptiste. After seven years of relentless warfare, the French now found themselves so badly weakened in spirit and manpower that they were left with little choice but to withdraw from Spain.

In September 1813, the deputies were satisfied their task had been achieved. They resolved to move the Cortes to Madrid, the country's official capital, to await the homecoming of Fernando VII. This historic decision was motivated by factors quite apart from a sense of mission accomplished. It was, in fact, carried out as a matter of urgency. Cádiz was a crossing point for seamen and merchants from across Europe and Asia, as well as tens of thousands of African slaves shipped in from Africa under shockingly unsanitary conditions. It is therefore no wonder the city was highly vulnerable to waves of contagious diseases. Cádiz had known numerous occurrences of yellow fever in the past. The most recent outbreak took place in 1810, while the Cortes were still in session. At that time, the authorities did their best to cover up, or at least minimise, the gravity of the situation, so as not to demoralise the armed forces or the inhabitants of a densely populated city under siege. When Cádiz was hit by a second yellow fever epidemic in January 1814, the deputies wasted no time in proclaiming Madrid the seat of national government. They hastily removed themselves northward, ostensibly to hail the arrival of the monarch.

No sooner had Fernando VII, now released from confinement by Napoleon, crossed the border, than it became apparent why the Desired One was to earn his title of the Traitor. There had even been warnings in the Cádiz press about the threat of reestablishing tyrannical rule. The paper that bore the quaint title of El Duende de los Cafés (The Elf of the Cafés) launched a hard-hitting attack on royal absolutism and the dangers it posed to all the reforms achieved by the Cortes. In 1813, the newspaper was confiscated and burnt in public by Spanish troops stationed in Cádiz, while shouting in unison, 'Long live our sovereign Fernando VII!' A mob of sympathisers stormed the paper's editorial offices and proceeded to thrash the staff.

The voices of reaction were in an uproar over their centuries-old privileges having been usurped by the liberals at Cádiz. Traditionalist voices – the army, members of the clergy incensed over the dissolution of the Inquisition and confiscation of monastic property, and the landed gentry – all found an attentive

1812 AND ALL THAT

ear in the reinstated monarch. Fernando VII lost no time in responding to their grievances, which they portrayed as a threat to his royal powers.

The liberal deputies in Cádiz had agreed to recognise the king on the condition that he swore a solemn oath to uphold the Constitution of 1812. Fernando was by nature not predisposed to have his royal prerogatives placed under restraint. There were two deciding factors in his defiance of the liberals' demands. On the one hand, he could count on the reactionary army General Francisco Javier de Elío, who offered the support of his troops to uphold Fernando's traditional rights. The king was also given a document known as the Manifesto of the Persians, in reference to the all-powerful rulers of ancient Persia. This letter was signed by ninety-six conservative deputies of the Cortes of Cádiz, mostly clergy, great landholders and members of the armed forces, in favour of the restoration of absolutist power.

It was from that moment foreseeable that the king's first decree would be to abolish the Cortes of Cádiz and declare the Constitution null and void. Fernando set forth the feeble justification for this volte face by casting doubt on the legality of the Cortes, which he said had taken this action while he was in exile and without his permission. The monarch resumed his autocratic powers and then attempted to recover control of Spanish America, now partly independent. It was never to be, chiefly because the poorly trained and ill-equipped Spanish Army units stationed in America were too ineffectual a force to contain the growing rebellions by independence fighters. During the Peninsular War, Wellington himself had expressed contempt for his Spanish military allies and maintained that the guerrillas were a far more effective fighting force than the regular army.

CÁDIZ

The Trienio Liberal

In 1820, Cádiz once again took centre stage in a tumultuous period of Spanish politics. Fernando VII refused to accept the shocking reality that Spain's overseas possessions were to become independent countries. The king was determined to prevent the empire from crumbling under his rule. In 1819, he raised an army of ten battalions to fight in the Spanish–American wars of independence.

One of these units, the Asturian Battalion, was placed under the command of Lieutenant Colonel Rafael del Riego, who was sent to Cádiz to assemble his troops for departure to America. Riego's men and those of the other battalions in Cádiz had an antipathy to risking their lives in what they deemed to be a pointless war. Six American colonies had already declared their independence after a period of bitter fighting. Only Cuba and Puerto Rico remained under the Spanish flag in the Americas, along with the Philippines and Guam in Asia. Much of the Spanish Army rank and file were disinclined to defend the monarch's delusion of colonial reconquest.

In January 1820, Riego staged a mutiny to call off the planned military operation in the name of the abolished Constitution. At the outset the uprising remained an act of sedition, contained to Cádiz and seemingly doomed to failure. Then quite suddenly, an anti-war revolt erupted, first in Galicia, followed in quick succession by military insurrections in Barcelona, Zaragoza and Pamplona. The bulk of the army remained non-committal for two months, until inspired by the Cádiz rebellion, the armed forces threw their weight behind the rebels.

The liberal spirit of Cádiz once again prevailed when On 7 March 1820, the Royal Palace in Madrid was surrounded by troops led by General Francisco Ballesteros, a soldier with a grudge against Fernando VII. Ballesteros had been sacked from his post as minister for war and banished to Valladolid for his outspoken opposition to royal absolutism. Hence the general's decision to throw his weight behind Riego's Cádiz insurrection. Ballesteros' men swiftly overpowered the palace guard and three days later, he forced the king to sign a decree relinquishing his absolutist powers and reinstating the Constitution of 1812.

Spain's new political order issued in three years of constitutional leadership came to be known as the Trienio Liberal (Liberal Triennium) of 1820–23. During that short-lived period of enlightened government, power rested in the hands of the *doceañistas*, who from the outset found themselves embroiled in an unremitting battle with both radicals in the Cortes and conservative elements in the army. Their efforts to unite the country were plagued by disenchantment and frustration, while the crown and its allies did what was in their ability to frustrate these attempts to bring together Spain's divergent factions. The king, who still occupied the throne, refused to work with ministers responsible to the Cortes or support any form of constitutionalism. Historian Raymond Carr notes:

> Without funds, without arms, royalism could not defeat the regular army, still loyal to the revolution it had made. The sole hope of success lay, therefore, in the French help for which royalist exiles had been angling since 1821.[16]

France, along with other European monarchies, saw Spain as a threat to absolutist monarchy. In response to Fernando's appeal for help to restore his former powers, France's Bourbon King Louis XVIII mobilised 'an army of salvation', nicknamed the 'Hundred Thousand Sons of Saint Louis'. The fateful event that marked the beginning of the end for the Cádiz-inspired rule of liberalism took place on 7 April 1823. The French Army under the Duke of Angoulême crossed the Pyrenees almost unopposed, predictably with the support of the middle classes and part of the urban population. The following month, the liberals forced Fernando to abandon the Royal Palace in Madrid and removed him to Cádiz.

Riego took command of the Third Army and put up a determined defence against the invaders. Sporadic skirmishes were fought across Spain until 31 August when the French, marching south, assaulted and captured Trocadero Fort, which controlled access to Cádiz. The French took nearly two thousand prisoners, and once the garrison was subdued, Angoulême turned the batteries of the nearby Fort San Luis on Cádiz itself. The city held out for three weeks despite relentless bombardments but was forced to surrender on 23 September 1823.[17] The liberals realised there was no option but to dissolve the Cortes and give back absolute power to Ferdinand VII and release the monarch to the French. On 30 September Cádiz surrendered, and four days later more than 4,600 French troops landed at its port. Fernando was freed, and his enemies were not to wait long before the humiliated monarch lashed out with a campaign of reprisals against all who had supported the constitutional government. The army rounded up and imprisoned all the rebels within their grasp. No sooner had the king been restored to his throne in Madrid, than Ballesteros fled to Cádiz, where he embarked on a British ship for France. Riego was less fortunate: he was captured, accused of high treason and sentenced to death for his role in depriving the king of his absolutist powers. On 7 November of the same year, despite his open repentance and impassioned plea for clemency, Riego was hanged in public at La Cebada Square in Madrid.

Fernando VII was to impose a reign of absolutist despotism on his country for yet another decade, until his death in 1833. The monarch bequeathed to his subjects a legacy as an instigator of civil strife. His last decree, as he lay dying in the Royal Palace, was to proscribe the Salic law. This statute, which came into force in 1700, would have made his brother Carlos, with whom relations had been deteriorating, the rightful heir to the throne. Fernando was instead succeeded by his infant daughter, who came to rule as Isabel II. In 1843, Fernando's widow the Queen Regent María Cristina stepped aside and Isabel, now of age, began her reign under the shadow of palace intrigues, barracks conspiracies and military pronouncements that exploded into open warfare.

6

IN THE EYE OF THE STORM

Cádiz, the birthplace of Spanish liberalism, was to serve as the staging ground of political upheaval in what became known as Spain's Glorious Revolution of 1868. In the interim period of peace, Cádiz took advantage of a radical piece of legislation to set in motion a long-overdue redevelopment of the city, much of it left neglected after many years of siege and bombardment.

In 1837, Finance Minister Juan Álvarez Mendizábal, who by coincidence happened to be a native of Chiclana on the Bay of Cádiz, issued his Desamortización Eclesiástica (Ecclesiastic Confiscations). This highly polemical law was bitterly condemned by conservative politicians and, needless to say, the Church and its followers. Many of Mendizábal's opponents were quick to ascribe the motives for issuing this law to the fact that he was Jewish. He flatly rejected this accusation, saying that the proceeds were needed to fight the dynastic war with the Carlists, who opposed the reign of Isabel II.

The Desamortización was the wholesale expropriation and sale by public auction of properties belonging to the Catholic Church. The lands were termed 'dead hands', in reference to their alleged lack of productivity. These were parcels of land across all of Spain that had come into Church ownership through donations and inheritances from people who died without heirs.

Cádiz was a beneficiary of the new law, which set into motion a major overhaul of the city's infrastructure along with the creation of new spaces for public leisure. Historian Manuel Bustos Rodríguez cites as an example the conversion of the fruit garden belonging to the Franciscan convent into the Plaza de Mina, in the heart of the old district. 'Once the square was completed, it was enclosed by a number of stately homes...Neoclassic in style, especially the Fine Arts Academy, now partly converted into a museum. One of these houses was the birthplace of the composer Manuel de Falla.'[1]

The centre of the square was originally occupied by a monument to a hero of the War of Independence General Francisco Espoz y Mina, hence the name. A bandstand was later installed which, in turn, was removed when the square was last remodelled in 1991. This latest rehabilitation respected the nineteenth-century aesthetics that characterise the square. Without doubt, its most prominent feature is a gigantic kapok tree, whose buttress roots give it an almost unearthly appearance. A short walk south toward the bay leads to the Plaza Candelaria, built on the grounds once occupied by the convent of the same name. A popular spot for evening relaxation, the square's most notable monument is the statue of Emilio Castelar, a native of Cádiz, historian and writer, who served in 1873 as president of the First Spanish Republic.

The Plaza de Abastos (literally: Supply Depot) adjacent to the central market was originally the location of the San Diego Convento, which was later demolished. Today this is one of the liveliest areas of the city, bustling with morning shoppers taking a break from the market stalls to indulge in the cafés and snack bars that line the outdoor colonnaded walkway.

IN THE EYE OF THE STORM

An economic renaissance

It was imperative at this time to revitalise Spanish sea power, which had fallen into a badly weakened state in the early nineteenth century. This was most notable after the Battle of Trafalgar, a veritable coup de grâce for Spain's naval forces. The country found itself in a near permanent state of conflict, and during the Peninsular War the Spanish Navy was all but non-existent as a fighting force. The late nineteenth century ushered in an era of intense activity for Cádiz's shipbuilding industry, the backbone of the city's industrial life. The opening of the Vea-Murguía shipyard on 23 July 1891 marked a day of jubilation, bringing as it did the promise of renewed prestige and prosperity for a city recovering from the loss of all but a handful of Spain's colonies. On that day, Cádiz took on a carnival atmosphere: government buildings were festooned with banners and foreign consulates flew their national flags in celebration of the momentous event. Rear-Admiral Miguel de Aguirre y Corveto, a hero of the colonial wars, presided at an official banquet complete with rounds of congratulatory speeches and toasts to the prosperity of Cádiz. Shops shut their doors that day to allow staff to join the crowds of cheering citizens who made their way to the port for the official inauguration ceremony.

The Vea-Murguía enterprise brought the number of shipyards and repair docks in the city to four. The oldest of these was La Carraca Arsenal, at the service of the Spanish Navy since 1717, the year the Casa de Contratación was transferred from Sevilla to Cádiz. In 1840, the British engineer and shipbuilder Thomas Haynes built a second shipyard in the Puntales district. Upon his death in 1882, the company adopted the name Sons of Thomas Haynes. Haynes's descendants were considered skilled craftsmen, building steam ships of all descriptions and torpedo boats for the Spanish Navy.

The Matagorda dry dock started life in 1878 on the Trocadero islet 3 miles east of the city's main shipbuilding area. At the outset, the company specialised in maintaining a fleet of mail vessels owned by the shipping magnate Antonio López, the Marquis of Comillas, whose statue stands at the top of a tree-lined promenade bordering the historic city centre. The shipyard was later renamed the Astillero de Puerto Real, which after extensive enlargement work extended to nearly eleven million square feet in 1972, which made it Spain's largest shipyard and the second-largest dry dock in Europe, after Nigg in Scotland.

The Factoría Naval Gaditana was founded in 1888 with capital from a group of local investors, which included members of the Vea-Murguía family. The plan was to make use of the Lacassagne dock, which had recently hosted an International Maritime Exhibition. The success of this enterprise depended on the company being awarded a government contract to build three cruisers, put out for tender by Secretary of the Navy José Rodríguez de Arias. Having failed to win the contract, the company was dissolved a few months after its inauguration.

One of the most important motivators of urban improvement was the railway connecting Cádiz to the rest of the country. The first train to (almost) reach the city arrived at the newly built station on the island of Trocadero in September 1859. From there, passengers were obliged to make their way to the city centre by boat, a crossing of little more than a mile. The station was built in colourful Italianate style, with brick and oyster stone walls, chessboard design floor tiles and an ornamental garden behind the building, still visible today. The railway connected the all-important Matagorda shipyards with the Puerto Real industrial zone on the bay. Travel by rail became a vital component of the city's commercial life. It was now possible to transport large quantities of construction material to building sites in a relatively short space of time, as well as labourers from outlying areas to their daily workplace.

Cádiz was getting back on its feet after years of economic stagnation. The first factory to produce gas for commercial and consumer use began operating in 1845. The problem of drinking water was addressed two years later, when the town hall sanctioned a project to set up a system running supplies from springs in the Valle de la Piedad. Given the growth in population in a city that experiences on average 300 days a year of sunshine, the need to ensure a reliable reserve of water could not be overestimated. Banks began to establish themselves to finance the surge in business activity and attend to an increasingly affluent population. The Banco de Cádiz opened its doors in 1846, followed in 1869 by Crédito Comercial de Cádiz and a year later the Compañía Gaditana de Crédito. Hopes of a sustained economic renaissance proved to be illusory. By late 1857, the port of Barcelona had taken the lead position from Cádiz in volume of trade. Cádiz was likewise hit by a sharp drop in exports of sherry wine, due to poor harvests. A decline in imports from the colonies was another heavy burden to bear. The city made an attempt to regain its former commercial prominence by applying to Madrid to grant it free port status, but the request was turned down.

Cádiz underwent a number of other changes in the days before the outbreak of civil strife. On the death of Fernando VII in September 1833, his Queen María Cristina became regent and had to navigate the succession between those who supported her daughter Isabel's accession to the throne as queen, or those who supported the late king's brother under Salic law, which excluded females from succession. Despite the political turmoil at the highest level, the government undertook a major reform of the territorial division of Spain at the provincial level, which remains largely in place to this day. The influential Liberal Party politician

Javier de Burgos came to the fore as the driving force behind the overhaul of Spain's administrative structure as secretary of state for development. Burgos pushed through legislation to set up a structure of loyal regional governments as part of an effort to create a centralised government. To this end, in 1833 Cádiz was designated the capital city of the newly formed province of the same name, thus taking on the role of the region's administrative centre.

Carlists, Isabelines and liberals: Spain's decades of upheaval

On a September afternoon in 1862, three years after the railway's inauguration, a thirty-two-year-old woman alighted at the Cádiz station, bearing with her a retinue of servants and bodyguards. Queen Isabel II had already reluctantly agreed to restore the Constitution of 1812, a promise that never actually came to fruition. She had occupied the throne upon coming of age in 1840 and had embarked on this official voyage to thank Cádiz and its people for their donations and defence of her legitimacy against the rival Carlists, who were waging war to oust her from the throne. The Carlist Wars was the name given to three series of battles waged between 1833 and 1876 by militants backing Fernando VII's brother, Infante Carlos, as the rightful heir to the throne. Cádiz was far more of a bystander than a belligerent during these campaigns, despite the brief uprising of a clique that supported the Carlist challenger to the throne. This never amounted to more than small contingents of guerrilla fighters in the hills, who were easily overcome by troops loyal to the queen. Only one military engagement of significance took place in Cádiz province. This was the battle of Majaceite in 1836, fought near Arcos de la Frontera, which ended in a clear victory for the Liberal Party forces that supported the queen. Cádiz's only other role in the Carlist Wars, which ended with the defeat of the insurgents, was to provide medical assistance for wounded Liberal soldiers and as a processing station for Carlist prisoners. The city's prisons became perilously overcrowded and this raised health concerns among the authorities, though fortunately there are no records of the city being stricken by disease.

The Carlist Wars were fought mainly in Navarre, the Basque Country and Cataluña, the regions most vehemently aligned with the insurgents determined to depose the queen. Cádiz, though not a direct participant, came to play a pivotal role in these anarchic years of civil strife. The decisive moment came in September 1868. A showdown between Carlists and liberals took place at a bridge near Alcolea, a village in the province of Córdoba on the banks of the Guadalquivir. A liberal army of ten thousand men fought under the command of Cádiz-born General Francisco Serrano. He was an influential figure at court who had backed the queen against her uncle, the pretender Carlos. Serrano was banished from court in 1873 when he became leader of the Liberal Union party.

The political inspiration for the liberals taking up arms came from two resolute opponents of Isabel II. Juan Prim, a prominent politician who the following year was to briefly serve as prime minister, was leader of the Progressive Party. Juan Bautista Topete was a Spanish Navy admiral who would occupy the post of prime minister after Prim's assassination in 1870. At the Battle of Alcolea they faced off a similar number of troops led by General Manuel Pavía y Rodríguez who, like Serrano, happened to be a native of Cádiz. Once hostilities began, Pavía launched a frontal attack but despite his superiority in artillery, Serrano vigorously repelled the assault. To inspire his demoralised troops, Pavía took command at the frontline, where he fell wounded by shrapnel. He was replaced by his chief of staff, Colonel José Jiménez de Sandoval, who by nightfall realised the hopelessness of his army's situation and negotiated a surrender.

CÁDIZ

In the prelude to insurrection, liberal activists in Cádiz had kept in close contact with Prim, exiled in London after inciting an abortive attempt at rebellion in 1866. He was known to be one of the chief architects of the forthcoming conflict. In August 1868, Prim, along with his associates the future Prime Minister Práxedes Mateo Sagasta and leader of the Radical Democratic Party Manuel Ruiz Zorrilla, boarded a steamer in London that was to take them to Gibraltar. From there, the three revolutionaries made their way by frigate to Cádiz. There was no shortage of politicians prepared to join forces with the conspirators, who could count on the help, if it came to that, of a friendly squadron of Spanish warships anchored in the harbour and prepared to mutiny against the crown. Residents of the city's San Fernando district likewise came out to join the revolt against Isabel. Lieutenant General Rafael Primo de Rivera, one of the signatories of Prim's proclamation, spearheaded the campaign.[2]

Prim was a fiery orator who could raise people's passions to boiling point, as happened to be the case when he issued his Cádiz proclamation on 18 September 1868. With the Spanish Navy anchored at port, Prim, with Topete steadfastly by his side, denounced the reign of Isabel II as well as the Bourbon dynasty. The army detachment garrisoned in the city, along with a crowd of armed citizens, stood firmly behind what had in a few hours become a general uprising. Their war cry was 'Long Live Spain, With Honour!'

The army moved on the Cádiz government headquarters, where they expelled the mayor and the rest of the city councillors and provincial officials, who were replaced by members of the Junta by unanimous consent of the people. Heady with the spirit of rebellion, that same week the juntas expanded their political hegemony to surrounding towns. The new governing bodies of Cádiz province were quick to assure an alarmed central government that the maintenance of public order and respect for private property were two of the juntas' guiding principles. In Tarifa, the revolutionary leader Francisco Alba Fruzado, a firebrand lawyer who in later life suffered a gunshot wound in a duel, on this occasion issued a call for 'the peace and tranquillity so necessary for freedom', while telling the people cheering on his speech that 'no revolution should be tainted with blood.'[3] In a bid to gather public support, the Cádiz Junta ordered a twenty-three per cent cut in the price of tobacco and seventy-five per cent in the case of salt. The widely despised *impuesto de consumos*, roughly equivalent to today's VAT on consumer goods, was summarily abolished.

At first, a popular outcry against the priesthood from certain sectors gave the impression the Church was doomed to become a casualty of anti-religious militants. Most of the latent hostility towards the Catholic Church and its prelates took place in Lower Andalucía, the region that includes Cádiz, the country's poorest region, in which the Church was seen as the redoubt of a privileged clique of clergymen. The government feared a resurgence of the anticlerical riots that had broken out in 1835. At that time, the wave of unrest was triggered by the Church's support for the Carlist pretender to the throne. It is true that the Cádiz region saw the destruction of several churches, while a number of juntas decreed the expulsion of the Jesuits. On the other hand, areas like Chipiona or Tarifa displayed a complete lack of radicalism toward the Church. In all, the established religious order suffered minimal hostility under the juntas.

The government disbanded the juntas in 1873, with the proclamation of the First Republic. They had come under fire from different political factions as a threat to democratic rule. In some, such as Cádiz, the juntas were in fact forerunners of modern democratic principles. The city bitterly opposed the order to abolish its junta, whose officials pointed to the project to introduce universal suffrage. This caused a head-on collision with other townships, who took the easier path of agreeing to the government ruling. Cádiz, in this case, was sixty years ahead of its time for it was not until 1933 that Spain introduced the free vote for all citizens. In the interim, the revolutionaries had declared Cádiz a Federal Canton within the framework of Spain's newly proclaimed First Republic, which was to enjoy a lifespan of less than one year. The familiar sight of army patrols in the streets by now incited little interest among the general populace, who went about their daily business of shopping at the market and enjoying drinks at the cafés that were becoming a familiar feature of the city's landscape.

Isabel II happened to be holidaying at her summer palace in San Sebastián at the time of the uprising. But after the defeat of her forces at the Battle of Alcolea, she realised with dismay that the revolution was sweeping not only across Andalucía, but the rest of Spain as well. With a heavy heart, she embarked on the fifteen-mile journey across the border into self-imposed exile in France, where she remained until her death in 1904. The deposition of the queen in 1868 came to be known as the Glorious Revolution. Two years later in 1870 the queen abdicated in favour of her eldest surviving son, the thirteen-year-old Alfonso, who would become Alfonso XII. Spain's political leaders now faced a dilemma, in that the queen had been ousted but the monarchical system was officially still enshrined in law. A new sovereign would have to be found.

Concerned that the young prince would be dominated by his mother and inherit her flaws, the conflict-ridden, multiparty provisional government that had ruled since Isabel's ousting refused to accept Alfonso as the legitimate king of Spain. Ministers had proposed several other candidates for the throne, but all either declined the offer or were rejected by the government. In 1870, the Cortes came up with Amedeo di Savoia, the younger son of King Vittorio Emanuele of Italy. No sooner had Amedeo been enthroned in November 1870, he fell victim to several assassination attempts. Three years after ascending the throne, Amedeo told the Cortes he found the Spanish people ungovernable. He abdicated with grace and in 1873 left for his native Italy.

Several hours later the government declared the short-lived First Spanish Republic under Francisco Serrano, the hero of the Battle of Alcolea. Finally, in December 1874, the army Captain General Arsenio Martínez Campos rose against the Republic and pronounced in favour of the restoration of the monarchy. These riotous years were brought to a climax that same year with the return of the Bourbon dynasty to the throne of Spain, in the person of Isabel's son Alfonso XII.

'Cádiz, sweet Cádiz!'

For most foreigners, Spain's violent dynastic disputes and the country's state of political chaos over the nineteenth century would have been enough to mark it a no-go area in most people's European travel guides. This was not the case with George Gordon Byron, or Lord Byron as he was known, who in 1809, at the age of twenty-one, embarked on the Grand Tour, then a customary part of the education of young noblemen. His journey paved the way for many distinguished (or in some cases not) foreign travellers who were to follow in his footsteps. Byron's timing could not have been less judicious, setting foot as he did on Spanish soil shortly after the outbreak of the Peninsular War.

Impervious to the conflict raging around him, Byron travelled south to Sevilla and from there to Jerez de la Frontera, where he visited the sherry winery of his friend Charles Gordon, to quaff at the fountain head of the drink that enjoyed an immense popularity in Britain. Brooding on war, peace and merriment, from there, in 1809 he moved on to Cádiz. It was love at first sight. Byron saw Cádiz as a city of enormous charm, one that replaced Sevilla in his affections. 'Cadiz, sweet Cadiz! is the most delightful town I ever beheld, very different from our English cities in every respect except cleanliness,' he wrote.[4] He accepted invitations from the local aristocracy to attend the opera, accompanying a certain Admiral Luis de Córdova, a distinguished officer celebrated as commander of the Spanish fleet that in 1780 captured an entire convoy of British merchant ships. This single act was a major blow to British sea trade. The fact is that Byron expressed little interest in Córdova's heroic tales, for he only had eyes for the admiral's daughter. In another letter, Byron extolls the behaviour of the Spanish married woman, whom he insists was happy to entertain a 'proposal which in England would bring a box on the ear.' Byron's Spanish biographer was the politician and writer Emilio Castelar, who served as president of the First Republic. He fully understood that Byron had expressed great praise for Spanish men, but he was at a loss to understand why he had depicted women of the country in a manner so at odds with his own observations. Byron gradually worked his way into the Spanish consciousness, particularly in his role as European literary celebrity and champion of their cause. No less a figure than Benito Pérez Galdós included a Byronesque noble in his depiction of the city in his historical series *Episodios Nacionales*. In this narrative, Lord Gray is portrayed as a rakish Englishman sporting an ambivalent, hedonistic manner.

So besotted was Byron with the women of Cádiz that before leaving the city for his onward journey to Greece, he penned a verse in praise of their exquisiteness. The first two verses of *The Girl of Cádiz* speak eloquently of his passion for the ladies he so admired.

> O never talk again to me
> Of northern climes and British ladies;

IN THE EYE OF THE STORM

> It has not been your lot to see.
> Like me, the lovely Girl of Cádiz.
> Although her eyes be not of blue,
> Nor fair her locks, like English lassies,
> How far its own expressive hue
> The languid azure eye surpasses!
>
> Prometheus-like, from heaven she stole
> The fire that through those silken lashes
> In darkest glances see us to roll,
> From eyes that cannot hide their flashes;
> And as along her bosom steal
> In lengthened flow her raven tresses,
> You'd swear each clustering lock could feel,
> And curled to give her neck caresses.

Byron's contemporary, William Jacob, was an early nineteenth-century British parliamentarian and businessman, whose London firm of J&W Jacob was keen to seize a share of Spain's trade with its South American colonies. To this end, in 1809 Jacob embarked on a reconnaissance voyage to southern Spain, seeking the best way to exploit what was widely seen as the decline of the Spanish Empire. The letters he wrote describing his experiences in Cádiz reflect astonishment with a city sparkling with merriment and colour, such as he had not experienced elsewhere on his travels.

Jacob recounts that he was 'greatly struck' by the extraordinary scene around him: 'I could have imagined almost that I had suddenly been dropped from the clouds into the midst of a huge masquerade. The variety of dress and characters, the swarms of people, the height and externally clean appearances of the houses...all produced feelings I never before experienced and which no language can describe.' He goes on to extol the dress and personal ornaments of the people he encounters: 'Both the men and women are very extravagant, especially the latter. I am told that the money expended on a lady's silk stockings and shoes alone (for they never walk out twice in the same) is enormous.'[5]

An intrepid nineteenth-century British traveller who showed remarkable tenacity on his voyage to Cádiz was Richard Ford, a writer specialising in books on Spain. In his classic tale of Spanish adventures, *Gatherings from Spain*, he recounts the almost 'medieval' navigation system on the Guadalquivir River, which he describes as 'scarcely practicable for sailing vessels of a moderate size even up to Sevilla. Passengers, however, have facilities afforded them by the steamers which run backwards and forwards between this city and Cádiz.'[6]

On disembarking at Cádiz in 1835, accompanied by his ailing wife Harriet, Ford marvels at what he terms retracing the steps of antiquity:

> Thus still on the banks of the Bætis [Roman waterway between Córdoba and Sevilla] may be seen those dancing girls of profligate Gades, which were exported to ancient Rome, with pickled tunnies, to the delight of wicked epicures and the horror of the good fathers of the early Church, who compared them, perhaps justly, to the capering performed by the daughter of [Princess] Herodias. They were prohibited by Theodosius, because, according to St. Chrysostom, at such balls the devil never wanted a partner. The well-known statue at Naples called the Venere Callipige is the representation of Telethusa, or some other Cádiz dancing girl.[7]

According to Hispanist Jimmy Burns, 'Ford drew a historical link between Andalusian dancers and the *puellae Gaditanae*, the dancing girls of Phoenician Cádiz, who were so celebrated by ancient Rome...At one of his own dinners, [the Roman satirist] Martial bemoaned not having enough money to pay for "girls from wanton Gades, who with endless prurience swing lascivious loins in practised writhing."'[8]

Ford's near contemporary George Borrow was equally impervious to the perils that might await the unwary traveller. All the more so in his case, as Borrow was on a mission from the British and Foreign Bible Society to sell copies of the Bible translated into Spanish (akin to the King James Bible which underpinned the Protestant faith in Britain). This activity gathered much opposition from the Catholic Church in Spain, as well as from many politicians. Borrow was impressed at his first sight of a city which he declared to be unlike any he had seen in the Peninsula. His descriptions of the symmetrical layout and narrow streets intersecting at right angles is a feature that will reverberate with any modern visitor. So too, what remains of the walls and battlements still visible in the modern city. 'It is not without reason that Cádiz has been called a strong town,' he notes. 'The fortifications on the land are perfectly admirable and seem impregnable. Toward the sea it is defended as much by Nature and art, water and sunken rocks being no contemptible bulwarks.'[9]

On first entering the city in 1838, Borrow perceives the prevailing atmosphere of instability. 'Numerous bands of the factions were reported to be hovering in the neighbourhood. An attack was not deemed improbable and the place had just been declared in a state of siege.'[10] Borrow took up lodgings in a French-owned hotel and went for a walk about town. He visited several coffee houses, where in his words 'the din of tongues was deafening',[11] citing one place in particular in which six orators were simultaneously haranguing on the state of the country and the probability of a military intervention on the part of England or France. Continuing on his stroll through the city's streets, Borrow, a highly talented linguist, struck up conversations with passers-by, who expressed ideas on religion that were 'anything but satisfactory' for him.[12] He stopped off in a bookshop and produced a copy of the translated Bible he carried in his case.

CÁDIZ

The bookseller pronounced it unsaleable in Cádiz. This echoed the response he received during his stay from all other potentially interested parties. Later in 1838, Borrow returned to London, having failed to achieve a single convert.

At around the time that Ford and Byron were on their Spanish sojourns, the future Prime Minister Benjamin Disraeli took a two-year break from politics to do some travelling abroad. Together with his sister's fiancé, William Meredith, in May 1830 Disraeli left London on the steamer HMS *Shannon*, bound for Falmouth. This was the departure point for the monthly steam packets for Malta, their destination after paying a visit to Andalucía. Disraeli and Meredith departed England on the HMS *Messenger*, a sloop that took them to Cádiz, aware that this was 'an excursion of hourly peril for our purses and perhaps our lives.'[13]

Andalucía was a destination of personal interest for Disraeli. He persuaded himself that he was descended from the Sephardic community of Jews driven from Spain in 1492 by the Catholic Monarchs. There is in fact nothing to substantiate Disraeli's belief that his family origins lay in medieval Spain, much less in Cádiz. The city did have a Jewish settlement, which increased in importance when the island on which Cádiz was situated became linked with the mainland by silt from the Guadalquivir. At the time of the expulsion in 1492, about 8,000 Jews left Cádiz, mainly for North Africa. Four centuries later, the city census showed 209 Jews in Cádiz, but there is no reference to what might have been Disraeli's ancestors. Nevertheless, Disraeli makes mention in his 1844 novel *Coningsby* of Sidonia, as in the Marqués de Medina Sidonia of Cádiz, who the author believed to be an aristocrat of Jewish origin persecuted by the Inquisition. The character of Sidonia is thought by some sources to be a cross between Lionel de Rothschild and Disraeli himself.

Disraeli, like Byron, found himself captivated by the women of Cádiz. In a letter describing his voyage he said it was like seeing 'Figaro in every street and Rosina in every balcony',[14] in reference to the characters from Rossini's *Barber of Seville*. He was equally impressed by the ladies he encountered out on their evening strolls along the promenades. 'Once out of their bowers, they amused themselves on the alameda, or public walk. All is now life and liveliness. Such bowing, such kissing, such fluttering of fans, such gentle criticism of gentle friends!'[15]

Alexandre Dumas must surely rank as the most flamboyant of nineteenth-century foreign travellers to Cádiz. With his Gallic jocularity and great piles of frizzy hair, the creator of *The Count of Monte Cristo* and *The Three Musketeers* would have certainly turned heads on his spirited promenades along the city's cobbled streets. In 1846, Dumas was approached by Narcisse Achille de Salvandy, minister of public instruction, who invited him to travel on behalf of the government to Algeria, to inform himself of the country that had just passed under French control. In all, Dumas spent two months in Spain hunting wild boar in Córdoba and writing letters from Sevilla to an enigmatic 'Madame', who might well have been a figment of Dumas's imagination. After all, he was the creator of the phrase '*Cherchez la femme!*' Dumas praised Sevilla's fifteenth century cathedral, La Giralda, as 'having no equal in the world' and he was mesmerised by its enormous paschal candle.

From there, Dumas travelled down the Guadalquivir River to cast anchor in the Port of Cádiz, 'dazzling white between the blue of sky and sea and crowded with sailing ships of every rig, size and nationality.'[16] He took lodgings in the now defunct Fonda de Europa, which had been recommended as the best hotel in Cádiz. His sojourn was cut short after two days – he was asked to leave for alleged 'unseemly behaviour.' This, he hints, may have been to do with his visitor, Julia, a woman he had met at a home that was 'not quite respectable.' Dumas himself acknowledged that his escapades had been the talk of all Cádiz. Despite his contretemps, he was overwhelmed by the city he described as the 'true daughter of the sun, bathed in a dazzling light, her only colours the blue of sea and sky, the white of her houses and the emerald green of her shutters. Cádiz is virtually an island, able to extend only upwards. The houses are very tall and seem to be standing on tip-toe to gain a view of the harbour, the water or even Tangier.'[17]

No less an enthusiast of Cádiz was the British novelist William Somerset Maugham. In his Spanish travelogue, published in 1905, Maugham speaks of Cádiz as the liveliest town in Andalucía:

> Spaniards have always a certain gravity. They are not very talkative and, like the English, take their pleasures a little sadly. But here lightness of the heart is thought to reign supreme and the inhabitants have not even the apparent seriousness with which the Sevillian cloaks a somewhat vacant mind. They are great theatregoers and as dancers, of course, have been famous since the world began. For those blithe people, it seemed that there was no morrow: the present was to be enjoyed, divine and various and the world was full of beauty and of sunshine. Merely to live was happiness enough. If there was pain or sorrow, it served but to enhance the gladness.[18]

Maugham also had praise for the city's sparkling appearance. He admired its well-kept streets and spacious rooms. He noted that the houses were taller than is usual in Andalucía, with a cared-for appearance just as those in a prosperous suburb of London.

The Disaster of '98

Cádiz regained some prominence in 1895 as the link with what little remained of Spain's colonial empire. Cuba had risen up in rebellion, demanding the overthrow of Spanish rule. Once

IN THE EYE OF THE STORM

again, the Port of Cádiz became the platform for dispatching army regiments to the western hemisphere, as had been the case during the independence campaigns of Spain's other former colonies.

The dispatch of the soldiers for Cuba bore all the trappings of a fiesta, a pastime so beloved by the people of Cádiz. The special send-off rations issued to the departing troops consisted of portions of Valencian rice and beefsteak, washed down with amontillado sherry wine and topped off with a Havana cigar plus, as a special farewell treat, a handful of coins. Vicente Calvo, the bishop of Cádiz, held a solemn Mass in the town hall square for the departing units, after which the columns were marched off to the awaiting ships to the accompaniment of the municipal band.[19] The Cuban revolt ended in a stalemate that failed to supress the Caribbean island's independence crusade.

What was left of the Spanish Empire, in terminal decline for many decades, collapsed conclusively after the Spanish–American War of 1898. Spain's defeat forced the country to relinquish sovereignty over Cuba, while ceding Puerto Rico, the Philippines and Guam to the United States. This dealt Spanish morale a heavy blow, and in the case of the economy of Cádiz, it placed the last nail in the coffin of what for centuries had been the lifeblood of the city's prosperity.

The debacle of 1898, as might well have been expected, propelled Spanish national pride into a tailspin. The future King Alfonso XIII was only three years old when the war ended, leaving the monarchy on shaky ground. Alfonso XII had died in November 1885, before his son was even born. His mother, the Regent María Cristina of Austria, was a foreigner, not well liked by the general public and reputed to be a person of less than average intelligence. The conservative Prime Minister Antonio Cánovas del Castillo had been assassinated by an Italian anarchist in 1897. To his successor, the Liberal Party leader Práxedes

Mateo Sagasta, fell the unenviable task of fending off a torrent of abuse from political enemies and sectors of the press for the country's defeat in the Spanish–American War.

Cádiz found itself in the grip of anti-British fever. People were fearful of a decline in trade with the loss of Cuba. It did not require much effort to persuade people that the country, which on so many occasions had turned its guns on their city, in some sinister way was behind the scenes in bringing about the Disaster of '98, as it came to be known.

Under the peace agreement negotiated in Paris between Spain and the United States, Spanish prisoners of war were released and sent home, not a few of them to Cádiz, which had supplied troops for the war in Cuba. Cádiz also began to welcome back those who had left during the years of turmoil to take up residence in more tranquil regions. They returned to find a city facing an economic void, its once thriving port no longer the Mecca of trade with the Caribbean islands and the Philippines.

Amnesty and regeneration

Upon reaching the age of sixteen in 1902, Alfonso XIII ascended the throne, putting an end to the regency of his mother. The government issued a general amnesty for political prisoners, and one of the most celebrated of ex-convicts was Fermín Salvochea, a former mayor of Cádiz who had served as president of the canton during the First Spanish Republic. With his neatly trimmed beard and thick spectacles, one would not guess that under this appearance of a gentle academic there raged the soul of an avowed insurrectionist. He had spent several years imprisoned on the orders of Pavía in Spain's North African territories on charges of anarchist agitation. Salvochea was one of the most colourful figures to emerge from Cádiz in the hectic days of anti-government insurgencies.

IN THE EYE OF THE STORM

No sooner had he been freed from jail, Salvochea lost no time in returning to Cádiz to busy himself with the spread of the anarchist gospel. His influence on radical politics spread from Cádiz to Madrid, where a few months after his release he helped to organise the general strike of 1902. His energetic propagation of anarcho-syndicalism was a driving force behind the founding in 1910 of the anarchist National Confederation of Labour (CNT) union, a vehement fighter for the Republican cause in the Spanish Civil War.

Salvochea did not live to see the fruits of his labour as a creator of the CNT anarchist trade union. He returned to Cádiz in 1907, where he renounced his family inheritance and donated all he possessed to the poor. He spent his final days in self-imposed poverty and died after falling off the wooden plank that he used as his bed.

Salvochea became a literary hero for celebrated Spanish novelists Vicente Blasco Ibañez and Jesús Cañadas. His bust adorns the wall of a building in Cádiz's Plaza de Argüelles and he is a familiar figure portrayed in the city's annual carnival. A grouping of the Cádiz Football Association calls itself Columna Salvochea while every year, on the anniversary of his death, the people of Cádiz lay flowers on Salvochea's grave.

The decade following the Disaster of '98 ushered in an era of political bedlam, with no fewer than fifteen prime ministers of the Liberal and Conservative parties holding office in that period. There was one reality that overshadowed a scenario of constant bitter sectarianism: the need to stem the rising tide of hopelessness and apathy afflicting the nation, precipitated by the loss of empire and Spain's status as a once-respected European power.

The catchphrase endorsed by the political classes was *Regeneración*, literally 'Regeneration'. In Cádiz, this translated into an ambitious public works programme, conceived by the municipal authorities and funded by the government and donations from local philanthropists. One such benefactor was the London-educated politician and wine merchant José Moreno de Mora. In partnership with his equally affluent spouse Micaela de Aramburu, in 1904 they financed the construction of the Hospital de Mora. This vast complex facing La Caleta beach now houses part of the University of Cádiz. When inaugurated, it was a veritable 'hospital city' in size that gave an architectural uplift to a neglected area of Cádiz. The Mora-Aramburu family also sponsored the San Miguel Arcángel Christian School, which in its day provided schooling for five hundred children of working-class families from the Santa María neighbourhood.

City officials were aware of the need to lift people's morale, so to this end an entertainment venue came into their planning strategy. The shipowner and Mayor of Cádiz Miguel Martínez de Pinillos Sáenz had sponsored the building of the Gran Teatro, to replace an earlier theatre which burnt to the ground in 1881. In 1884, the work began on building the new theatre, which was to take over the old theatre site, as well as the adjacent site of the former hospital. The building was completed in 1905, bearing the name Gran Teatro Falla, in honour of the celebrated Cádiz composer and pianist Manuel de Falla, although it was not fully ready for public performances until 1910. The building was designed by the architect Juan Cabrera Latorre, who conceived a façade of neoclassical inspiration with a balcony in the centre flanked by large Ionic attached columns. Elements of cast-iron architecture are used in the inside, where the Imperial-style stairs form a connection between the two main rooms. It is now one of the city's most stunning attractions, built of red bricks in the Mudéjar style. The interior, also in the Moorish-Spanish style, is noteworthy for its richness and colour.[20]

The hospital and theatre are but two monuments of the new century to be admired by the visitor to Cádiz. By the sea wall, the somewhat pretentiously named Real Academia Hispano Americana de Ciencias, Artes y Letras de Cádiz ('Royal Hispanic-American Academy of Science, Art and Letters of Cádiz') was founded in 1875 as an institute devoted to the study of Spanish science and literature. In 1909, Mayor Cayetano del Toro, who was eager to celebrate the cultural achievements of Spain's former colonies, arranged to purchase a building for the society. It was at this time the academy acquired its current title and role. The mayor also arranged for the purchase of another building within the Old Town to create the Museum of the Cortes of Cádiz to commemorate the forthcoming centenary of the Constitution of 1812; this was in Calle Santa Inés, right next door to the historic church of the Oratorio San Felipe Neri, where the Cortes had held its debating sessions in the city.

Cádiz launched three of what might be defined as urban renewal projects in the early years of the twentieth century. One of these enterprises was an attempt to expand the city beyond the limits of a monumental bastion at what was the gateway to metropolitan Cádiz. The Puertas de Tierra, adjacent to the Plaza de la Constitución, was built in the eighteenth century around remnants of the old defensive wall. The towering marble-glazed structure flies the purple flag of Cádiz to signal the entrance to the city proper.

It became obvious to town planners that the port, which throughout its history had stood as Spain's foremost link to global trade, had gradually decayed into a shambles. This inspired the authorities to create the Junta del Puerto in 1906, which was to provide a blueprint of port renewal. Six years later, thousands of high-spirited citizens turned out to cheer the unveiling of Reina Victoria dock, the first of several that were built at the port. Whatever social or political vicissitudes Cádiz has gone through since that time, the port, with its 6,500 feet of quay, has continued to retain its importance in city life.[21]

An undertaking of more debatable benefit to Cádiz, one that sparked a great deal of controversy, was the decision in 1906 to demolish part of the city's ancient defensive walls. It was obvious that the loss of the walls would bring a radical change in Cádiz's appearance, yet Mayor Cayetano del Toro made this one of his pet urban development schemes. The day before the wrecking balls moved in, Del Toro announced to the crowds gathered below the town hall balcony that this would be celebrated as a solemn festivity. He asked people to hang lamps from their houses and give bits of bread to beggars so that their 'tears of gratitude will irrigate the soil on which the walls are seated.' The mayor claimed that razing the walls was a long-standing aspiration of the citizens of Cádiz, who wanted nothing so much as to open up new space to expand the city. In effect, the disappearance of the walls, whether or not a symbol of progress, did allow for the construction of new housing along the strip today known as Paseo de Canalejas.

Another round of demolition work took place six years later, in what is today the Plaza de España, to mark the centenary of the Constitution of 1812. As Manuel Bustos Rodríguez notes:

> With the disappearance as well of the fortified wall that protected this area...a few years later, in 1918, the city erected one of the city's most famous monuments, dedicated to 'the Cortes, Constitution and Siege of Cádiz'. It is filled with deep symbolism, the empty throne of Fernando VII, statues of the deputies and the steps of the semi-circular chamber, a tribute to the Constitution, prosperity and the [Napoleonic] war. It is a celebration of the Cortes and the proclamation of the Constitution of 1812.[22]

The decision to pull down the bulk of the city walls had been decried by many as a criminal act that obliterated centuries of glorious history as the city defended itself against successive waves of combatants. Supporters argued that it was a necessary step forward in taking Cádiz into the twentieth century. Soon after the job was done, the newly opened land became a building site. This was to be a working-class housing district called Barriada Obrera. City planners had the foresight to appreciate the need for transport to take workers not only to the city centre, but to Carraca, Chiclana and other localities across the bay. To this end, in 1906 the Cádiz tram came into service, the first surviving urban rail system in Andalucía. This was a box-like contraption on wheels that rumbled noisily through the city's flagged streets, clanging its bell at pedestrians and broughams, the driver and conductor formally turned out in white uniform and cap.[23]

Transport and tourism

Coinciding with advances in the city's urban rail transport system, Cádiz began to experience its first mass influx of foreign tourism, rather than intrepid single travellers. France and Italy were the traditional destinations on the European tourist itinerary. These two countries were well-established as a must for their famous monuments and fine cuisine. Spain was for most people a blank space on the map, thought of in the prevalent imagination as a land of cruelty and violence. True enough, bullfighting for the non-aficionado is in itself a metaphor for brutality. Spain has also been the European country most ravaged in contemporary history by warfare and internal strife. There was also the perceived poverty of its cuisine, unable to match the refinement of French or Italian cookery, along with a dearth of tourist accommodation of a high standard. These were the disincentives seen by those on the Grand European Tour, mostly Britons, as the reasons for not adding Spain to their travel programme.

Perhaps encouraged by the exotic accounts of Lord Byron or Washington Irving's *Tales of the Alhambra*, or even Gioachino Rossini's *Barber of Seville*, it was now time to take the plunge into the dark, unexplored land south of the Pyrenees. The most intrepid were to venture beyond the somewhat familiar environs of Madrid and Barcelona, to the great Andalusian capitals of Córdoba and Sevilla. A few of these voyagers carried on even further, to explore the mysteries beyond these great historic cities. Regardless of what might have been the enticement, by the early twentieth century city officials were beginning to take notice of the trickle of foreign visitors arriving in Cádiz. This was viewed as a source of badly needed income to alleviate the financial crisis. In 1906, the Vista Hermosa seafront was enhanced with a boardwalk and leisure services that drew crowds of holidaymakers to the beach. A year later, the Gran Balneario Reina Victoria spa welcomed its first holidaymakers. A newly opened tram line followed the Alameda Apodaca promenade, and visitors could purchase a combination ticket for the journey and spa entry. A six-piece orchestra was at the gates to welcome nearly six hundred people who visited the spa on its opening day.

The city had appointed José Romero Barrero to design this huge facility. Barrero, an acknowledged maestro of the modernist style, also took on the task of rehabilitating the stately home of the landscape artist Manuel Mayol Rubio, in the heart of the old city. The Tourism Information Office, conveniently located by the dock that was the disembarking point for many tourists, was another of Barrero's creations.

The Reina Victoria spa was exclusively a sanctuary for the city's bourgeoisie. Likewise, the recently renovated casino, a splendid specimen of Moorish revival architecture, whose brilliant white walls illuminate the Plaza San Antonio. The eighteenth century building was originally the home of the Marqués de Pedroso. It was sold in 1848 to a consortium of Cádiz businessmen, who set up the casino as the equivalent of a gentlemen's club for the upper echelons of Cádiz society. Alongside these venues for high society, the city's middle classes and growing proletariat needed a source of entertainment. To this end, the Cádiz Club de Fútbol was founded in 1910. It was a relative newcomer to the league of Spanish football clubs. The Cádiz club traces its origin to a morning in 1903, at a meeting of supporters in La Hoyacana bullring, the site of today's Mirandilla stadium, where it was agreed by popular acclaim that the city needed a team to compete against established clubs like Huelva, which in 1899 became Spain's first, with Bilbao, Madrid and Barcelona following in quick succession.

The future was looking brighter as Cádiz approached the centenary celebrations of the 1812 Constitution. When the great day arrived on 25 August, the entire population hung banners from their balconies and kept their lights on throughout the night. The ceremonies commenced that morning with a Te Deum at the cathedral with the music of Spain's master composer of choral music, Miguel Eslava. The municipal authorities marched into the square carrying maces – symbols of victory. On that day, great throngs poured into the streets to indulge in an afternoon and evening of dancing and singing, unsuspecting that in the not distant future the city would be struck by its worst disaster since the Battle of Trafalgar.

7

CÁDIZ AT WAR

As the Disaster of '98 gradually faded from memory Cádiz began to seek new opportunities for breathing life into an economy, one historically centred on shipbuilding and trade with Spain's colonies, that had been flatlining for more than a decade. These were not days that encouraged much optimism. Amongst other problems, Cádiz, like the rest of Spain, was grappling with a downturn in tourism influenced by the First World War and exacerbated by the 1918–19 so-called Spanish flu.[1] Labour unrest in the wake of the Russian Revolution of 1917 plagued the manufacturing and industrial sectors. The most badly affected areas of Spain were the poorer regions of the south. Cádiz was no exception, though to a lesser extent than in the country's large cities. The general strike of 1917 saw hundreds of thousands of workers of the socialist and anarchist unions take to the streets to protest the impact the European war was having on inflation, wages, unemployment and supply shortages. Industrial action brought the country to a standstill and sparked a rash of violence that left more than two hundred dead and injured.

CÁDIZ

Green shoots

In spite of these obstacles to economic recovery, the early years of the twentieth century on balance brought signs of green shoots. The city was now clearly on the European tourism map, ready to take advantage of the post-First World War turnaround. No longer would visitors from abroad be obliged to hold up in one of the grubby inns so disparaged by the likes of Lord Byron and Alexandre Dumas. By 1930, Cádiz was able to offer lodgings in twenty hotels of a high standing. The previous year, the city had inaugurated its parador, facing La Caleta beach, whose grand promenade closely resembles Havana's Malecón. One of the hotel's early guests was King Alfonso XIII, who in 1929 had inaugurated in Álava province the first of the country's ninety-seven paradors. The monarch spoke admiringly of the hotel's charm, though Alfonso made it clear that he was less impressed by the demolition of the city walls. The Cádiz parador later joined with the luxury Hotel Atlántico, which featured the novelties, unheard of in those days, of a private bathroom and fireplace in every room.

One visitor who was not able to enjoy the new luxury accommodation was the English writer Laurie Lee, who had left his Cotswold village in 1935 to discover Spain, playing his violin to earn his way. Lee had landed at Vigo in northwest Spain and gradually worked his way south, mostly walking through the countryside, stopping at towns and cities, where his stay depended on whether there was a living to be made through his playing. Arriving in Cádiz after three months of wandering, his initial view was of 'a city of sharp incandescence, a scribble of white on a sheet of blue glass, lying curved on the bay like a scimitar and sparkling with African light.'[2]

However, the police told Lee he was forbidden to play music in the streets for money, so he was limited to the poorest accommodation, 'an evil old posada whose galleries were packed with sailors, beggars and pimps. There was little to do all day except sit round in the dust while the scorching winds blew in from the Atlantic.'[3] Lee recalls meeting an array of poverty-stricken inhabitants and hearing tales of those who were even worse off, living in the drains of the city and surviving on scraps of shellfish from tavern floors. He did not linger long in Cádiz but moved east along the Andalusian coast.

Although it was hard times for the poor of Cádiz there was good news on the industrial front. The Ford Motor Company chose Cádiz as the location of its Spanish assembly plant. The US automobile firm had considered Barcelona, which seemed the logical choice given the size of the Catalán capital's well-established manufacturing industries. Henry Ford, the company's founder and arch-conservative, harboured some doubts about Barcelona and its political instability, being a city with a unionised and combative working class. Cádiz, despite its stormy history, was at the time seen as a quieter and more manageable headquarters for Ford's Spanish business. Its strategic geographical position and free zone were additional incentives, as were the extensive tax exemptions granted by the local government. These were enough reasons to convince Henry Ford, who in September 1919 gave the green light to setting up the Ford Motor Company SAE Cádiz, which from 1920 began turning out ten thousand Model T cars a year, earmarked for domestic sales and export.

The Cádiz shipbuilding industry provided a morale-booster with the launch of the *Juan Sebastián Elcano* in 1927, the four-masted topsail schooner that became the Spanish Navy midshipmen training vessel. The ship is named after the Spanish navigator who in 1522 completed the first circumnavigation of the globe on the Magellan expedition to the Spice Islands. The *Elcano*, as it has become popularly known as, was built in the Echevarrieta y Larrinaga shipyard, later to become Astilleros de

Cádiz and from 1969 Astilleros Españoles. The original shipyard was set up by Horacio Echevarrieta, one of Spain's most ambitious and resourceful businessmen. Until the start of the Spanish Civil War in 1936, the unstoppable entrepreneur Echevarrieta also founded Iberia airlines, electricity companies like Iberdrola, cement factories, mining and timber firms, as well as building and insurance enterprises. Echevarrieta amassed a great fortune in the First World War by transporting desperately needed iron ore and other war material to Britain and France. His Cádiz-based shipyard also built a replica of the *Santa María*, one of the three galleons that took Christopher Columbus on his first voyage to the New World.

Prospects for an economic comeback were looking brighter than at the start of the century. A general feeling of cautious optimism meant that more people were able to turn their thoughts to leisure pursuits, such as entertainment. The 1930s denoted the birth of Hollywood's golden era, with Cary Grant, Katharine Hepburn and other stars of the screen packing in spectators around the world, including Spain, whose major cities had opened movie theatres as early as 1896. Cádiz was now to partake in the cinema craze sweeping Europe. The long-vanished modernist-style Cine Gades, designed by municipal architect Antonio Sánchez Esteve, occupied an entire city block in the old town when it opened its doors in 1932. Before each screening, more than six hundred spectators sat enthralled by a spectacle of light and music in an auditorium lavishly equipped with Zeiss projectors and a Marconi sound system. On the gala opening night, an audience that had for the most part never set foot in a cinema was treated to the Spanish-language version of the 1931 Fox Film thriller *Charlie Chan Carries On*.

Given the political turmoil sweeping Spain in the early 1930s, the city maintained a remarkable air of surface calm. The audience leaving Cine Gades would have gone for a stroll along the nearby

Avenida del Puerto promenade or dropped into a tavern for an aperitif before making their way home or to a restaurant for supper.

The Second Republic

General Miguel Primo de Rivera had installed himself as dictator in 1923 after staging a successful military coup, with the tacit blessing of the king. He ruled for seven years, until being ousted in a putschist plot led by General Manuel Goded, who was himself to become a central figure in the July 1936 army uprising against the Second Republic. The king, who had been discredited by his support for Primo de Rivera's coup, ordered General Dámaso Berenguer to form a new government. But Berenguer's *dictablanda*, or soft dictatorship, failed to provide a viable alternative, and in April 1931 the new cabinet called municipal elections for the first time in nine years. The elections, widely recognised as a plebiscite on monarchy, brought a clear warning of impending violence. Forty-one of Spain's fifty provinces returned a vote in favour of leftist Republican candidates. Cádiz was one of the thirteen that voted for parties that supported the monarchy. It may appear odd that Cádiz, with its manifold economic and social problems, turned its back on the Republican cause. The province elected to office 484 monarchist candidates, compared with 166 for the Republican and Socialist parties. Cádiz was the only province in Andalucía to vote overwhelmingly for the monarchist alliances. On the surface, this may seem inconsistent with the region's large working-class population. The electoral history of Cádiz, across the province as well as in the capital, reveals a propensity for the common people to do the bidding of the oligarchy. Many civil servants as well as blue-collar workers owed their livelihoods to those who held power, be they the great landowners of Jerez de la Frontera and the countryside, shipyard owners, or mayors like Ramón de Carranza, who participated in the 1936 coup that overthrew the Republic.

The elections sounded the death knell for the monarchy. Shortly after the results were announced, Alfonso XIII followed in the footsteps of his grandmother Isabel II and left for exile in France, while on 14 April 1931, contrary to prevailing fears, Spain peacefully proclaimed the Second Republic.

When the news reached Cádiz that Spain had once again become a republic, those who had voted for the leftist candidate Emilio de Sola gathered en masse outside his rented flat in Calle Adolfo de Castro, near the Alameda Gardens, to shout their congratulations to the man who would become the city's first mayor under the new Republic. In a further show of esteem, the crowd placed some forty copies of works of art, curiously enough almost all religious paintings by Zurbarán, Murillo, Tintoretto and other classic artists, outside his house. From there, they marched across the city to the city hall to raise the Republican flag. The municipal band paraded through the streets playing 'La Marseillaise' while a hydroplane circled overhead dragging in tow a Republican tricolour flag.

Amid this outpouring of jubilation from those who welcomed the Republic, few were to appreciate the storm clouds moving in from the very day in April 1931 Niceto Alcalá-Zamora was sworn in as the Second Republic's first prime minister. The republic had inherited a country still convalescing from decades of political and social unrest. The greatest danger sign was a growing demoralisation in the army. This had come to the fore in the wake of the Disaster of 1898, to which in 1921 was added what became known as the 'Tragedy of Annual'. The expression refers to a stinging defeat of the Spanish Army at the hands of Berber tribesmen in the Rif War of 1920–27. Spanish Army units were sent to Morocco to supress a tribal uprising in what was at that time a Spanish protectorate. The war ended in a hard-won and bloody victory for Spain, whose army sustained 43,500 casualties and left the country in control of Spanish Morocco until 1958. In the view of Hispanist Raymond Carr,

> The military disasters of 1921 in Morocco made the army feel at the same time insecure and indignant: indignant in that it sensed the politicians had deprived it of the material base of glory, insecure in that it feared that the same politicians would once more turn the cry of 'responsibility' against an army to which their parsimony had denied the sinews of victory.[4]

The first serious spate of political violence under the republic was a massacre that happened in Casas Viejas, a small farming village in Cádiz province, some 30 miles south-east of the capital. In January 1933, anarchist revolutionaries took hold of the town. The insurrectionists were led by members of the CNT trade union, many of whom had travelled from Cádiz and elsewhere in the region to partake in the uprising. What ensued on that day in Casas Viejas was nothing less than a dress rehearsal for the outbreak of strife and hatred that was to engulf Spain for three tragic years.

The anarchists seized control of the streets in a matter of hours. They were at first unchallenged, leading them to imagine themselves the forerunners of a revolution that would spread to the rest of the country. It was not long before the Assault Guard and Civil Guard were called in to stamp out this naïve dream. Some of the revolutionaries were armed and in an exchange of gunfire, two of the paramilitary officers fell wounded. Some of the anarchists barricaded themselves in the straw and mud cottage of a CNT militant. The guardsmen then poured petrol over the house and set it alight. One man carrying a baby was the only person to emerge alive from the inferno, in which sixteen people were incinerated. The guardsmen then arrested anyone found carrying a firearm. The prisoners were marched to the smouldering ashes of the hut, where they were summarily executed. In all, twenty-four people died that day in one of the main episodes that was to fuel a breach in the Republican coalition.

The tragedy of Casas Viejas stands as one of the defining moments in the history of the Second Republic and is often credited as one of the events that set Spain on the path to civil war. As historian Raymond Carr explains, 'It was the long-term effects of Casas Viejas which destroyed [Manuel] Azaña's government in September 1933. [Azaña had become prime minister in October 1931 after the resignation of Alcalá-Zamora.] The cycle of disorder and repression not merely alienated the proletarian forces but put a weapon into the hands of malcontents on the right – corrupt, incapable of preserving public order, yet violent.'[5]

In Cádiz, as in the rest of Spain, political schisms were stoking a division within all ranks of society, splitting them into opposing factions. On the one side stood the traditionalists, mainly the orthodox middle classes, angered by what they perceived to be a breakdown in law and order. These people had good reason to be appalled by the attacks on their Catholic religion. In 1931, shortly after the Second Republic was installed, anticlerical rioters torched four of the city's oldest churches: Santo Domingo, Santa María, Iglesia del Carmen and San Francisco. After a period of calm, shortly before war was declared in 1936, anticlerical provocateurs were again on the rampage. The churches of La Merced and Santa María were destroyed, while San Pablo, La Pastora, the seminary and other religious edifices were badly damaged by the mob.

The coming storm

The self-proclaimed revolutionaries of Cádiz – to say nothing of the political rivals of the Second Republic, perpetually bogged down in suicidal infighting – would have done well to heed the plot being hatched by a coterie of high-ranking army officers to overthrow the government. Most Spanish generals had fought in the wars of Morocco. They embraced the idea of a Spain unfettered by partisan politics and free of what they scorned as non-Spanish values, namely socialism, communism and anarchism, in their view the ideological diseases that had poisoned the government.

A number of top military commanders looked on in alarm at a Popular Front coalition of socialists, communists and other leftist parties that had come to power in the February 1936 general elections. Among the disgruntled military there figured a small, pudgy and squeaky-voiced general from Galicia. Francisco Franco was a veteran of the Moroccan campaigns, who in 1936 had been banished to a remote posting in the Canary Islands by the government which considered him – quite rightly, as history was to prove – a danger to the Republic. Franco and other senior officers were at this time actively discussing a plot to overthrow the Popular Front.

The incident that spurred the conspirators into action occurred in Madrid on 13 July 1936. A party of Civil Guard and Assault Guard officers, with the tacit permission of the Republican Government, assassinated José Calvo Sotelo, a prominent figure in the monarchist movement. This was in revenge for the previous day's killing of the Assault Guard and Socialist Party member José Castillo, shot dead by gunmen of the Falange, the right-wing party modelled on Benito Mussolini's Fascist Party.

This was the final straw for the putschists, the pretext they had been waiting for to make their move. The government had been aware of a real threat from disgruntled generals since at least 1932. In that year, General José Sanjurjo, one of Franco's co-conspirators, was arrested and sent to Cádiz military prison for having attempted an uprising in Sevilla. Two years later he was granted amnesty and went into exile in Portugal. When the military rebellion in Morocco finally got underway, Sanjurjo boarded a private plane in Portugal to fly to Spain and assume command of the revolt. He was killed when his small biplane crashed near Estoril, allegedly having been warned by the pilot that he was carrying an excessive amount of heavy luggage. This was Franco's cue to step in as leader of the insurgency.

The conspiracy began to take root in Cádiz in late April 1936 through contacts set up between the plotters and the army garrison. General Emilio Mola was leader of the rebel forces in the north of Spain, while Franco operated from North Africa. Mola was thought of as the plotter most likely to head a future Nationalist government but like Sanjurjo, he was to die in an air crash, in suspicious circumstances in 1937. Nevertheless, Mola acted as chief tactician of the Cádiz revolt and sent an emissary to Cádiz to explore the local units' readiness to take part in an act of treason. This was Colonel Francisco García Escámez, a native of Cádiz, who was cleverly deployed to his home territory. He reported back to Mola that in his opinion, the officers he met with showed some reluctance to back a general insurrection – he was to be proven wrong.

The main thrust of the uprising came on the morning of 18 July 1936. The geographic proximity of Cádiz, being the city closest to the army of Morocco's base of operations, along with its large naval base and sizeable armed forces taskforce, made it a crucial target for Franco's planned invasion. The city authorities had received news the previous day that *tercios* (regiments) of the Foreign Legion and Moorish Regulares were being kitted out and briefed for an invasion of the mainland.[6]

A swift victory for the rebel forces was never a foregone conclusion. Franco's initial successes were patchy and inconclusive. Hispanist Paul Preston notes, 'When war broke out, the military forces in the Peninsula, approximately 130,000 men in the Army and 33,000 Civil Guards, were divided almost equally between insurgents and loyalists. That broad stalemate was dramatically altered by the fact that the entire Army of Africa was with the rebels.[7] The first forty-eight hours were a cliffhanger, as Franco struggled to find a way to convey his army across the Strait of Gibraltar. Before the official outbreak of hostilities on 18 July, the Spanish destroyer *Churruca*, two merchant steamers and a ferry boat were all the future Caudillo could muster to carry 220 men from Africa to Cádiz. More discouraging for Franco was the mutiny staged by the crew of the *Churruca* against their rebel officers. The bulk of the Spanish Navy had refused to back the invasion. The crew of the *Churruca* arrested the ship's officers and handed over the destroyer to the Spanish Republican Navy. Two other destroyers anchored off Melilla, the *Almirante Valdés* and *Sánchez Barcáiztegui*, rushed their officers and overpowered them. They then elected a ship's committee, bombarded the insurgent bases of Melilla and Ceuta and returned to the loyal naval base of Cartagena. The rebels thus had only one destroyer and one gunboat, the *Dato*, to start ferrying the badly needed reinforcements from the Army of Africa across to Cádiz.[8]

Franco had a stroke of luck in that General Alfredo Kindelán, founder of the Spanish Air Force, happened to be in Cádiz when news reached the city of the uprising in Melilla. In a telephone conversation, Franco appointed Kindelán head of his embryonic air force, thus gaining a useful asset in organising transport to Cádiz and Sevilla. Progress remained slow, as the Nationalist advance met with stiff resistance from loyalist defenders in Madrid, Barcelona and other strategically important cities. The solution to Franco's predicament appeared in the person of Adolf Hitler. Franco maintained cordial relations with the führer, who understood it was in Nazi Germany's interest to have a right-wing military regime ruling Spain, rather than a leftist government that might enter the war on the Allied side. To this end, shortly after the outbreak of the Civil War in 1936, Hitler agreed to supply Franco with twenty bombers, a gesture that was to bring a turnaround for what was starting to look like a failed coup. A fortnight after the revolt, ten Junkers carrying military fittings for all twenty bombers were loaded onto ships and embarked by sea from Hamburg to Cádiz. The other ten, disguised as civilian transport aircraft, flew directly to Spanish Morocco. This was followed up in October 1936 by the arrival of a complete German battle group, the notorious Condor Legion. In all, by the end of November twelve thousand German soldiers had landed in Cádiz, along with artillery and armoured transport.

The Germans were able to deploy arms and troops to Cádiz unopposed for the simple reason that the city had succumbed to the rebels almost immediately. The morning of 18 July found city government hierarchy in frantic meetings called to organise their defence tactics. Spanish troops garrisoned in Cádiz had joined the rebellion, led by General José Enrique Varela, a native of the city and staunch Franco confederate. Civil Governor Mariano Zapico, who a few days later was to be put in front of a Nationalist firing squad, ordered Varela's arrest on suspicion of plotting with the insurrectionists. His incarceration in Santa Catalina military prison was a short-lived affair. He was freed in a matter of hours by soldiers of the local garrison who had joined the uprising. The insurrectionists then marched to government headquarters, spurred on by Varela leading the column, when they came under fire from workers hidden on rooftops in the Santa María district and Puertas de Tierra bastion. These republican loyalists were swiftly put out of action by the heavily armed artillery and infantry brigades. The insurrectionists then surrounded the building where Zapico was holding out, backed by a small contingent of Assault Guards.

The army split into several formations to surround the civil government headquarters, the town hall and the post office, each of which was manned by loyalists. With total disregard for the hopelessness of the situation, Zapico and the other city hall defenders refused to lay down their arms. The insurgents let loose with a fusillade of automatic weapons that went on unabated until the following dawn. The army launched an attack on other enemies who had barricaded themselves inside four churches, two schools and the Catholic Workers' Centre. When the troops from Morocco disembarked in the port on the morning of 19 July, the defenders realised they had no choice but to lay down their arms to avoid a massacre. The military coup against the Republic had triumphed in Cádiz. While it is true that the city was in the hands of Franco's army, a small number of army detachments and citizens loyal to the Republic held out for several months in the Santa María quarter. Once the resistance was quashed, the reprisals were terrible. Even today, mass graves of executed supporters of the Republic are being unearthed in and around Cádiz. The walls of the Puertas de Tierra monument, built in the eighteenth century to guard the city entrance, began to bear witness to daily executions of city officials who had opposed the uprising, as well as Popular Front, socialist and anarchist union activists. In the first month alone after the fall of Cádiz, 111 people were stood before firing squads.

Cádiz life during the war

The sort of life the citizens of Cádiz, along with those of other cities that had fallen into Nationalist hands, could look forward to under the new regime became chillingly clear on the morning of 23 July 1936. On that day people of Cádiz switched on their radios to hear the terrifying harangue of a debonair, ruthless army general who had once been arrested for challenging a foe to a duel. General Gonzalo Queipo de Llano, the army officer who would be directly responsible for the execution of the poet

Federico García Lorca the following month, was a veteran of the Spanish–American and Rif wars. Shortly after the uprising, he recorded a radio broadcast ordering all citizens to return to their places of work and for retail establishments to open for business as usual. Transport workers were told to ensure the buses and trams were working and ready to take people about their normal daily routines. Queipo de Llano then launched a vicious diatribe against those who had supported the Republic: 'Our valiant Legionnaires and regular troops have taught the red cowards what it means to be a real man. This is totally justified because these communists and anarchists espouse free love...They will not be spared, regardless of how they shriek and stomp their feet.'[9]

Queipo de Llano also made it menacingly clear that women who opposed the Franco forces were not to be spared from the reign of terror. He endorsed the rape of Republican women and insisted they were not exempt from receiving the death penalty. A renowned female victim of Francoist brutality was Milagros Rendón, a typist from Cádiz and communist activist, who was taken prisoner after the Francoist uprising and charged with terrorist offences. The night of the July coup, Rendón and her father, the owner of a watch shop, joined the pro-Republican units that were securing government headquarters. Her father and husband were later arrested and executed after a summary court martial. Rendón was taken prisoner and raped by Moorish troops. She was then condemned to death by a military tribunal, accused of having shot the army bugler Rafael Soto Guerrero, the only soldier to have died in the attack on the government stronghold. Escorted to the Puertas de Tierra wall, she was placed between two male victims, whose hands she held when the order was given to fire. Rendón left a year-old daughter, who died shortly afterward. There is now a street in Cádiz named after Milagros Rendón, near the watch and costume jewellery shop owned by her father.

CÁDIZ AT WAR

Although the insurrectionists had effectively taken control of Cádiz in the space of twenty-four hours, this did not mean the city was placed safely outside the war zone. Sporadic attacks by Republican Air Force bombers served as a reminder that active resistance to the rebel advance was still very much alive. The Port of Cádiz became a transport point for Francoist forces making their way from Andalucía to battlegrounds in Galicia, Asturias and the Basque Country. Detachments of the Army of Africa, including the Foreign Legion, were ferried across from Morocco, where they regularly came under fire from Spanish Navy ships patrolling the Strait of Gibraltar.

Nearly ninety years after the capitulation of Cádiz, as in the rest of Spain, not a few issues remain plagued by controversy. On the night of the 18 July coup, with the city's administrative centres under siege, groups of marauding vandals set fire to many businesses and homes. The rebels predictably claimed the attacks had been orchestrated by Zapico and his cohorts in order to distract the rebel troops in the streets. The first victim, as might be expected, was a firearms shop near the docks in Calle San Francisco. This took place while armed groups were gathering at the nearby cathedral square, where shopkeepers began pulling down their shutters in expectation of imminent violence. The next victim was an ironmongers in Calle Sagasta, after which the arsonists torched several other shops around the cathedral area. The burnings carried on unchallenged late into the night, leaving nearly fifty businesses and private homes reduced to ashes.

A debate continues to this day on whether the riots had been the spontaneous work of socialist UGT and anarchist CNT unionist supporters of the Republic, or if the orders to go on the rampage had come from the besieged authorities. 'There is evidence to support the second theory,' according to historian Joaquín Gil Honduvilla. 'There are [personal] testimonies to suggest that the orders were given by Zapico. As might be expected, once the crowds had been overpowered, the police began to work on identifying the culprits.'[10] One of the suspects under investigation confessed from his hospital bed that instructions to carry out the arson attacks had indeed come from official circles. After their emphatic victory over the loyalists in Cádiz, Franco's rebels in the south and Mola's in the west advanced through the country, capturing most of Spain's northern coastline by 1937 and laying siege to Madrid and its surrounding areas. The fiercely Republican province of Cataluña held out until January 1939, but its eventual fall to the Nationalists left Madrid and a few other scattered loyalist strongholds isolated. By the end of March 1939, Madrid too had been occupied, the remaining loyalist forces had surrendered, and Franco proclaimed his victory in a radio address on 1 April. The war was over, and the Republican cause had been crushed.

Repression, reprisals and resistance

Cádiz, like the rest of Spain, lapsed into a state of war-weary lethargy after Franco's army marched triumphantly through the streets of Madrid on 1 April 1939. The country's shattered economy had ground to a standstill, scarcity of food and widespread poverty left millions having to endure daily hunger, while Spain could expect no aid from other European nations, which were fighting their own war of survival.

Cádiz had the relative good fortune of possessing a dockyard and shipbuilding know-how to save the city and its region from total collapse. Gradually, European countries like the UK and France, as well as the United States, abandoned their trade embargos with Spain, which had been in force during the Civil War, to establish diplomatic relations with the new regime. It had been imperative for the Nationalist war effort to maintain control of the Bay of Cádiz, given that the bulk of the Spanish

Navy had remained loyal to the Republic. Despite the war, Cádiz's shipyards had carried on a respectable level of construction work during those three years.

While there was some economic stability for the city, on the political front the wave of deliberate killings of anti-Franco militants continued during and after the Civil War, in particular members of the outlawed Spanish Communist party (PCE). Summary executions of regime opponents in Cádiz carried on for at least fifteen years after the Nationalist victory. Official figures speak of more than three thousand deaths by firing squad across the country between 1936 and 1952, with an even greater number of leftist militants serving time in jail.

For Cádiz, the incidents of court martials and firing squads continued intermittently through the post-Civil War years. A case in point was the summary execution in 1941 of Daniel Ortega, a physician who happened to be brother-in-law of the executed communist militant Milagros Rendón. He was condemned to death by a military tribunal for alleged communist sedition. Ortega's death, added to the extensive list of those executed in the post-war years, confirms that active resistance to the Franco regime meant putting one's life on the line.

No one was more acutely aware of this risk than the Spanish maquis, guerrillas who had fled across the border after the Civil War to join the French Resistance during the German occupation. The name 'maquis' refers to dense scrub underbrush, symbolic of the undercover war conducted by these guerrillas. The mission of these irregulars was to weaken the enemy through harassment and sabotage. Many of the Spanish insurgents who survived the First World War returned clandestinely to Spain to launch a campaign of guerrilla warfare against the dictatorship.

Spain is Europe's second most mountainous country after Switzerland, which makes it a natural habitat for guerrilla bands. Their objective was to incite unrest and demoralise the forces of repression, mainly the Civil Guard, which was tasked with patrolling rural areas. They naively believed that if people were made aware of an armed opposition to the Francoist tyranny, there was every chance of stirring up anger and non-cooperation with the government.

The maquis took as their main bases of operation the great northern mountain ranges, with smaller groups moving south to Andalucía and eventually the Cádiz hillsides. They incited a degree of tension in the region in their efforts to destabilise the governing forces with bombings and armed attacks on official institutions. 'Given the difficulties involved, in order to survive they at times would resort to theft, kidnappings and other criminal activities,' says historian José Luis Millán Chivite. 'These were semi-autonomous units with limited coordination between them, given the difficulties of maintaining mutual contact.'[11] Six groupings quickly established themselves in Cádiz's densely wooded hill country. Unlike their colleagues who had experienced combat in France, these were guerrillas who had held out in Spain after the Civil War. They made their presence known in January 1940 with an attack on Civil Guard headquarters, which prompted the commandant to move the barracks to the more secure township of Medina Sidonia. These guerrilla units were securely entrenched in their isolated mountain hideouts. Hence, they were able to hold out for ten years or more, before most of them disbanded in the 1950s, while a few held out even longer. One of the most notorious of these bands, at least from the authorities' perspective, was the so-called Stalingrad Group of some fifty guerrillas who planned their attacks from a base in the Cádiz hills. This nest of insurgents was so well-concealed that the group managed to hold out until 1976, a year after Franco's death. The worst of the violent state repression had ended by the early 1950s, when Spain emerged from blockade and diplomatic isolation. The US lifted its trade embargo after the Civil War and diplomatic relations with Madrid were restored in 1950. The dictatorship needed to reform its policy of bloody reprisals in order to secure the international aid needed to reactivate the impoverished country's economy.

Crucial redevelopment

The poverty and hunger stalking Cádiz in the early post-war years left people largely indifferent to the cause of armed resistance to the dictatorship. The crucial issue of the day was to earn a wage to put food on the table. The Cádiz shipyards continued to be vital to the local economy. The Empresa Nacional Bazán de Construcciones Navales Militares, headquartered in San Fernando on the south side of the bay, was set up in 1942 under the auspices of the newly formed state industrial agency Instituto Nacional de Industria (INI), with a mandate to produce warships. Likewise, Empresa Nacional Elcano was founded in the same year to build oil tankers and cargo carriers. Other operators were kept under private ownership, such as Matagorda y Echevarrieta y Larrinaga, which continued to construct ships for Spain's merchant fleet. So it was, until the business came crashing down, quite literally, on the night of 18 August 1947. That date continues to send a shiver down people's spines, especially those few who witnessed the disaster at 9.45 pm that night, as well as the many who regard it as an episode as devastating to Cádiz as the 1755 Lisbon post-earthquake tsunami. More than 150 died and some five thousand were injured – about five per cent of the population – in the explosion of the San Severiano underwater arsenal. Every year on that fateful day, people gather to lay wreaths at the site of the blast, while in the Santa Catalina Castle the town hall has erected a permanent exhibition documenting the event.

The disaster quite understandably gave rise to an outcry of grief and horror, but also frustration for no one dared point the finger at the responsible party. Experts prior to 1947 had quietly expressed concern about the perils of keeping 2,228 anti-submarine mines, deep-water bombs and torpedoes in a storage facility that was situated next to the city's residential area. No one in the regime heeded the tenuous forewarning. The munitions were placed in the armoury some years previously to prepare the city's defences against an attempted Allied landing in southern Spain. These fears, of course, were rendered redundant after the 1943 invasion of Italy, yet the armaments remained in storage. The munitions disaster triggered an official enquiry in the wake of the catastrophe, which was unable, or more likely unwilling, to reveal what had caused the explosion. A Spanish Army investigation in 2010 points to the presence of nitrocellulose among the weapons stored underwater and places the blame for the blast on this highly unstable and combustible compound. Nitrocellulose is the main ingredient of modern gunpowder and needs to be stored in a low-humidity environment, which was obviously not the case in the subaquatic arsenal. The San Severiano explosion was a clear-cut case of delinquent negligence. However, in Franco's Spain an incident that was so clearly linked to the military was not to be open for full public investigation.

Witnesses spoke of an ear-splitting detonation that cast a red glow over the entire city. Nothing survived of the shipyard founded by Horacio Echevarrieta, located alongside the arsenal. Many buildings, including the cathedral and Manuel de Falla Theatre, were damaged in the blast. Much of the historic centre was spared the worst of the calamity, as it was shielded from the blast by the Puertas de Tierra bastion erected around the city's old defensive walls.

One of the most vital development areas needed for Cádiz was to enable working-class families and the growing middle class to find a place to live in a city facing an acute housing shortage. The city's population density ranked as one of the highest among Spanish provincial capitals. Cádiz experienced a growth in population of nearly forty per cent between 1950 and the late 1960s, from some 100,000 to 136,000 in less than twenty years.

The urban redevelopment of Cádiz was in large measure owed to the efforts of José León de Carranza, who served unchallenged as mayor from 1948 until his death in 1969, a record for the city. Carranza was a man of avuncular appearance, an unwavering Franco ally who despite his now discredited politics, was acutely aware that the key to economic recovery was intrinsically coupled with Cádiz's port. Carranza was appointed to office a few months after the 1947 arsenal explosion, and it fell to him to devise a plan for reconstructing the zone devastated by the blast. He focused most of his efforts on modernising the bay and overseeing the completion of a free port. One of his most visible achievements was the bridge over the bay, inaugurated in 1969, which made it possible for the first time to travel directly across the bay and avoid the circuitous land route. The 4,600-foot steel bridge over the Bay of Cádiz is one of Europe's longest and it marked the first step in creating what is today the greater metropolitan area joining central Cádiz to Puerto Real, El Puerto de Santa María and Jerez de la Frontera. This project alone played a key role in boosting the city's economic growth. It is now the older of two bridges linking Cádiz to the mainland. The newer one to the north is the Puente de la Constitución de 1812, popularly referred to as La Pepa, which opened in 2017. That was the year the name of the Avenida de Ramón de Carranza was changed to Avenida 4 de Diciembre, in remembrance of the day in 1977 when Andalusian separatists took to the streets to demand independence for their region. Despite protests by groups seeking to erase all references to the Franco dictatorship, the Carranza Bridge has so far retained its name. His name has also been adopted in songs heard in Cádiz's annual carnival, which he was instrumental in reviving. The Estadio Ramón de Carranza, the football stadium that is the home ground of Cádiz CF, did not survive the purge. Its name was changed in 2017 to Estadio Nuevo Mirandilla. The latest move to discredit Carranza came in 2023, when he was posthumously stripped of the Gold Medal for Work Achievements he had been awarded by the Franco government for his labours in rebuilding the city. In 1970, Carranza's family had placed a plaque with the former mayor's bust on the wall of his ancestral home in the Calle Cánovas del Castillo. This was taken down in 2019 on the orders of the municipal authorities, who claimed it was in violation of Spain's Historical Memory Law.

It is nearly half a century since the death of Generalísimo Francisco Franco was announced in the early hours of 20 November 1975, and Spaniards still struggle to come to terms with thirty-six years of autocratic rule, which few dared to defy. Germany and Italy emerged from the Second World War as free nations, liberated of the tyrannies that had left their countries in ruin. The obvious difference is that Germany's and Italy's totalitarian regimes had been defeated and eradicated after plunging their countries into conflict, while in Spain it was the military, having squashed a democratically elected civilian government, that took power after the Second World War. The post-war period is not a comfortable topic of conversation in Spanish society, even after so many years of reconciliation within a strong democracy embraced by political parties across the spectrum. Yet there exists a certain degree of bad conscience, for want of a less unkind epithet, that has given rise to a manifestation of what in today's parlance would be labelled 'cancel culture'. The Historical Memory Law is a piece of legislation enacted by the Spanish Parliament in 2007, which ostensibly recognises the victims on both sides of the Civil War and the removal of symbols that exalt the July 1936 uprising against the Republic. This has been a contentious statute from the day it was ratified by the Congress of Deputies. The law specifically states that all insignias, plaques and other objects commemorating the military uprising, the Civil War or the regime's repression are to be removed from public buildings and spaces. Opponents of the law argue that almost no account has been taken of the atrocities committed by Republican troops and militia during the war.

Cádiz can be singled out as an example of the law's alleged lack of impartiality. The city is a soft target, having fallen to the Nationalists almost immediately and swiftly used by the Franco war machine. The burning of churches and other religious monuments was the only notable act of criminal violence attributable to the resistance fighters. This has passed into the distant recall of history, with no visible reminders of these acts of political vandalism. The campaign to obliterate the memory of Ramón de Carranza is another matter. Carranza was an unapologetic advocate of Franco and maintained a close personal relationship with many of the regime's most powerful figures. He stood on what is now regarded as the wrong side of the political fence, but this does not invalidate his accomplishments in laying the groundwork for Cádiz's future development.

During Carranza's twenty-one years in office, he endorsed plans for an airport, today a small aerodrome offering sightseeing flights over Cádiz and its region. He upgraded the city's antiquated water supply system, modernised port facilities and provided grounds to build educational facilities, including the city's first state-run schools. Carranza made possible the first direct phone connection with the Canary Islands with the laying of an underwater cable from Cádiz to Tenerife. He set up a summer university lecture programme that put Cádiz's name on the country's cultural map by bringing in renowned figures like journalist Luis María Ansón, scientist Gregorio Marañón, philosopher Rafael Calvo Serer and newspaper editor Torcuato Luca de Tena. Carranza oversaw the construction of the José María Pemán Theatre, where the public could enjoy a variety of shows, from classical concerts to pop music by the 'Beatles Gaditanos'. Carranza took a personal interest in reviving Cádiz's flamenco scene and the city's time-honoured February Carnival, with its flamboyant Queen of the Carnival and *chirigota*, or choral folksong, competitions.

By the time of Carranza's death in office in 1969, Cádiz had shaken off the grimness and gloom that had characterised city life in the late 1940s. His altruistic spirit was taken up by his successor, Deputy Mayor Jerónimo Almagro, who on the eve of All Saints' Day would hold a vigil at the San José Cemetery to lay flowers on the graves of victims of the Civil War, regardless of their political affiliation.

8

CÁDIZ IS RISEN

Throughout its more than three thousand years of history, Cádiz and the sea have always been as one. Maritime trade and shipbuilding have formed the bedrock of the city's economic life, hence the bulk of the commercial infrastructure has traditionally been centred around the port. In recent times, however, Cádiz has had to face a number of challenges in areas where it once reigned supreme. The past thirty years have seen the deep-water Bay of Algeciras, located in Cádiz province but about 60 miles from the city proper, emerge as a strong contender for maritime traffic. The fishing industry was dealt a blow by the loss of privileges in July 2023, which Spain had enjoyed for nearly fifty years under the now obsolete fishing ground agreement with Morocco. The city was highly dependent throughout the 1960s and 1970s on its shipyards. This crucial source of income went into a tailspin with the 1986 oil crisis that saw crude prices plummet by fifty per cent, a setback worsened by geographical shifts in the world shipbuilding industry. Production at Cádiz's shipyards since then has fallen below capacity, due to dwindling worldwide demand and stiff competition from foreign challengers, notably China and South Korea, which rank number one and number two in the global ranking of ship building countries. In 2024, Spain did not make the top ten, with competitors in Europe, Italy, Germany and France all having a larger profile in the industry. However, the sector is still an important player in the country's economy, worth over €4 billion. The Spanish state-owned ship building company Navantia runs seven shipyards with four of these and its training facility in the Bahía de Cádiz. Since 2021 the company has invested €3 million to modernise the yards and their facilities. The Navantia yard at San Fernando has one of the largest dry docks in the world, able to accommodate vessels up to 500 metres long. Navantia builds warships, from patrol ships up to aircraft carriers as well as submarines; they specialise in refitting cruise liners, and design and build ship engines and other marine equipment.

In terms of other industrial activity, Cádiz fares better than might be expected on a national scale, good news for a region once so highly dependent on shipbuilding. By the end of 2023, the region ranked fourteenth among Spain's fifty provinces in total exports and ninth in value of imports. The region has long been associated with food and wine production, but its top two export items are refined petroleum and stainless steel. Alongside these exports, the shipyards still manage to pull their weight in the export ranking, coming third owing to the construction of warships.

Despite these signs of relative growth in the local economy, Cádiz still suffers from a high level of unemployment, which has the effect of being a social, as well as an economic, depressant. This has been the case for nearly half a century. Not counting the North African territories of Ceuta and Melilla, Andalucía, with an unemployment rate of 18.6%, tops Spain's list of seventeen autonomous communities with the highest rate of unemployment. Within Andalucía itself, the unemployment rate for Cádiz, at

Fig. 28: The Battle of Trocadero, 1823.

Fig. 29: Portrait of Lord Byron (1788–1824).

Fig. 30: Ornate streetlamp in Calle Ancha celebrating the Cádiz maritime tradition.

Fig. 31: Enemy canon repurposed to protect the building corner from passing traffic, Plaza San Augustín.

Fig. 32: Murals by Goya in the Oratorio Santa Cueva, Cádiz.

Fig. 33: The Cádiz city arms in stained glass at the town hall.

Fig. 34: Mudéjar-style courtyard of the Casino Gaditano, founded as a gentlemen's club in the nineteenth century.

Fig. 35: Statue of nineteenth-century politician Emilio Castelar in the Plaza de la Candelaria, Cádiz.

Fig. 36: Portrait of Isabel II, 1859, by Dionisio Fierros Álvarez.

Fig. 37: Ornate nineteenth-century door knocker at Calle José del Toro, 13, Cádiz.

Fig. 38: Gran Teatro Falla.

Fig. 39: 'Merry hours with the pretty senoritas of Cadiz'. Image from a nineteenth-century stereograph souvenir.

Fig. 40: One of the impressive old trees of the Alameda Apodaca.

Fig. 41: Balneario de la Palma Spa.

23.4% in 2023, puts it well above the regional average. There is some optimism that this rate may decrease, as the numbers employed in the local labour market grew by 3.5% in 2023, with the rate expected to increase at a more modest 1–2% per year over the coming few years. There is still a large gap however, which will require many thousands of jobs to be generated and sustained across different sectors of the local economy before the unemployment rate shows a substantial decrease that can be maintained over time. 'While Cádiz province shows encouraging signs of generating employment, as is shown by the number of people signed up to social security, it is not sufficient to absorb the working population,' says Javier Cabeza de Vaca, chairman of the Cádiz Association of Professional Economists. 'The unemployment rate remains above 20%, which is double the national average.'[1]

Cádiz, tourist destination

With shipbuilding and traditional industrial sectors facing an uncertain future, tourism has emerged as the undisputed hope for economic prosperity in Cádiz. Recent years have seen a considerable amount of effort and capital investment put into this sector, with a strong emphasis on sustainability and promotion of local cuisine, among other themes. This is the main reason that Cádiz saw a higher rate of economic growth in 2023, not only above the rest of Andalucía, but on a national level as well.

The cruise line industry is extremely important to Cádiz both in terms of the shipyards and tourism. The Navantia shipyard is one of the biggest centres in the world for the refurbishment and refitting of cruise liners. These are lucrative contracts; for example, the refitting of one of the Carnival Cruise Line ships, the *Carnival Radiance*, was worth US$200 million in 2021. The work on the ship included fitting new cabins, refurbishing the public areas across the ship and many technological improvements to the engines, navigational equipment and lighting. The yards employ a vast range of skilled craftspeople, engineers and technicians to carry out this work. At the end of the Covid-19 pandemic, as the cruise industry was set to relaunch itself, the Navantia shipyards had a record number of eight cruise liners in dock at one time for refitting.

The port of Cádiz is also a major stop on the cruise itineraries. The massive liners are a common site in the Old Town, where they moor by the Plaza de San Juan de Dios, looking like a skyscraper that has been built overnight at the end of the square. Cruise ship arrivals reached record figures in 2023. The number of ships docking in that year grew by 15% to 347, while disembarking passenger figures increased 72% to 680,000. These visitors are not officially classified as tourists to the area, and it is debatable how much of a positive contribution they make to the local hospitality industry, as many cruising visitors will merely disembark for a stroll around the Old Town before returning to the ship for lunch and refreshments, as their cruise ticket includes all meals. Undoubtedly, some of the cruise visitors will be net contributors to the tourism economy, patronising the cafés and buying souvenirs in the town or joining local day trips to the sherry bodegas of Jerez de la Frontera or Sanlúcar de Barrameda, or visiting some of the nearby Pueblos Blancos, such as Arcos de la Frontera.

Tourism now accounts for a hefty 12% of Cádiz's GDP and has in recent years become one of the region's most important economic sectors, along with farming and livestock. The tourism industry provides employment for fifty thousand people. Industry figures for 2023 showed a record number of visitors from abroad as well as other regions of Spain. Manuel de la Varga López of the Cádiz Tourism Board explained, 'This exceeded the 2019 figures, which had been the best ever. Numbers for the pandemic years of 2020 and 2021 were flat, as might be expected, but a strong recovery took off in 2022. We had 2.8 million visitors in 2023, of which 1.9 million were Spanish and 866,000 from other countries, mainly the EU and Britain.'[2]

At the time of writing, Germany provides by far the greatest number of foreign visitors of any single country. But healthy figures have been reported for tourists from other EU nations and Britain. All-year tourism is growing, particularly with visitors from the Nordic countries tending to travel abroad in winter, which in the past was a slow season for Cádiz. The winter sunshine and the lack of summer crowds are a draw, along with newly built facilities for golf and water sports. Areas that have been developed in recent years have eschewed the skyscraper hotels of the 1970s to early 2000s built along the Cádiz isthmus shadowing the Playa Victoria and Playa Santa María del Mar.

New developments such as the luxury resorts at Sancti Petri or Conil, both a short distance from the city centre, are part of a drive by the Cádiz tourism authorities to encourage holidaymakers to explore the wider region. The Novo Sancti Petri is a sustainable tourism luxury resort, located between the dunes and waters of La Barrosa Beach, with a golf resort designed by Severiano Ballesteros, all just a few minutes south of Chiclana de la Frontera, today itself practically a suburb of Cádiz. The resort is next to one of the most ancient archaeological sites in the region, the remains of the Sancti Petri Castle. This structure was built on the site that is believed to be a sanctuary erected in honour of the god Melkart, a reminder of the region's Phoenician past.

In this same district the Spanish property firm Grupo Soluciones is building four new five-star hotels on the coast. The company is investing €250 million in the project, which will increase capacity by a thousand new rooms and provide employment for some two thousand people over the next five years. In all, Cádiz now has over six hundred hotels, guest houses and hostels spread throughout the region's towns and rural resort areas.

Carnival and Semana Santa

Visitors are attracted by the beaches, the natural beauty and the historic interest of Cádiz and the surrounding area. Not least of the attractions is the world-famous Cádiz Carnival, celebrated here, as around the world, to mark the days of feasting before the abstemious Christian Lent period begins. Visitors to Carnival are likely to remark on the almost total absence of religious, namely Catholic, motifs in the processions that march through the city in February. This is not surprising given that this festival traces its origins back to ancient Greece, or even earlier according to some sages, as a festival celebrating the cycles of Nature and the Universe. Carnival was later celebrated by the Romans in honour of the deities Bacchus, Saturn and Pan.

It is a rare day that local Carnival enthusiasts and members of the different carnival clubs, or *compañías*, fail to devote some of their time to preparing for the yearly festival, designing costumes, rehearsing their songs and putting together the carriages that will carry their group of singers along the streets for the ten-day celebration.

Carnival in Cádiz has not been without its political vicissitudes. A street sacred to revellers is Calle Valverde, a narrow passageway that winds its way through the heart of the city centre. It is named after Mayor Juan Valverde, one of Cádiz's most revered politicians, who in 1861 officially recognised Carnival as part of the city's cultural heritage. Valverde was the driving force behind an extensive list of urban improvement schemes. During his mandate, he promoted the construction of the Cádiz-Sevilla railway, refurbished the cathedral, provided the entire city with gas lighting, paved the streets with cobblestones, built the Plaza de la Merced and renovated the Plaza Mina. Valverde hosted Leopoldo O'Donnell, a fellow Liberal Union member, in his home on the prime minister's two official visits to Cádiz.

Carnival lights went out in 1937, with the Civil War raging across the country, when General Franco issued an order banning the celebration of any type of carnival or street festivities in Spain. In the immediate post-war years, the ritual was so deeply mourned that every February, in wine bars and food shops, people would gather to swap memories of Carnival nights and sing their choral favourites. The outright Carnival prohibition was relaxed to some extent in 1948, after the terrible disaster of August 1947. The civil governor, Carlos María Rodríguez de Valcárcel, decided that allowing some elements of Carnival would help to raise the spirits of the city, still in shock after the blast. The authorities decided to allow aficionados to sing 'La Piñata Gaditana', one of the festival's classic tunes. Once that door was opened there was no reining in the general outcry for a full resurrection. The festival returned to the streets under the vigilant eye of the government censors, to prevent anything that could hint at an anti-Franco protest. In keeping with the regime's perverse policymaking, the only stipulation was that the ban was to remain in force on using the word 'Carnival'.

Two years later, the authorities at last felt it was safe to ease the restrictions another notch by sanctioning what was called the Fiestas Típicas Gaditanas, a kind of decaffeinated carnival. This remained the official position until 1977, two years after Franco's death, when Cádiz finally recovered its traditional February Carnival in full name and glory.

Carnival has continued to grow and is one of the best known in Spain, attracting huge numbers of domestic and international visitors. Unlike other carnivals that focus on glamour and spectacular shows, the heart of the Cádiz Carnival is the humour of the songs belted out by the different groups, making clever use of wordplay and parody. Many of the songs are satirical, choosing for their targets political and celebrity figures from the local, national and international scene. The music performed by the groups of Carnival companies packed into open-top lorries is alien to the musical individualism of Andalucía. It is always a group effort that is entertaining, opinionated and often somewhat subversive in character. There are several types of singing groups, the main four being the *chirigotas* (folk tunes), *comparsas* (folk dances), *coros* (choirs) and *cuartetos (*quartets) which, oddly, are as likely to have three or five members as the expected four. The groups sing choral folksongs that originated in Cádiz. They are more deeply influenced by samba and Afro-Cuban rhythms than music native to Spain. The songs are accompanied by guitars (but in a vastly different style to flamenco), with drums and kazoos, and augmented by some simple percussion from objects like scrapers, metal bowls and home-made wooden flutes.

The *comparsas* are possibly the most serious groups, focused on writing the cleverest, most satirically biting songs. The groups compete fiercely in the months leading up to Carnival in the annual song competition, with the finals held at the Gran Teatro Falla. Along with their songs, the *comparsa* will design a new flamboyant group costume each year, which all the members wear while performing, often brightly coloured identical suits with tailcoats and extravagant matching top hats. Each *comparsa* has a wide repertoire of songs, which they sing in the streets and squares, and at open venues organised by the carnival clubs throughout the festivities.

To the casual visitor, the *chirigotas* appear very similar to the *comparsas*. They are groups of about ten (usually men) belonging to one of the Cádiz Carnival clubs. They all wear a group design of brightly coloured costumes and together perform a repertoire of original songs and compete in the annual song competition. The difference is that their songs are more humorous, with a happier style than those of the *comparsas*, even though they may be about the same topical subjects.

The *coros* are larger groups who travel Carnival streets on lorries and floats, accompanied by their band, which usually includes guitars and lutes as well as drums and percussion. The *coros* may adopt a humorous theme for their costumes, linked to their songs, such as pirates or clowns. Lastly, the *cuartetos* are small groups of three to five, performing comic sketches and songs accompanied by clacking sticks, gourds and reed whistles.

Many of the songs have been inspired by modern inventions of the day. Some of the most famous ones date back to the nineteenth century, such as the 'Electricity' ditty, sung to a tango rhythm in 1889, whose opening lyrics go:

> In the current era, there is nothing more fluorescent than electricity, the telephone, the microphone, the so very singular phonograph.

Other *chirigotas* find their inspiration in natural phenomena, such as the 1935 melody about an almost unheard-of snowfall in Cádiz.

> When snow fell on Cádiz we noted certain singularities in the streets. People strolled along the seafront, paying little heed, as oblivious as had they been in Nice.

Still others ring with political satire, such as this one from 1963 about ongoing work on the Carranza Bridge across the bay, which opened in 1969.

> The day that Cádiz has its bridge, we will make it in a leap to Puerto Real and will you look at this, how little children oh so quickly make their way across to the city.

Following on from Carnival in the religious calendar of festivals, after the days of Lent, Cádiz is plunged into the spectacle of Holy Week – Semana Santa – which goes for ten days in the city, from the Thursday before Palm Sunday, through to Easter Sunday. This is when nearly thirty brotherhoods of musicians and tableaux bearers, along with long columns of penitents in pointed caps and white gowns – some ten thousand participants in all – parade through the city streets. Different groups are linked to the different churches in the city and the thirty *cofradias*, or brotherhoods, have set days to parade, each with their special route, starting from their assigned 'penitence station'. Each group is responsible for a set of wooden sculptures, many of them hundreds of years old, depicting a certain episode in the story of the passion or a spiritual aspect of Jesus or the Virgin Mary. The group parades the statues on huge wooden platforms, supported by ten to twenty members of the brotherhood, depending on the size and weight. They have an even harder job than those in other Easter parades around Spain, as the tradition here is to proceed at a very slow pace. Cádiz's Holy Week celebrations share many traditions with the rest of Andalucía, in their vivid colour, liturgic music and outpouring of religious fervour. There are several factors that distinguish the celebrations in Cádiz from those of the greater region. For one thing, the bay is never more than a ten-minute walk from the city centre, hence most fraternal associations choose the cathedral by the sea as their place of penitence. This usually takes place late in the day, to benefit from the spectacular moment when the sun seems to dip into the sea as a backdrop for the dramatic ceremony.

During Holy Week one very particular style of flamenco can be heard sung from balconies as the religious processions go by. Historians trace the origin of this singular music to the triangle formed by Sevilla, Jerez de la Frontera and Cádiz. The specific type of flamenco heard during the Cádiz festival is the *saeta*, a form of religious song even revered by modern musical greats such as Miles Davis in his *Sketches of Spain*. Saetas are songs of strong, mournful emotion, usually sung a cappella by a single voice, the *saetero*. The style is believed to stem from Jewish traditions of reciting the psalms, with the Catholic practice dating from the sixteenth century. The modern *saeta* may be sung to a simple syllabic melody or it can be a highly ornamented style, which incorporates key elements of flamenco singing. The plaintive songs carry a dramatic intensity, performed as the religious statues proceed along the narrow streets, addressing the statue of Jesus as the Man of Sorrows, the crucified Christ or the suffering of the Virgin Mary. The devout Catholics of Andalusia have a tradition that one must speak to God during Holy Week and the singing of *saetas* are a powerful expression of this aspiration.

During Holy Week, the haunting soul-felt melody of the *saeta* echoes from balconies and around the streets, which fall silent as the singers express their religious devotion. The throbbing heart of the *saeta*, a place where hundreds of aficionados gather, is the Santa María district, home to the celebrated flamenco *peña* (club) La Perla de Cádiz.

Santa María

Santa María embodies the soul of flamenco, the Mecca of an art form that has hosted performances by legendary dancers, singers and guitarists from across Spain. The district crosses the city centre, from Puertas de Tierra to Plaza San Juan de Dios and the ancient Pópulo quarter. Like many parts of Cádiz, Santa María in the 1980s benefitted from an urban renewal programme aimed at bringing new life to areas that had experienced decades of neglect. The process kicked off in 1981 when the city, which had now become the capital of the Cádiz urban semi-autonomous region, was able to enact and implement its own legislation, which previously required the consent of the centralised Franco dictatorship. The flamenco heartland had fallen victim to two grievous problems, namely drugs and a deterioration of private housing.

The campaign that finally put an end to the drug trade was spearheaded by a group of militant neighbours, the Tres Torres Association, led by José Rodríguez Vázquez, who in 2023 was awarded the Residents of Cádiz Award for his successful campaign to rid the streets of dealers and addicts. 'We began by clearing the neighbourhood of what was something like a supermarket of illegal drugs,' says Rodríguez. 'Then we took on the task of repairing and restoring many buildings that were in sorry shape.'[3] Needless to say, the award ceremony was enlivened by the music of flamenco guitarist Joaquín Linera, or Niño de la Leo, along with singers Francisco Reyes and Nuria Carrasco. Before action was taken, it was common for passers-by to give Santa María a wide berth when strolling through the city centre. Rodríguez and other neighbourhood association members set up guard posts on street corners to intervene in a persuasive manner whenever a pusher was spotted doing a deal. The association relied on support from town hall authorities, who provided muscle back-up when required.

Many residential properties in the neighbourhood were in a very poor state of repair. This neglect was in no small measure a reflection of Santa María's reputation as an unsafe area in which to live. The Tres Torres Association carried out a house-by-house assessment of the degree of decay. In 1995, the town hall agreed to expropriate and rehabilitate those buildings in most urgent need of restoration. The renovation work was a joint effort enlisting expertise and funding from official bodies and private property promoters. Santa María underwent a radical transformation and today there remain only a handful of buildings still to be fully renovated. It is now a delight to stroll down the main hill, the Cuesta de las Caletas, toward the Plaza de San Juan de Dios and take in the neighbourhood's many historic sights. On the port side stands the early nineteenth-century tobacco factory, today the city's main conference centre. The district is bisected between the port and the city by the Calle Plocia, a hub of sixteen of Cádiz's best-known restaurants and taverns. Since action was taken to redevelop Santa María, Calle Plocia has become the city's most pleasurable pedestrian area to enjoy a drink or meal at an outdoor terrace.

Santa María has taken a great leap beyond urban renewal. The Plaza de la Merced is the district's main square, and it is here that in 2006 the Centro de Arte Flamenco opened its doors to the public. The complex hosts concerts and exhibitions, while flamenco aficionados are offered classes in flamenco guitar, singing and dancing. The town hall has also endowed Santa María with a sports centre, the Mirandilla, along with the la Casa de Iberoamérica cultural centre, housed in what was formerly the royal prison.

Cádiz, and most notably the Santa María district, has given the world some of Spain's top flamenco dancers. Juana Vargas, known by her stage name of Juana la Macarrona, ranks as one of the outstanding historical figures. She was born in 1870 in Cádiz's next-door neighbour Jerez de la Frontera. During her career, she put the name of Cádiz on the map in countries as far afield as Germany and Russia and was even said to be a favourite of the shah of Persia. Antonia Gilabert, who rose to fame as La Perla de Cádiz, was an early twentieth century native of Cádiz who became a star of Madrid's flamenco *tablaos*. Another nineteenth-century celebrity from Jerez de la Frontera was Mercedes Fernández Vargas, who took the stage name Merced la Serneta. As well as being a renowned dancer, it is her singing and compositions that are particularly remembered. She was a famous creator and performer of songs in the *soleá* style during what is regarded as the golden age of the *soleá*, the last quarter of the nineteenth century, at the time when the *café cantante* (musical café) was the preferred venue for flamenco artists. Most of the *soleá* melodies we know today have been attributed to singers such as Merced, who were active at that time.

The best-known contemporary name among flamenco dancers is Lola Flores, born in 1923 in Jerez de la Frontera as María Dolores Flores Ruiz. She was an all-embracing artist: a *bailaora* of genius but also a renowned singer and actress. Throughout her career, she became a household name in Spain, as well as in Mexico and South America. The name that stands out among male flamenco singers is José Monje Cruz, professionally known as Camarón de la Isla, in reference to his birthplace in Isla de San Fernando across the Cádiz Bay. Camarón's flamenco heritage was impeccable: his father was a gypsy blacksmith, whose ancestors made horseshoes and arquebus shells for the Catholic Monarchs at the time of the conquest of Granada. Camarón's mother was said to have burst out in flamenco song when she gave birth to José, the seventh of her eight children. Camarón was considered by many to be the greatest flamenco singer ever, a veritable gypsy god of flamenco.

There is a growing international interest in flamenco, which brings audiences to Cádiz, as well as musicians and dancers from Spain and internationally to attend flamenco courses.

Beauty beyond the city

The Bay of Cádiz is the repository of three millennia of history. It has been the gateway to the Atlantic for Mediterranean seafarers, merchants and explorers alike. The Roman theatre, the many grand buildings and monuments towering over ancient leafy squares – all these make for a fascinating sojourn. Yet there is much to be discovered and enjoyed beyond the lively streets and bustling taverns. This is a region rich in biodiversity to be found only a few miles south of the urban centre. The city is home to Europe's most extensive wetlands. The 26,000-acre Cádiz Nature Park, encircled by the municipalities of San Fernando, Chiclana de la Frontera, Puerto Real and Puerto de Santa María, is a treasure trove of marshland beaches, pine woods, dramatic waterspouts and dunes. Its shrubbery hides rocks covered with moss and salt, which the Phoenicians used as a food preservative. Later civilisations inherited their shrewdness and used the Nature Park for aquaculture to breed and harvest fish, shellfish and aquatic plants.

The park boasts a vast array of birdlife. The wetlands here, together with those of the Doñana National Park, 35 miles north of Cádiz, form one of the most important wetland habitats in Europe, home to more than fifty thousand birds of some 150 species, some resident, most of them migratory. It is not uncommon to find the elegant white plumes of the gregarious wading roseate spoonbill and the black stork, which is listed as an endangered species, along with flocks of flamingos. With luck, the visitor might also spot an eagle overhead, spying its prey in the water. The salt harvesting days in the estuaries marked the opening of the fishing season, done with small net barriers, known as *almadrabas*, to trap species passing through these waters, primarily tuna migrating from the Mediterranean to the Atlantic. Today the catches include seabass, sole, lobster and prawn.

The park has a network of signposted trails, starting at Isla del Trocadero, which can be followed on foot or bicycle. One of the sights of interest along the way is the remains of a fortification seized by the French in the Peninsular War. Further south, the trail passes the Punta del Boquerón, a sandy headland listed as a natural monument with a wide representation of the park's flora and fauna.

Another wonderful area of natural beauty to explore is the Alcornocales Natural Park, 35 miles southeast of Cádiz. A unique day-long winter outing for visitors to the park focuses on the bountiful and varied mushrooms that grow in the area. The excursion starts with breakfast as a warm-up for the fascinating walk through an area of the park that provides the opportunity of collecting and classifying different varieties of mushrooms native to the Cádiz region.

One of the wonders of the Cádiz region are the Pueblos Blancos, the historic, pretty white villages of the hill country, mostly clustered around the mountains and valleys of Sierra de Grazalema Natural Park, their whitewashed walls glimmering in the brilliant sunshine. The Pueblos Blancos offer an alternative or add-on to winter beach holidays. Many of these villages have their own culinary specialities, such as the much sought-after *payoyo* goat's cheese from the Grazalema hills region. The villages are fast becoming one of the Cádiz region's most popular short break, or even day trip, destinations. The names of several of these towns bear the suffix *de la Frontera* (of the Frontier), as in Arcos de la Frontera, Vejer de la Frontera and Jimena de la Frontera. This tag was added to denote that between eight and five centuries ago they were the defensive fortifications marking the advancing, retreating and advancing again frontier between Christian Spain and the Moorish Al-Andalus.

Medina Sidonia is one of the closest of these villages to Cádiz, lying only 26 miles by road east of the capital. The town traces its origin to Phoenician settlers from the Lebanese city of Sidon. *Medina* is derived from the Arabic *madina*, meaning 'city', which became its definitive name after the town was conquered by Alfonso X in 1264. Some two centuries later, it became part of the feudal estate of Juan Alfonso de Guzmán, the first Duke of Medina Sidonia and bearer of Spain's oldest title of nobility, Conde de Niebla. The town has been designated a Historical-Artistic Monument; its white streets filled with Andalusian charm almost invariably lead to ancient remains and religious edifices, of which the Church of Santiago is an outstanding example of a fourteenth century hermitage. Winter offers some of the best attractions in Medina Sidonia. The festivities of the town's Patron Saint, Nuestra Señora de la Paz, take place on 24 January, followed shortly by the town carnival and Holy Week, which is enlivened by a street procession on Maundy Thursday.

One of the most splendid of these towns is Arcos de la Frontera, an ideal starting point for a tour of the white villages, given its proximity to Cádiz. The historic old quarter has been designated a National Monument in recognition of its exceptional architecture and impressive location. Arcos is perched atop La Peña, a rocky limestone ridge, the town's whitewashed houses and stone castle walls coming to an abrupt halt at a sheer cliff face towering over the Guadalete River. Legend has it that the settlement was founded by Brigo, a grandson of the prophet Noah. What is known is that it was inhabited successively by Phoenicians, Carthaginians and Romans. The Moors converted it into a fortress and laid out the streets more or less as we know them today. One of the outstanding features of Arcos is the variety of its vegetable-based cuisine, like the classic *alboronía*, made of tomato, pumpkin and chickpeas, or *ajo molinero*, a cold soup made of tomato, bread, olive oil and garlic.[4] Arcos is also renowned for its traditional handicraft, most famously its shoes, baskets and writing paper produced from *esparto* grass. Local artisans also produce carpets woven on eighteenth century looms.

Continuing on for 35 miles from Arcos in a northeasterly direction, the route leads to Zahara de la Sierra. The road is winding and slow-going, but well worth the effort. Upon approaching Zahara, a dazzling village of some 1,500 souls comes into view and appears to be precariously joined to a rocky bluff, rising more than 3,600 feet above a valley and artificial lake. The setting is nothing short of breathtaking. The remains of the twelfth century castle, basically the keep, sit on top of a rocky promontory overlooking Zahara. During the days of the Reconquista, the garrison could maintain eye contact with fellow Christian soldiers in three other nearby castles to warn of approaching Moorish forces.

A truly imposing sight is Zahara's *abies pinsapo* (evergreen conifer) forest, on the edge of the Sierra de Grazalema Natural Park, which has been declared a UNESCO World Biosphere Reserve. This is one of the few places in which the *pinsapo*, which can grow to a height of 100 feet, remains more or less as it stood in prehistoric times.

In an upland valley beyond Arcos de la Frontera lies Ubrique, a small village whose name resonates with few people, unless, for instance, you happen to be in the know with Louis Vuitton, Gucci or Loewe. These are three of the fashion design houses that employ the skilled craftspeople working in Ubrique's famed leathergoods industry to make the high-end handbags that are the cornerstone of these businesses' global sales. The village is one of the most picturesque of the Pueblos Blancos, nestled below the Cádiz sector of the Serranía de Ronda mountain range. As early as the eighteenth century Ubrique was manufacturing leather products for export to France, the Netherlands and Germany, from tobacco pouches to military accessories. It is almost certain this handicraft was thriving in Ubrique in much earlier times: researchers have discovered Roman testimonials to the town's leather products.

Ubrique leather was kept almost a house secret until the early twentieth century, when several astute entrepreneurs realised its potential and encouraged the town's leather craftsmen to begin marketing their goods more widely to other regions of Spain and internationally. 'The industry is still in the hands of artisans and today there are more than thirty factories producing goods from shoes, belts and rucksacks to handbags and wallets,' according to travel writers Rafael Arjona and Lola Wals. 'To avoid forgeries of these high-quality goods, the Association of Leathergoods Craftsmen has designed a label with a chip that guarantees the authenticity of the product.'5 The town has a leather museum, housed in a converted seventeenth century convent, displaying traditional leather-working machinery and examples of beautiful, historic hand-tooled leather objects.

Jerez de la Frontera

Other visitors are drawn in by the focus on Spanish gastronomy, which has revived traditionally made dishes from local ingredients, overtaking French cuisine as a favourite of European foodies. The local wine business is thriving in both the continuing tradition of the sherry bodegas and the development of high-quality table wines immediately in the Cádiz district. The region was awarded Vino de la Tierra status in 2005 and is working on its application for promotion to Denominación de Origen (DO) status, for its white wines, which have been winning approval from tasting experts. There is thus optimism for the future prospects of the city as a hub for cultural and gastronomic tourism. A major incentive for wine lovers to pay Cádiz a visit lies a short train journey 30 miles north of the city. Jerez de la Frontera is the sherry capital of the world and has been for centuries. It was known as *Ceret* by the Romans, *Shera* under the Greeks, *Seret* at the time of the Visigoths and *Scherich* during the Moorish occupation. Wines in many other parts of the world borrow the denomination, but the only true sherries come from this part of Spain, where the term is strictly geographical. Jerez is part of the sherry triangle, which includes Sanlúcar de Barrameda and El Puerto de Santa María, cradle of the region's most cherished wines. Between them they produce virtually all the sherry that is exported to the rest of the world. Depending on preferences of taste, the enthusiast can sample classic varieties like fino and amontillado in Jerez and

Puerto de Santa María. Sanlúcar de Barrameda is rather special, in that its famous variety is manzanilla.

In the first quarter of the twenty-first century, sherry has returned to its position as a high-quality, specialty fortified wine, with an established place on the wine lists of restaurants and bars around the world and in the cellars of wine connoisseurs. The sherry industry maintains a balanced situation in terms of production and sales. The chairman of the Sherry Denomination of Origin Council, Beltrán Domecq, recalls the days, not that long ago, when sherry's future looked frankly bleak:

> The 1970s and 1980s marked a negative parenthesis of excess production. We are now back to 7,000 hectares of vineyard, about the same as in the 1960s. Uncontrolled expansion towards the end of the twentieth century had led to a trebling of vineyard area, which in turn brought on a disaster in overproduction. Producers were struggling to sell at any price they could obtain. The turnaround started in the mid-1990s and we are now in a far more competitive position.[6]

Far more than a mere variety of wine, sherry is and has been throughout the ages a sacrosanct drink, long associated with the world of arts and letters. In eight of William Shakespeare's works, the Bard makes more than forty mentions of this wine, which was known as sherry sack. From the time of Ben Jonson in the seventeenth century, it was customary to fête a newly named English poet laureate with a barrel of wine from Jerez. And Charles Dickens placed a glass of sherry in the hands of various characters in his novels.

Jerez de la Frontera is the ideal setting to enjoy the drink, and a good time to do this is during the first fortnight of September. The production as well as the drinking of sherry is enveloped in an aura of near holiness, as is made manifest in the grape harvest festival, known as the Fiesta de la Vendimia. The annual celebration's star attraction is the inauguration, known as Pisa de la Uva, or Treading of the Grapes. The ceremony, open to the public, is held in front of the cathedral to the accompaniment of flamenco singing and rousing music of the municipal band. Wicker baskets of grapes are carried up the cathedral steps to a vat, where in the time-honoured tradition they are crushed by foot and the *mosto*, or must, is blessed by the dean of the cathedral.

The city's airport, a thirty-minute cab journey to Cádiz, has gained international status and now offers direct flights to London. It speaks volumes of the predominant nationality of foreign visitors to Jerez and Cádiz that the other three European cities served by the airport are Dusseldorf, Frankfurt and Hanover. Jerez has become a year-round tourist destination, owing to a multiplicity of attractions. The superstar of most of these fiestas is the Andalusian horse, as intrinsic a part of Jerez's history as sherry wine itself. The beginning of each year kicks off with the ceremonial 'Blessing of the Horses', today a secular albeit still colourful exhibition of horses and carriages paraded through the González Hontoria Park. Barely have the steeds been escorted back to their stables, the town erupts with its own version of the February Carnival.

Around the same time, Jerez has a renowned Flamenco Festival, celebrated for two weeks around the end of February and early March each year, an occasion when the most authentic facets of flamenco converge as the city beats to the rhythm of flamenco music and dancing. The city opens its architectural heritage during the festivities: mansion houses, wineries, flamenco peñas and the Villamarta Theatre accommodate the general public, enthusiasts and lovers of the art of flamenco. Next comes Jerez's Holy Week, which begins before Palm Sunday, and is one of the most brilliant and powerful displays in Andalucía of religious fervour that commemorates the Passion, Death and

Resurrection of Christ. It is celebrated each year at the time of the paschal full moon.

The Jerez Horse Fair, known as the *Feria del Caballo*, dates from 1284 when it was a livestock market. The fair has evolved over the centuries and is now a yearly jamboree of regional cuisine, sherry and, of course, a display of thoroughbred Andalusian horses and festively adorned carriages, with participants turned out in full traditional Andalusian dress. The event is held in the first half of May, with some two hundred *casetas*, or tented stalls, offering regional food and drink specialities. The stands are decorated with colourful paper lanterns, known as *farolillos*. Each day as the sun sets, the fairground takes on a dramatic quality with a total of 1,360,000 lights, including 206 archways, a hundred halide lamp projectors and hundreds of garlands displayed in the *casetas* and across the fairground.

The most pleasurable and certainly the fastest way to return from Jerez de la Frontera to Cádiz is by train. The starting point itself is a rewarding experience: the hemispherical railway station is one of the loveliest in Spain, a 170-year-old listed building of whitewashed walls, rich blue tiles, red brickwork and Moorish arches flanked by pilasters. It is worth arriving a bit early to take a seat at a table in the richly adorned station café and watch the world go by. The rail journey of little more than half an hour, or forty-five minutes on a slow train, offers splendid views of the bay between San Fernando and Cádiz. Before passing El Puerto de Santa María, the Toruños Park looms into view, 2,500 acres of tidal marsh classified as a nature preservation area. The sixteenth century Monasterio de la Victoria, once a convent that also served as a prison until the 1980s, can be spotted from the train near El Puerto de Santa María railway station. The restored building now hosts cultural events, the most emotive in recent years being the farewell ceremony in 1999 for Rafael Alberti, the local poet and militant Marxist who fled into exile after the Civil

CÁDIZ IS RISEN

War and was esteemed as one of Spain's foremost anti-Franco literary figures.

Cádiz has enjoyed half a century of peace since the dictator's death and the city, like the rest of Spain, has benefitted from the country's membership in 1986 of what was then the European Economic Community. Yet the city has had to face some serious adversities since the 1980s. There has been a steady decrease in population, from around 160,000 in 1980 to less than 120,000 in 2024. With the decline of shipbuilding and other heavy industries, young people have been forced to migrate to seek employment elsewhere. As of the end of 2023, the region of Cádiz's twenty-three per cent unemployment level was the fourth highest of all Spanish provinces.

There are signs of a trend toward stability and gradual improvement in the economic outlook. For one thing, tourism is making a post-pandemic comeback, a key factor in a city that has come to depend largely on the services sector for future growth. Despite the uncertainties ahead, the prevailing air in a city that has withstood 3,000 years of invasion, bombardment and siege reflects a consensus that Cádiz will surmount the hurdles ahead.

It is a five-minute walk from the Cádiz railway station up the hill to the Santo Domingo Church, now a luxury hotel located at the start of Calle Plocia. The street's multitude of outdoor cafés and taverns have earned it the title of Cádiz's Golden Mile of cuisine. It is a lively reminder that Cádiz is a vibrant, modern city built on millennia-old foundations. Therein lies the city's seductive charm. The contrast between Old World customs and contemporary stylishness is everywhere to be seen. On a sunny morning, one can hear the knife-grinder on his bicycle announce his presence by piping up and down the scales on his tin whistle. Residents appear from the Andalusian patios of ancient homes, knives in hand, an image that calls to mind a scene from a *zarzuela*, the Spanish operetta. In an all but lost tradition, their blades are honed on the bicycle's grinder wheel while they sit at the outdoor terrace of a chic café, sipping a *café con leche*. They can accompany their morning coffee with typical Pan de Cádiz nougat from the Sabor a España confectioners near the cathedral, a favourite haunt for those with a sweet tooth for more than a century. They lounge contentedly, basking in the light breeze from the sea, which is never more than a short stroll away.

LISTINGS SECTION

Sights

Catedral de Cádiz, Plaza de la Catedral

The splendid Catedral de la Santa Cruz de Cádiz is the New Cathedral, also called the Cathedral of the Americas, as it was planned at the height of the prosperity brought to Cádiz through trade with the New World. Building started in 1722 with a baroque design, but the building work was delayed due to lack of funds and went through several changes of architect. It was not completed until 1853, with a reduced design, in the neoclassical style, with the dome and towers to a smaller scale than the original plans. Despite not being built to its original planned glory, the cathedral is a beautiful landmark in the city, with its golden dome and twin white towers. Inside the cathedral are the tombs of two of the city's most famous sons, the composer Manuel de Falla and the poet and novelist José María Pemán.

A glass case in the crypt is the reliquary of Santa Victoria Mártir. Local legend has it that this young girl suddenly collapsed and died on her way to her first communion. It is not known whose remains are really in the reliquary. In 1816 a mummified body from an ancient Roman tomb was shipped to Cádiz from Rome, by Cardinal Giulio Maria della Somaglia, secretary to the Inquisition, in what seems to have been a move to bolster local faith against ongoing incursions of liberalism.

Outside in the Plaza de la Catedral, don't miss the white marble tiles, which set out a plan of the cathedral in the paving of the square.

Roman Theatre, calle Mesón, 11–13, southern end of Calle San Juan de Dios

One of the highlights of Cádiz, the Roman theatre, was only rediscovered in the 1980s. It attests to the importance of Cádiz in Roman times that this is the second-largest Roman theatre excavated in Spain and almost certainly the earliest, dating from around 70 BCE. Visitors can walk through the gallery under the seating area and out into the theatre remains. Here, a section of about two-thirds of the full seating area is exposed up to about the twentieth row, with a view down to the front portion of the stage. Later buildings cover most of the stage area. The high back wall of the stage, which would have been decorated with archways and statues, has to be left to the imagination to overlay onto the wall of an apartment block that now stands there. Entrance to the theatre is free; the visitor route goes through a well laid-out and informative multimedia exhibition, prior to entering the ruins. It's not the easiest site to find but it is well worth a walk through the Barrio del Pópulo to locate it.

Tavira Tower, calle Marqués del Real Tesoro, 10, near the corner with Calle Sacramento

The Tavira Tower is the only one of the unique watchtowers of Cádiz that is open to the public. The tower is part of the Palacio de Recaño, which is now owned by the Cádiz Council. It is situated at the highest point of the Old Town, so that the top of the tower is 45 metres above sea level. Because it was the highest tower in 1778 it was made the official watchtower for the city and is named after the first official watchman appointed, Lieutenant Commander Antonio Tavira. The role of the watchman was to share information on major shipping movements with the other official watchtowers along the coast at Torre Alto in San Fernando and Torregorda in between.

Now, as a tourist attraction, visitors can see exhibitions about the history of the town in the rooms on different floors and a view across the rooftops from the outside terrace at the top. The tower also houses a camera obscura, giving a panoramic 360º view over the Old Town and the Bay of Cádiz. The top of the tower is reached via 173 steps, and as of 2024 there is no lift, although planning permission to install one has been sought.

Gran Teatro Falla, Plaza Fragela, 11003 Cádiz

Built in neo-Mudéjar style, the theatre's red brick arched doorways and windows make it one of the city's finest architectural treasures. It was constructed on the site of the former Gran Teatro de Cádiz, which was destroyed in a fire in 1881. Work began in 1884 but was beset with funding problems, so the building was not completed until 1905. There were then further delays to get it up and running, with the theatre opening to the public for the first time in 1910. In 1926 the name was changed from Gran Teatro to Gran Teatro Falla, after the famous composer Manuel de Falla, born in Cádiz. The building can be admired from the outside in the handsome Plaza Fragela and occasionally from inside if there is a performance on.

It is well worth getting a ticket to a performance at the Gran Teatro Falla. The theatre is famed for its acoustics and opulent interior, with gilded boxes and a ceiling painted with an allegory of Paradise by Felipe Abarzuza y Rodríguez de Arias. The theatre hosts a sporadic programme of plays, dance and classical music events, as well as the finals for the famous singing groups of the Cádiz Carnival (February/March), with their topical musical parodies. During the Cádiz Carnival the theatre hosts the fiercely contested competition of the local singing groups, who compose and perform new satirical songs every year. The tickets for the competition tend to sell out, so if visiting for the carnival it is worth trying to book tickets in advance.

Monument to the Constitution, Plaza de España

This monument was commissioned in 1912 as part of the centenary celebrations of the 1812 Constitution. The competition for the design was won by the architect Modesto López Otero, with elegant sculptures by Aniceto Marinas. The monument was unveiled in 1929. It includes a multitude of figures symbolising the ideals and ambitions of the Constitution. The central female figure represents the Constitution, flanked by allegorical figures symbolising wisdom, justice and strength, with group sculptures representing citizens and agriculture. Relief carvings at the base depict scenes from the drafting and signing of the 1812 Constitution. On the far edges of the monument are bronze figures representing peace on one side and war on the other. At the lower level beneath the allegorical figure of the Constitution is a central empty throne indicating the absent monarch, Fernando VII. Around the plinth, bronze sculptures represent significant figures from Spanish history.

Phoenician dock at Cueva del Pájaro Azul, Calle San Juan 37–39

In this cave below the city streets, it is possible to see piers of the Phoenician dock, which dates from the third century BCE, together with an area used as a dry dock for ship repair, excavated from the natural rock. This shipyard would have been an essential asset for the Carthaginians to maintain their fleet during the Punic Wars with Rome.

The dock would have continued in use through the Roman period but later fell into disuse, as the geography of the waterways changed over time. It was rediscovered in the 1950s by a local winemaker, Manuel Fedriani Consejero, who initially used the cave as a wine store and later transformed it into a famous venue for flamenco. It is now possible to visit the atmospherically lit, archaeological site for a 45-minute tour. A maximum of fifteen people can visit at one time, and it is essential to book at: https://cuevadelpajaroazul.com/

Yacimiento Arqueológico, Calle de San Miguel, 15 (inside the theatre)

This is another spot where it is possible to view some of the Phoenician remains of Gadir. The archaeological site has a video introduction explaining the history, in Spanish with English subtitles. Visitors then take a guided tour around the fascinating underground ruins. The site is free to visit but booking is essential as only twenty-five people are allowed at a time, but it is not possible to book days in advance or online. The best way to organise a visit is to go when the site opens and get tickets for your preferred timeslot that day.

Museums and galleries

Museo de Cádiz: Archaeology, fine arts and ethnography museum, Plaza de Mina

The main museum of Cádiz is divided into three distinct sections. The archaeological collection on the ground floor includes artefacts from the earliest inhabitants of the region, through the

Phoenician settlement, Roman period and the Arab city. Some of the most spectacular items on display are the two Phoenician sarcophagi, presented here as a couple but actually discovered in disparate parts of the city, along with beautiful jewellery recovered from Phoenician gravesites. There are Roman sculptures from the theatre in the city and the wider area, together with huge pottery amphorae, which tell of the important trade in wine and olive oil from Cádiz to the eastern Mediterranean and later across the whole Roman Empire.

In the fine arts section, the museum has a wonderful collection of Spanish Masters of the sixteenth to the twentieth centuries, including works from Zurbarán, Murillo, Rubens, Zuloaga, Sorolla and Miró.

The ethnography collection is centred on the collection of one of the oldest puppet companies in Spain, Los Títeres de la Tía Norica. The finely crafted puppets are over 200 years old and were originally presented in a play known as *Nacimiento de figuras de movimiento* (Birth of Figures in Motion). Characters included historical personages in the popular presentations *Isabel II* and then *Libertad*, as well as the old lady character, Tía Norica (Aunt Norica), who gave the shows and the theatre their popular names. An even larger collection of puppets can be seen at the Cádiz Puppet Museum – see below.

Museum of Las Cortes De Cádiz, Calle Santa Inés, 9

The Museum of the Cortes of Cádiz was initiated by the then mayor, as part of the centenary celebrations to commemorate the Constitution of 1812 and the Cádiz Parliament, which was in session throughout the Napoleonic siege of the city and its daily bombardments. The parliamentary debating sessions took place in the baroque Oratorio de San Felipe Neri church, next door to the building that now houses the museum. It is a fine neoclassical-inspired construction, with imposing Ionic columns at the entrance and a grand iron staircase as the main feature of the entry hall. The museum collection displays numerous objects linked to the portentous events of 1812: flags, weapons, portraits of the personalities involved. It includes a large canvas of the proclamation of the constitution by Salvador Viniegra and various historic documents, including one of the copies of the final constitution. Among the most interesting exhibits is a beautiful 1:252 model of Cádiz in the late eighteenth century, made from precious woods obtained from the trade with the Americas – mahogany, ebony and peroba – with the cathedral in marble. From the model we know that the street plan of the Old Town has changed little since that time.

Casa de Iberoamérica, Calle de Concepción Arenal, Antigua Cárcel Real

The Casa de Iberoamérica, of the Cádiz Society for 1812, is located in an eighteenth century building that once housed the royal prison. The building is considered one of the best examples of the neoclassical style in Andalucía. It underwent several renovations throughout its history as a prison, but when the inmates were relocated in 1966, the building was abandoned for twenty years. In the 1980s this neglect was reversed, and the building was renovated as the regional courthouse from 1991 to 2006. On its return to the city council, another major refurbishment was undertaken for it to become the Casa Iberoamérica, inaugurated in January 2011, to provide a focus for cultural and arts activities celebrating Cádiz's links with Central and South America.

There is a permanent exhibition of works by Juan Luis Vassallo, gifted to the city of Cádiz by the artist's family, including drawings, portraits and smaller sculptures. In one room the sculptor's studio is recreated, while the monumental sculpture *Gades* is on display alone in the courtyard. Temporary exhibitions by twentieth century and contemporary Central and South American artists are a mainstay of the arts programmes. There is also a musical and lecture programme, so it is well worth checking out what is on during your Cádiz visit.

Cathedral Museum, Plaza Fray Félix

The museum is in a separate building from the cathedral, housed in a group of structures that stood around the tower of the old cathedral. From the entrance, the first room is a small gallery of religious paintings. What stands out is *La Inmaculada Grande* from the late sixteenth century Madrid school of religious painting. From the gallery visitors cross a courtyard to reach the Patio Mudéjar, where larger Roman and medieval carved stone remains are on display. The next series of rooms show treasures of the cathedral including crosses, chalices, candelabra and other works of gold and silver, mostly from the seventeenth and eighteenth centuries.

Puppet Museum – Museo del Títere, Puertas de Tierra, Bóvedas de Santa Elena

A part of the massive land gates to the city and its barracks complex have been converted into a museum to display a unique international collection of puppets, which was gifted to the city by Ismael Peña, an avid collector of folklore artefacts. The entrance to the Puppet Museum is through the courtyard of the old fire station, leading to eighteen of the vaults over the ground and first floor, which display over 500 puppets and marionettes, together with the puppet stages and props used in shows around the world, from Mexico to Ghana, China, Italy and Thailand. The puppets include a wide range of moveable figures, including shadow puppets, glove puppets and finger puppets, while the marionettes, which are always operated by strings or wires, are more complex. The most sophisticated of the puppets, including the oldest set, the Austrian Marionettes, were left in hock at the Teatro de Tívoli in Barcelona, by a company that could not pay its bills.

Notable buildings

William Somerset Maugham decried the travel guide approach to Cádiz: 'I prefer to wander in old streets at random without a guide-book, trusting that fortune will bring me across things worth seeing...often I discover some little dainty piece of architecture, some scrap of decoration that repays me for all else I lose.'[1]

Throughout the Old Town there are numerous interesting architectural and decorative features to delight the observant wanderer. We suggest a combination of the two approaches to reveal the best of Cádiz. Here are some of the buildings and features to look out for as you stroll around the streets of the Old Town. Sadly, most of these buildings aren't routinely open to the public, but many of the architectural details can be viewed from the street.

Casa del Almirante, Plaza de San Martin, 3

The Admiral's House in the Barrio del Pópulo, around the corner from the *Ayuntamiento* (town hall), was built at the end of the seventeenth century as the town palace of the Admiral of the Fleet of the Indies and thus one of the wealthiest and most important people in the South America and West Indies trading enterprise. The four-storey house has a magnificent marble archway around the main entrance, surmounted by the coat of arms of Admiral Diego de Barrios. Inside the entrance there is a typical colonnaded patio, with a staircase ascending under an elliptical dome, with the main reception rooms being on the double-height second floor. The building is topped by two watchtowers to look out for the returning fleet, the oldest preserved watchtowers in the city. There have been plans since 2008 for the building to be restored and refurbished as a luxury hotel, but at the time of writing this project has not yet been completed.

Casa Palacio de Mora, Calle Ancha, 28–30

Found on the main pedestrianised shopping street, Calle Ancha is the stately home of Manuel Moreno de Mora, head of a successful family wine business with bodegas in Jerez, El Puerto and Sanlúcar. The house was inaugurated in September 1862 by a ball in honour of the visit to Cádiz of Queen Isabel II and her husband Francisco de Asís. The building is a very fine example of nineteenth-century neoclassical domestic architecture. The elegant façade is adorned with intricate ornamentation, including corbels of Carrara marble, large windows either side of the grand entrance and balconies over the street on the first floor. Inside, it is the only historic house in Cádiz that has retained all its original interiors, with a mix of styles including Gothic arches, Moorish tilework and Renaissance elements. The reception rooms on the first floor are filled with antique French and Italian furniture, artworks including paintings by Bianchi and Zurbarán and exquisite chandeliers, all as they were for Queen Isabel's ball. It is possible to book a tour of the house. At the time of writing, these are available on Wednesdays.

Casa de las Cinco Torres, Plaza de España, 7

This distinctive four storey building runs along one side of the Plaza de España, just in front of the Monument to the Constitution. It is actually a terrace of five baroque-style merchants' houses built around 1771. At the rooftop level, each house has a watchtower

LISTINGS SECTION

with a small dome and a decorative parapet. Four are in the 'sentry-box' style, while the one above 5D is polygonal.

There are well over a hundred other surviving **tower houses** in the streets of the Old Town. Good places to view some of these are **Plaza Mina**, which has watchtowers at numbers 4, 5, 6, 8, 9 and 10. The **Casa de las Cuatro Torres** with its highly decorated towers is at the corner of Plaza Argüelles 3–4 and Manuel Rancés 27–29. Towers can be seen on many of the buildings along **Calle Sagasta**, at numbers, 1, 2, 5, 31, 33, 63, 91 and 93.

Casa de las Cadenas, Calle Cristóbal Colón, 12

This building has been remodelled many times since 1692 when, during a Corpus Christi procession torrential rain came down, and the merchant owner invited the bishop of Cádiz to take refuge inside with the sacred sculpture. In remembrance of this act of piety, an inscription was engraved, 'I praise and give thanks to the Holy Sacrament of the Altar', and King Carlos II granted the privilege of having decorative chains on the façade of his house. Although the chains have long since gone, the name remains. The magnificent baroque entrance is flanked by two sinuous double columns of marble with an inscribed tablet over the door. On the roof is a square watchtower, with a fancy balustrade. Over the centuries the building has been a merchant's house, a convent, a pharmaceutical warehouse and a hotel. It now houses the provincial historical archive.

Casino Gaditano, Plaza San Antonio, 15

This lovely eighteenth century townhouse was built as the palace of the Marqués del Pedroso. In 1848 it was sold to become the headquarters of the Casino Gaditano, a gentleman's club for the Cádiz bourgeoisie, which also carried out charitable work. As the casino, the building was remodelled to give it its wonderful grand staircase, with a sculpture of a woman holding the crystal chandelier and the magnificent neo-Mudéjar courtyard patio, which today is open to the public as a restaurant.

Castillo de San Sebastián

The Castle of San Sebastián is a significant feature of the fortifications constructed after the 1596 sacking of Cádiz by the English and Dutch, to protect the city from future attacks. The castle is on an island, joined to the city by a long causeway called Paseo Fernando Quiñones, after the poet Fernando Quiñones Chozas (born in Chiclana de la Frontera, 1930–1998), whose statue is seen at the beginning of the walkway. When the fortress is open, it is possible to walk around the parapets and across the water-filled moat by drawbridge to reach the north-west part of the island where the fifteenth century chapel and the tower-lighthouse, built in 1908, are located.

Baluarte de la Candelaria

This fortification at the Punta Candelaria, the northernmost point of the Old Town, was built in the seventeenth century to protect the entrance to Cádiz Bay. The roughly triangular shape is built up around the north and west with battlements and corner viewing points, with the south side open towards the city. In the 1990s there were plans to develop a Museum of the Sea in the interior space, but the museum never came to fruition, although the building is occasionally used for temporary exhibitions.

Correos de Cádiz (main post office), Plaza Libertad/Plaza de las Flores

The main post office is a fine 1930s structure in the neo-Mudéjar style, with terracotta and tile decoration on the outside of the building. It is one of the post offices that still uses the traditional

LISTINGS SECTION

lion's head posting boxes set into the outer wall on the Plaza Libertad side of the building. Putting your hand in the lion's mouth to post your letter is always a little thrill!

Cannon as street corner protection, Plaza San Augustín, corner of Calle San Francisco

This is one of the many corners in the Old Town where you will see enemy cannons set into the building walls on street corners, there to protect the building from cars (and in earlier times wagons and carriages) scraping it as the vehicles turn the corner. Once you start to notice the cannons, you will see them protecting many building corners in the Old Town!

Notable churches

There are many fascinating churches around the streets of the Old Town. Listed are some with the most interesting architecture, decorative features or historic associations.

Iglesia de Santa Cruz – the old cathedral, Plaza Fray Félix

The old cathedral, the Iglesia de Santa Cruz, can be visited in Plaza Fray Félix, between the cathedral and the Roman Theatre. This church is on the site of the Muslim Mosque, making it one of the oldest churches in the city. Little remains of the thirteenth century building, which was destroyed in the English-Dutch sacking of Cádiz in 1596, led by the Earl of Essex. The cathedral (as it had been) was one of the first buildings to be rebuilt, with the current church building completed in 1605.

Oratorio San Felipe Neri, Plaza San Felipe Neri

This baroque church is most notable for having been used as the debating chamber for the 1812 parliament. The church was rebuilt in 1755 in the baroque style, after the Lisbon earthquake and tsunami hit Cádiz. It has a very unusual elliptical floor plan, with seven chapels leading off from the main church. It was chosen as the debating chamber for the 1812 parliament due to its roomy oval interior and lack of columns impeding the internal view. Parliamentary sessions were held between February 1811 and September 1813, with the 1812 Constitution being drafted here. The members were seated around the main body of the church and the sessions were open to the public, who could watch the proceedings from the two levels of balconies. The church has many plaques on the exterior commemorating the 1812 parliamentarians. Inside, the altarpiece includes an Immaculate Conception by Murillo, considered one of his finest works.

Oratorio de la Santa Cueva, Calle Rosario, 10

The Oratorio de Santa Cueva is an absolute gem in the neoclassical style, unique among the religious buildings of Spain. It was built by the Congregation of the Christian Retreat, a religious society formed by prominent figures in Cádiz society around 1730. One of them, the Marquis of Valde-Íñigo, used a large part of the family fortune amassed from trade with Mexico to fund the construction of the church. *The interior* is divided into two chapels: an underground one dedicated to the passion and death of Christ and an upper one dedicated to the exaltation of the Eucharist. The lower chapel was built first in 1783, designed as an austere enclosure suitable for penitential prayer where the image of Calvary stands out. The Marquis of Valde-Íñigo commissioned Joseph Haydn to compose his work *The Seven Last Words of Our Saviour on the Cross* for this chapel. The ceremony of the Sermon of the Seven Words takes place every Good Friday, accompanied by a string quartet performing Haydn's work. *The upper or sacramental chapel*, completed in 1796, is intensely decorative, giving an intentional contrast with the penitential area. The glorious paintings include three by Francisco de Goya, which represent the miracle of the loaves and fishes, the parable of the wedding guest and the Last Supper, in what is considered one of his most successful religious-themed ensembles.

Iglesia del Carmen, Alameda Marqués de Comillas

This very pretty white church, with terracotta-coloured highlights on the exterior, was built between 1743 and 1762 in the baroque style. Its most striking feature are the two gracefully curving white belfries on either side of the main façade. Due to the location of the church, close to the north-western tip of Cádiz, the interior enjoys abundant natural lighting, which brings out the beauty of the gilded wood altarpiece, presided over by an image of the Virgin of Carmen.

Parks and beaches

Alameda de Apodaca

This lovely promenade is a popular place to stroll on summer evenings, to enjoy the refreshing breeze coming off the Atlantic. Among the impressive trees and plantings of evergreen shrubs there are several commemorative sculptures. These include one to the Marqués de Comillas, Claudio López, head of the Compañía Trasatlántica Española, one of the driving forces behind the prosperity of Cádiz, together with a monument to Ramón Power y Giralt, a famous mariner and member of the 1812 parliament for Puerto Rico. There is also a sculpture of the twentieth century writer, Carlos Edmundo de Ory, who appears to have stepped off his pedestal and is himself taking a stroll along the promenade.

LISTINGS SECTION

Balneario de la Palma, Playa de la Caleta

The only beach that is actually in the Old Town, Playa de la Caleta, is dominated by this wonderfully quirky Art Nouveau building, which opened as a spa in 1926, providing changing rooms and lockers for bathers, as well as spa facilities. In common with many of the historic buildings of Cádiz, it has had a chequered history. Commandeered as a boarding school for naval cadets in the Civil War, the building then reopened after the war as a municipal spa but was later sold off as a banqueting venue. The building fell into disuse and disrepair to the extent that there were proposals to demolish it in the 1980s. Campaigners were successful in turning this decision round and the municipality restored the building, but with no clear plans for its future use. It has since become the offices for the Cádiz Department of Underwater Archaeology, so at least it has some connection with the ocean, but it seems a shame that such a charming building is not open for the public to enjoy its light airy spaces and wonderful views out to sea.

Parque Genovés

This beautifully laid out area is the largest green space in the Old Town, right at the western edge of Cádiz facing the Atlantic. The gardens were first planted at the end of the eighteenth century and were extended several times. The current park was opened in 1892 with the additions of fountains, an ornamental pond, a bandstand and an open-air café, along with varied botanical species. The gardens have some of the rarest and oldest trees in Cádiz, including the famous Dragon Tree, native to the Canary Islands and one of the largest of its species in Europe. The name comes from the reddish sap that oozes out of the bark and was believed to have healing properties.

LISTINGS SECTION

Entertainment

Flamenco

Along with Sevilla and Córdoba, Cádiz is one of the best-known centres for flamenco in Spain. The city has played an important role in the development and evolution of this musical style over the centuries, and several of the towering artists of the genre are from Cádiz. Here are some of the best venues to see authentic flamenco guitarists, singers and dancers, rather than the chorus line shows of tourist venues. Artists also appear at other venues in the city, including bars and the arts centres, so look out for posters advertising these performances. The city's flamenco festival is held in September each year, featuring some of the best artists from around the world.

Taberna Flamenca La Cava, Antonio López, 16, 11004 Cádiz

Offers nightly performances of an authentic flamenco show by the La Cava company, in the intimate setting of a traditional tavern, decorated with memorabilia of famous flamenco artists. The Taberna serves typical cuisine, with dishes from Cádiz and the region. Book online through the website: https://flamencolacava.com/en/

Peña Flamenca la Perla de Cádiz, Calle Concepción Arenal

The 'Pearl of a Cádiz' is a flamenco club which runs classes and competitions for local dancers as well as putting on events by national and international flamenco artists; these are on a roughly monthly basis. Check out the website to see what is coming up: https://www.perladecadiz.com/noticias/index.php

Tickets can be booked by email: pflaperla@gmail.com.

LISTINGS SECTION

Tablao Flamenco Cueva del Pájaro Azul, Calle de San Juan, 37

This is the same venue as the archaeological site of the Phoenician dock. One of the city's longest running flamenco shows is hosted here, celebrating the ancient history of the city and authentic flamenco. At the time of writing, shows are at 9 pm on a Friday. Check the website for details and to buy tickets: https://cuevadelpajaroazul.com/?lang=en

Peña Flamenca Juanito Villar, Paseo Fernando Quiñones, 2

This traditional flamenco club is right by the sea, at the Caleta Beach end of the Castillo de San Sebastián causeway. The small venue focuses on the traditional flamenco styles of fandango and bulería.

Festivals

The dates for the two most popular spring festivals in Cádiz vary year to year as they are linked to the dates for Shrove Tuesday and Easter.

Carnaval de Cádiz, usually February/early March, Old Town throughout the streets

The Cádiz Carnival is one of Spain's most vibrant festivals as the streets of the Old Town burst into life for ten days of celebrations including parades, music, singing, dance, food giveaways, competitions, street shows and fireworks. It is the largest carnival celebration in Spain, attracting visitors from all over the world. The roots of the carnival can be traced back to the sixteenth century, closely tied to the influence of the Italian traders and sailors, who brought the traditions from the Venetian Carnival to Cádiz. Over the centuries, it has evolved to include unique Spanish elements, particularly those reflecting local culture and satire.

LISTINGS SECTION

The festival is renowned for its spontaneous nature. Unlike other carnivals that focus on grand parades, the Cádiz Carnival is more about impromptu street performances. Much of the crowd wears fancy dress, especially on the first weekend of the Carnival. Friends often decide on a group theme and go to enormous lengths to perfect their home-made costumes, from a circus menagerie to six lads going as a pack of beer.

The defining feature of the carnival is the clubs of singing groups, which are classified into different types by the number of members and the style of their songs. Each group has a theme for their matching costumes, and they compose original satirical songs to perform for the carnival. The songs are shaped by current affairs and mock prominent figures in Spanish life. The groups, called *comparsas* (slightly more serious in approach) and *chirigotas* (singing humorous songs with lots of double meanings) sing in the streets and squares, at improvised venues like outdoor staircases or archways, and in established open-air *tablaos* organised by the carnival clubs. There is an annual competition among the groups with the heats held at the Gran Teatro de Falla before the carnival. *Coros* are larger groups that travel through the streets on flat-bed lorries, singing their satirical songs along with lyrical homages to the city, accompanied by guitars. Their costumes are, by far, the most sophisticated and elaborate. Other groups of performers are the comic *cuartetos* that, oddly, can be composed of five, four or three members. They bang sticks to mark their rhythm and perform comic songs and improvised sketches.

There are two main processions during the carnival celebrations. On the first Sunday, the parade into the Old Town from Puertas de Tierra includes hundreds of motorised floats, costumed groups and singing groups, taking about four hours to parade along the 3 to 5 kilometre route. The second parade, known as the Humour Parade, is on the last Sunday, and moves through the historic centre of the city, with groups in elaborate fancy dress. Throughout the celebrations, the *coros* traditionally parade in the area around the Abastos Square, but the growth of the carnival has led to new routes being introduced taking in other streets and squares during the week.

Easter week processions, usually during March/early April, various routes to the cathedral

Semana Santa goes on for over a week in Cádiz, starting the Friday (Viernes de Dolores) before Palm Sunday and continuing until Easter Sunday. Easter is celebrated through the tradition of religious processions around the Old Town, with schedules for each day of Holy Week. There are more than thirty organisations called *cofradías penitenciales* – religious fraternities – usually attached to a parish church, which are responsible for the Semana Santa processions. Every group has a specific *paso* with a set day and route for their procession of painted wooden sculptures, each of which shows a particular scene related to the Passion of Christ or the Sorrows of the Virgin Mary. Some of the images are artistic masterpieces of great antiquity. The combined statues for a *paso* can weigh up to 6 tonnes and are carried on highly decorated floats, or on the shoulders of Penitenciales. The Semana Santa procession can be quite dramatic as each *cofradía* has its brass band playing mournful music, accompanied by *penitenciales* carrying enormous candles, wearing tall, pointed hoods and robes, with hundreds of people following each procession.

Other festivals in the region

Vendimia de Jerez, wine harvest festival, first half of September, cathedral, Jerez de la Frontera

The wine harvest festival includes a programme of celebrations across Jerez, including concerts and equestrian competitions. The formal opening of the fiesta is the charming evening ceremony of the Blessing of the Grapes on the steps of the cathedral (Iglesia Colegiata). The cathedral forms a wonderful backdrop and is an appropriate setting as the building was funded through special taxes on the wine and sherry industry.

Large baskets of grapes are ceremonially brought to the steps by beautiful young men and women from Jerez in traditional costume. A priest blesses the grapes as a choir sings and the town band plays. A young woman who has been crowned Queen of the Harvest occupies a seat of honour at the top of the steps. She and her attendants then pick up their baskets of grapes and empty them into a large rectangular wooden tank and a small group of men in pristine white shorts and shirts with red sashes proceed to tread the grapes wearing special studded shoes to crush the grapes (but not the pips and stalks), as they begin the first pressing of the vintage (*mosto*). As the cathedral bells ring out the official party is offered a glass of fino by a *venenciador* (wine pourer). During the next few days the city celebrates, with music and parties spilling out of bars into the streets day and night.

Horse racing, Sanlúcar de Barrameda, the beach at Sanlúcar, second and fourth weekend of August

These exciting horse races are held along the beach, so the timing may vary depending on the tides. The races are free to watch and take place in the evening. At around 6.00 pm the Guardia Civil move people off the beach where the horses race. The Sanlúcar de Barrameda races attract riders from all over Europe, with about eighty horses and riders taking part each year. The races officially date from 1845 when the Real Sociedad de Carreras de Caballos de Sanlúcar was formed. Before this the races were informal affairs, with locals racing the horses used for transporting fish from the local ports. There are four races each evening from 6.30 to 9.00 pm. It is a wonderful experience to watch the horses race as the sun sets over the river Guadalquivir and the Doñana nature reserve.

Where to stay

The main group of holiday hotels in Cádiz are along the Playa de Victoria beach. These are mostly large, modern tower block hotels; many have pools and all the expected amenities of three to five-star beach hotels. We have selected some of the characterful hotels right in the heart of the Old Town below, ranging from the most luxurious to homely comfort.

Áurea Casa Palacio Sagasta, Calle Sagasta, 1, 11004 Cádiz

Four-star hotel in a beautifully renovated eighteenth century baroque mansion on one of the main streets in the Old Town. The building was the British Consulate during the Peninsular War, hosting Sir Richard Wellesley, the Duke of Wellington's brother. The building has the traditional central patio and a lookout tower, used by later owner Don Benito Cuesta, a shipping tycoon and political leader in the nineteenth century. Rooms are spacious and well furnished. The hotel also has a spa and wellness centre (additional charges).

Casa Cánovas boutique hotel, Calle Cánovas del Castillo, 32, 11001, Cádiz

Another four-star renovation of one of the Old Town palatial buildings, which has become a small ten-bedroom family-run hotel. The hotel has a restaurant and bar, while each bedroom has been individually styled with unique furnishings and sumptuous decoration.

LISTINGS SECTION

Parador Atlántico de Cádiz, Avenida Duque de Nájera, 9, 11002 Cádiz

Four-star hotel, right at the tip of Cádiz's Old Town, by the Playa Caleta. The Parador is housed in a modern building, a ten-minute walk from the historic centre. The rooms are pleasantly furnished, many with a sea view and with contemporary-styled bathrooms. The hotel has a gym, spa and an outdoor pool with sea views.

Hotel Boutique Convento, Santo Domingo, 2, 11006 Cádiz

As the name suggests, this is a seventeenth-century Dominican convent that has been converted into a hotel. The building retains the feeling of austere peacefulness, with comfortable, simply furnished rooms arranged over two floors around the original chequerboard-tiled convent cloister. This is a great choice if arriving by train, as it's only a five-minute walk from the railway station and then a stroll along one of the main streets, lined with bars and restaurants, into the historic centre.

Hotel Casa de las Cuatro Torres, Plaza de Argüelles, 3, 11004 Cádiz

A chance to stay in one of the unique watchtower houses of Cádiz, from which the eighteenth-century merchants would look out to sea to scan for their ships returning with cargo from the Americas. This charming two-star hotel is in a refurbished neoclassical merchant's house on a quiet square offering a range of rooms, including small apartments, sleeping up to four people. The hotel has a rooftop deck, next to the tower, with an ocean view.

Soho Boutique Hotel, Calle Flamenco, 12, 11005 Cádiz

This small three-star hotel is an old townhouse that has been modernised with light, airy décor while retaining the old archways and character of the building. The hotel also has a small open-air rooftop pool and sunbathing terrace.

Food and drink

Cádiz is famous for its fish and shellfish, of which there is a rich variety including Sanlúcar prawns, shrimp tortillas, oyster soup, clams in fino sherry, and *pescaditio* – fried fish in bite-size pieces. The region also produces venison, wild boar and the local morcilla black sausage.

The best-known local wines are of course sherries, the fortified wine from Jerez de la Frontera: fino; oloroso; amontillado; rich, sweet Pedro Ximénez, drunk as a dessert wine; and dry manzanilla sherry from Sanlúcar de Barrameda. The other local wines to try are Chiclana white wine and the red from Rota.

Restaurants

La Candela, Calle Feduchy, 3

Very popular restaurant with quirky retro décor of mismatched glass lampshades, ceramic tile placemats and sewing machine table bases. The restaurant serves modern, creative Spanish food, using fresh seasonal produce with great flavours. La Candela serves possibly the best croquetas de jamón ever, as well as perfectly cooked fish, such as cod loin with avocado salsa. Booking is recommended as La Candela is a small restaurant and tends to fill up. If you don't book, you can join the queue that starts to form about thirty minutes before the restaurant opens for lunch or dinner, for a place to sit along the bar.

El Faro de Cádiz, Calle San Félix, 15

El Faro is a popular, traditional-style restaurant in the barrio de la Viña that has been run for over sixty years by three generations of the Córdoba family. Starting from a small taverna, decorated with fishing nets, it is now quite a formal affair. Famous for seafood, with a wide range of fish and shellfish, El Faro also serves a full menu of meat and some vegetarian dishes. We recommend the cheese and leek *friuritas*, savoury fried bites served with Pedro Ximénez sauce and the sea bass or sea bream cooked in salt, which beautifully preserves the moisture and flavour of the fish. The restaurant has a large dining room with a smaller bar section and booking is recommended.

Somnámbulo, Plaza Candelaria, 12

Modern-style industrial chic décor and friendly staff give a good impression before the food arrives, then things get even better. The menu has inventive takes on traditional ingredients and everything is beautifully presented. A good range of local wines are served, as well as some unusual regional wines from around Spain, along with favourites like Rioja, Ribera del Duero and Albariño.

Burlesque restaurant, Calle Amaya, 2, on the corner with Calle Plocia

Something a bit different for Cádiz, a restaurant that is as much focused on the décor, style and ambience as the excellent food. The venue is opulently decorated with subtle lighting from silk shaded lamps, bountiful branches of artificial blossom and photos of screen and music icons. The cocktail bar offers a range of classic and innovative mixes. The menu includes typical fish and meat dishes with a focus on tuna and steak.

Mesón Cumbres Mayores, Calle Zorrilla, 4

A traditional restaurant aiming for the style of a rustic inn, Mesón Cumbres Mayores is famous for its exquisite dishes of

Ibérico pork. The chef uses first class local ingredients to make authentic dishes from the Huelva region. It is recommended for its generous portions, good value and friendly service.

Bars and cafés

Café Royalty, Plaza Candelaria, corner with Calle Obispo Urquinaona

The beautiful early twentieth century Café Royalty is one of the best examples of a romantic era 'Gran Café' in Spain. A delightful spot for a break from viewing sights in the Old Town, the café was returned to its former glory, ready for its centenary in 2012. In the hundred years between opening and refurbishment it had gone from being the smartest café in Cádiz, from 1912 up to the 1930s, with nightly concerts and famous patrons from the arts, literature and music to an empty shell. It shut as a café at the end of the 1930s and over the next seventy years was used intermittently as a warehouse, then a cut-price bazaar, then it closed altogether. In the early twenty-first century it was rescued from this fate by the De la Serna family, who committed to a total restoration, using the original plastering, painting, woodwork and gilding techniques. The interior is a gem. Don't miss the wonderful ceiling painting of a Bacchanal scene, with cupid poised with his arrow and a cherub holding aloft a bottle of champagne.

The café serves great coffee, cakes and drinks all day and evening, with the most attentive staff. It also has a very fine restaurant serving lunch and dinner every day.

Taberna La Manzanilla, Calle Feduchy, 19

As the name suggests, this is the place for a light, dry glass of the region's famous manzanilla sherry, straight from the barrel.

The bar is nearly 100 years old, run by the grandson of the original proprietor. It is also known as 'the wine museum' due to the vast range of sherries available from different wineries. It is worth trying a few different types of sherry and of different ages to appreciate the subtleties of the wines. Olives, cheese and other cold tapas are available to have with your sherry but no hot food, as heat from cooking could interfere with keeping the ideal ambient temperature for the sherry!

Taberna Casa Manteca, Calle Corralón de los Carros, 66, barrio de la Viña

Established in 1953 in the popular barrio de la Viña, this small bullfight-themed traditional bar and restaurant is famed for its *jamón serrano* and *tortitas de camarones*, small, battered discs packed with shrimps, a speciality of Cádiz. Also serves a good range of tapas, as well as simple, traditional meals in the restaurant behind the bar.

Mercado Central de Abastos, Plaza de la Libertad

Recently restored, the Central Market of Cádiz has a wonderful food court, which now takes up the outer ring of stalls. The market offers a great range of tapas, particularly fried fish and shrimp tortillas, also sushi and hamburgers for variety, with stalls selling local wines and craft beers. It's a great place for a sunny lunch, soaking up the atmosphere of the historic market.

Café de Ana, Calle Nueva

One of the best options for breakfast in the Old Town, serving juices, good coffee, a variety of teas and a great range of baked goods, toasted sandwiches, pancakes, cakes and brunch dishes. The café is decorated in a cosy retro style with friendly and efficient service.

LISTINGS SECTION

Freiduría Las Flores, Plaza de las Flores

This bar, around the corner from the market and opposite the main post office, is reckoned to be the best place for traditional fried fish tapas served in paper cones. Try it with a cold beer or fresh white wine. Freiduría Las Flores always does a brisk trade at lunchtime, with a fast-moving queue.

Las Nieves, Plaza Mendizábal

A traditional no-nonsense café, said to be one of the oldest continuously operating in the city. Serves great coffee together with a full range of alcoholic and non-alcoholic drinks, tapas and larger portions of cheese, charcuterie and seafood, as well as a very reasonably priced *menú del día*. Note, the café is only open Monday to Friday.

Shops

Mercado Central de Abastos, Plaza de la Libertad

If you're in self-catering accommodation, the market is a great place to buy fresh fish and vegetables to cook in your apartment, much more atmospheric than the local supermarket. The market is open Tuesday–Saturday from 9.00 am through to 2.00 pm (although some of the fish stalls will be packing up before that).

Sherry Wine Shop, Stall 6, Plaza de Abastos – central market

The shop is in the outer ring of stalls in the market and is the best place in Cádiz to buy sherry. It stocks a huge variety from many of the local wineries in Jerez, from fino to amontillado and Pedro Ximénez, as well as the excellent vermouths from the Bodegas Lustau and manzanilla sherries from Sanlúcar de Barrameda.

LISTINGS SECTION

La Dulcería de la Rondeña, Calle Sagasta, 11 at the corner of Calle Ancha, 11001 Cádiz

A delightful traditional sweet shop, the branch of a family business established in Sanlúcar de Barrameda, selling *turrón*, glacé fruits, marzipan and artisanal Andalusian confectionery. Your choices are carefully wrapped in paper and parcel ribbon, giving a special feel to the purchase.

Sabor a España, Calle Compañía, 20

Another traditional confectioners, part of a small Andalusian chain, Sabor a España is found on the corner of one of the streets leading into the cathedral square. The shop sells traditional *turrón* (caramelised nuts and marzipan), along with cakes and pastries made with nougat, honey and nuts. All the sweets are made by the company, now run by the fifth generation, using the highest quality ingredients.

Quorum Libros, Calle Ancha, 27

A good general bookshop with the latest bestsellers, as well as children's books and a wide range of non-fiction. There is a small selection of works in English.

Librería Manuel de Falla, Plaza de Mina, 2

Charming traditional bookshop with many works on the history and culture of Spain, with a strong local focus on Andalucía. Also stocks Spanish classics and the latest literary fiction.

El Vestuario Boutique, Calle Valverde, 9

Exclusive, small boutique with a well-curated collection of party dresses, formal wear and luxe sportswear, plus handcrafted accessories, unusual jewellery, bags and scarves. One of the smartest places to shop in Cádiz and always worth a look for unique fashion that you won't find elsewhere.

Around Cádiz

The province of Cádiz has a wealth of interesting places to visit. Many of these are accessible within thirty minutes, while others are further afield, suitable for a day trip from Cádiz.

Doñana National Park – a vast area of wetlands, north along the coast from Cádiz, is one of the most important European biodiversity sites, with over 200 bird species, as well as being home to diverse types of fish, molluscs and crustaceans. The park is a labyrinth of channels, swamps and sand dunes. Guided tours can be arranged around the park on foot or by boat.

Puerto Real – is easily accessible across the bay by the Carranza Bridge, which has led to much development since the mid-twentieth century, but the origins of the town go back to Roman times and in the Middle Ages it was a centre for ship building. The main attractions these days are the fine beaches and the pinewoods of the Parque de las Canteras.

San Fernando – grew up around the Roman bridge Ponte Suazo and the fourteenth century Castle of San Romualdo, it is also known as the Isla de León. Since the eighteenth century it has been a centre for shipbuilding and marine activities. The Navy Museum here includes a collection of important historical ships and nautical artefacts, while the Pantheon de Marinos Ilustres celebrates the lives and deaths of intrepid sailors and maritime explorers. The Royal Naval Observatory is housed in a majestic neoclassical building on the highest part of the Isla de León. The observatory has a wonderful collection of eighteenth-

and nineteenth-century scientific instruments to observe the movements of the stars and planets, used to aid navigation.

El Puerto de Santa María – One of the most ancient settlements in the Bay of Cádiz is a short hop across the bay by catamaran ferry. Legend has it that it was founded by an Athenian king, although there have not been any archaeological finds to support this. It flourished from the time of Columbus's first voyage to the Indies and with the American trade, was known as the city of a hundred palaces in the eighteenth century. Many of these buildings remain, including the Casa Cargadores de Indias, the commercial exchange at the centre of the trade, as well as the thirteenth century Castle of San Marcos and the very fine fifteenth century late-Gothic Mayor Prioral Church.

Chiclana de la Frontera – was founded in the fourteenth century on the banks of the Río Iro, which still divides the town in two. A pleasant walk along the Alameda del Río provides views of the historic buildings, including the Church of San Juan Bautista, the ancient clocktower over one of the town gates and the seventeenth century church of Jesús Nazareno, which has a fine marble portico.

Sanlúcar de Barrameda – is another ancient port and trading centre that came to prominence in the fifteenth to seventeenth centuries under the dukes of Medina Sidonia, who were one of the wealthiest aristocratic families, owning huge tracts of land across the region. The outstanding historical sights are the Castle of Santiago, dating from the fifteenth century, and Medina Sidonia Palace. The town is famous for its beaches, seafood – especially prawns – and for the production of manzanilla sherry. Several wineries are open for visitors to observe the winemaking process and sample the results. The Manzanilla Fiesta takes place at the end of May to early June and includes carriage and horseback processions in traditional local costume, illuminations around the town and tastings of manzanilla.

Jerez de la Frontera – is famous as the home of sherry. There are many bodegas within and close to the city offering tours to show the unique process of making sherry by the solera system. A bodega tour offers the opportunity to sample and appreciate the different types of sherry and their special characteristics. Another famous attraction is the Royal Andalusian School of Equestrian Art, which gives a show for visitors every Thursday, a horseback ballet of breathtaking precision. On the outskirts of the town the Carthusian Monastery is one of the most important historic buildings of the province. Built in the late sixteenth century, the great entrance is in High Renaissance style and the interior includes splendid plateresque choir stalls.

Jerez is a very attractive town to walk around, with a wealth of historic buildings including the cathedral, the Church of San Miguel, the Chapterhouse that has a magnificent plateresque entrance, the city walls and the Alcázar, which conserves the mosque and the Arab baths. There is also the splendid twentieth century architecture of the 1929 Gallo Azul commercial building that dominates the junction of the main shopping streets and the neo-Moorish railway station from the same period with spectacular tiles, towers and terracotta detailing.

Los Pueblos Blancos – The cycling or driving route of the white villages takes you on a trip of three to four days through lovely scenery and some of the most beautiful villages in Spain. The traditional starting point is the small town of Arcos de la Frontera; the layout of the town with its narrow streets winding up the hill to the castle shows that it dates back to Moorish times. The town centre is listed as a Historic and Artistic Monument and includes one of the original gates from the city walls, the fourteenth century ducal palace and an outstanding fifteenth century church in the Gothic-Mudéjar style. From Arcos de la Frontera the route goes on through the villages of Bornos, Espera, Villamartín and Olvera, each of which is wonderfully preserved with whitewashed houses, ancient churches and a palace or castle, or the ruins of a keep, at the highest point.

ACKNOWLEDGEMENTS

First and foremost, we wish to express our gratitude to publisher and managing director at Hurst Publishers, Michael Dwyer, for commissioning this work, along with his highly efficient and helpful team: Assistant Editor Alice Clarke, Raminta Uselytė and Jess Winstanley in publicity, Production Director Daisy Leitch, Production Assistant Niamh Drennan and proofreader Lusana Taylor-Khan. Thanks are due to copyeditor Deborah Shaw, whose review of the manuscript with a 'fine tooth comb' vastly improved the narrative. We are hugely grateful to photographer Simon Roth for providing the wonderful array of images you will find in this book.

We were indeed fortunate to have the celebrated Spanish author and journalist Ana Romero Galán, a Gaditana to her marrow, write the foreword to this book. Her knowledge of Cádiz's past and traditions has been an invaluable aid. Many thanks indeed to the person who introduced us to Ana, the venerable Hispanist Sir Paul Preston, whose works form the foundation stone for research into all things Spanish. We would also like to thank our agent, Duncan McAra, now retired, who guided us safely to port on many voyages.

In Cádiz, our appreciation goes to all those whose knowledge has proved so invaluable in researching and understanding this

ACKNOWLEDGEMENTS

city's complex history. The historical works of Manuel Bustos Rodríguez and Juan Antonio Fierro Cubiella have been an invaluable aid throughout. Archaeologist Paloma Bueno Serrano and the team at the Historical Archive of Cádiz have been a source of extremely helpful information on the complex subject of Cádiz's remotest past. We are indebted to venerable mariner Diego Galán, for sharing his insightful historical expertise, along with Manuel de la Varga López and David Ibañez Montañez of the Cádiz Tourism Department and David Doña Guillón of the Provincial Government Office. Many thanks indeed to Beltrán Domecq in Jerez for his enlightening words about the wonders of sherry wine. Last but not least, we are grateful to the magnificent and glittering Café Royalty for providing an inspiration to explore the fascinating tale of the history of Cádiz.

NOTES

1. IN THE BEGINNING

1. Melville, Herman, *Moby Dick*, Oxford: Oxford University Press, 2022, p. 59
2. The Phoenicians built two major types of ships. Trading ships known as *gauloi*, or 'round ships', were constructed with rounded hulls and curved sterns. The *gauloi* had a giant rectangular sail in its centre, which hung from a yard and could turn to catch the wind. It used an oar-like blade, attached to the port side of the ship, to steer the vessel. Phoenician warships were slightly different; they were longer and narrower, in order to hold large numbers of soldiers. The warship carried two sails and coverings on the deck to hide officers. At the bow was the forecastle, an area used by bowmen or catapults during battle. The Phoenicians also created navigational tools that enabled them to maintain their sea power for centuries.
3. Williams, Mark, *The Story of Spain*, Málaga: Ediciones Santana, 1990. p. 23
4. Williams, *The Story of Spain*, p. 20
5. This was changed to *Plus Ultra* (Even Further) some decades after Christopher Columbus's voyages of discovery, to denote the expansion of the Spanish Empire under the Holy Roman Emperor Charles V, who ruled as Carlos I of Spain. It is today the official motto of Spain.

6. Harrison, Richard J., *Spain at the Dawn of History*, London: Thames and Hudson, 1988. p. 82
7. Mierse, William Edwin, 'The architecture of the lost Temple of Hercules Gaditanus and its Levantine associations', *American Journal of Archaeology*, Volume 108, Number 4, p. 545
8. Harrison, *Spain at the Dawn of History*, p. 124
9. The Punic Wars were a series of conflicts lasting 118 years between Carthage and Rome. When they began, Rome had nearly completed the conquest of Italy, while Carthage controlled north-west Africa and the islands and commerce of the Western Mediterranean. When the wars ended, Carthage had not even survived as a ruin, while Rome stood as the greatest power west of China.
10. In ancient Rome, a quaestor was a magistrate in charge of public revenue and expenditure.
11. García, Milagros Alzaga, *El patrimonio arqueològico subacuàtico en la evaluaciòn de impacto ambiental*, Boletindel Instituto Andaluz del Patrimonio Històrico, 2000, p. 98
12. Bueno Serrano, Paloma, 'Un asentamiento en el Cerro del Castillo, Chiclana (Cádiz)', Istituto di Studi Sul Mediterraneo, Antico (Rome), 2014, p. 225
13. Ibid.
14. Fierro Cubiella, Juan Antonio, *Historia de la ciudad de Cádiz*, Cádiz: self-published, 2004, p. 52

2. IN ROMAN HANDS

1. Cilician pirates dominated the Mediterranean from the second century BCE. Because there were notorious pirate strongholds in Cilicia, on the southern coast of Asia Minor, the term 'Cilician' was long used to generically refer to any pirates in the Mediterranean.
2. Quoted by Esther Macías in *La Voz de Cádiz*, 22 January 2010, p. 14
3. It is usually known as the Flavian Amphitheatre (Amphitheatrum Flavium), however there are no records of this being the name used under the empire. The reference is to the Flavia dynasty, during which time the amphitheatre was built. That said, the structure is normally referred to as the Colosseum.
4. Cañas, Jesús A., 'Spanish researchers discover possible location of

legendary temple of Hercules Gaditanus', *El País*, 17 December 2021, p. 16
5. Bustos Rodríguez, Manuel, *Recorrido por la ciudad de Cádiz y su historia*, Madrid: Sílex Ediciones, p. 22
6. Ibid.
7. An amphitheatre, such as the one built in Mérida in 8 BCE, is a full circle shape, as opposed to the half circle of a theatre. In modern terms they can be compared to a sports stadium versus a cinema.
8. Suárez de Salazar, Juan Bautista, *Grandezas y antigüedades de la isla y ciudad de Cádiz*, 1644, p. 48
9. García Vargas, Antonio (translator), *Rufus Festus Avenius, Ora Maritima*, Academia.edu, 2017, verse 27

3. MOORS ON THE COAST!

1. The Berbers are a diverse grouping of ethnicities indigenous to North Africa, mainly the Maghreb of Morocco, Algeria, Libya and, to a lesser extent, Tunisia.
2. Bustos Rodríguez, Manuel, *Breve historia de Cádiz*, Cádiz: Ediciones Mayi, 2021, pp. 47-8
3. Hispanist Jason Webster explains that for a long time the accepted version was that Al-Ándalus was the mispronunciation of 'Vandals'. Another theory is that the Muslims decided to name Spain after a system of land distribution used by the Visigoths, *landalauhts*, the place where land is distributed by lots. A third hypothesis is that Al-Andalus was derived from 'Atlantic'. The most recent theory is that it comes from the original, pre-Moorish name for the Tarifa peninsula. (Webster, Jason, *Violencia*, London: Hachette, 2019, pp. 89-92)
4. The garden scene in Toledo is depicted by the German portrait artist Franz Xaver Winterhalter in a nineteenth-century oil-on-canvas held in the Metropolitan Museum of Art in New York. Winterhalter wrote in a letter dated 1869 that his inspiration for the painting was a sixteenth century Spanish ballad entitled *La Cava*, and his painting follows the text closely.
5. Josephs, Allen, *White Wall of Spain: The Mysteries of Andalusian Culture*, Florida: University Press of Florida, 1990. p. 13
6. Bustos Rodríguez, *Breve historia de Cádiz*, p. 50. The *Almoravid*

dynasty was an imperial Berber line native to present-day Morocco. The *Almohad* Caliphate or *Almohad* Empire was a North African Berber kingdom founded in the twelfth century.
7. Ibid., p. 60
8. Ibid., p. 78

4. THE KING OF SPAIN'S BEARD

1. Fierro Cubiella, Juan Antonio, *Historia de la ciudad de Cádiz*, Cádiz: self-published, 2004, p. 123
2. The Anglo-Spanish War continued between 1585 and 1604 as an intermittent conflict that was never formally declared as war. The conflict began when England sent a military expedition to the Spanish Netherlands in 1585 in support of the Dutch, who were in rebellion against the rule of Spain. The Treaty of London ended the war in 1604, negotiated between Felipe III of Spain and James I as the new king of England.
3. Fierro Cubiella, *Historia de la ciudad de Cádiz*, p. 12
4. Fierro Cubiella, *Historia de la ciudad de Cádiz*, pp. 128–9
5. Bustos Rodríguez, *Breve historia de Cádiz*, p. 36
6. Quoted by Jesús Mejías in *La Voz de Cádiz*, 5 September 2021, p. 3
7. The Acts of Union between England and Scotland had been signed into law in 1707. However, the term 'England' was widely used at the time to refer to the United Kingdom. The British fleet that took part in the Battle of Trafalgar included significant contingents from Ireland, Scotland and Wales.
8. Williams, Mark, *The Story of Spain*, Málaga: Ediciones Santana, 1990, p. 154

5. 1812 AND ALL THAT

1. Cockburn, Lt. Gen. George, *Voyage to Cádiz and Gibraltar*, London: J. Harding, Vol. I, 1815, p. 11
2. Ibid.
3. Ibid.
4. The Spanish Cortes traces its origins to the Visigoth occupation of the Iberian Peninsula, roughly between the fifth and early eighth centuries CE. The Concilium was a ritual gathering of early Christian

bishops to discuss matters affecting the Church and society. The Cortes of Cádiz marks the first time non-clergy representatives sat in session to decide on political and civil issues.
5. MacDonell was one of several Irishmen who took up the Spanish cause against France. A great number had settled in Spain and some rose to positions of prominence. In the early years of MacDonell's lifetime, the prime minister of Spain was Ricardo Wall, of Limerick origin, and the finance minister was Bernardo Ward, a native of County Monaghan. MacDonell was a seasoned and disciplined military officer who had inherited, and was not averse to deploying, his Irish temper. At a bullfight in Cádiz, he got into a row with a Frenchman that ended with a sword attack. MacDonell was placed under house arrest by the Governor of Cádiz, Lieutenant Alejandro O'Reilly of County Meath, who had previously served as governor of Madrid. Finally, at the end of the war in 1814 MacDonell was appointed full-admiral and three years later, member of the Supreme Council of the Admiralty. He died in Cádiz in 1823.
6. Márquez Carmona, Lourdes, 'Recuerdos de un timonel', *Trocadero*, No. 20, 2008, p. 33
7. Longford, Elizabeth, *Wellington*, London: Abacus, 1969, p. 140
8. Carr, Raymond, *Spain 1808-1975*, Oxford: Clarendon Press, 1982, p. 51
9. Guzmán, Eduardo, *Cádiz 1812, Tiempo de Historia*, Issue Number 10, Madrid: September 1975, p. 29
10. In 1789 Jovellanos, having risen to a position of high social prominence, sat for a portrait by Francisco de Goya, a work now on display in the Prado Museum. He went to Madrid after Godoy's fall from favour and was appointed minister of justice. That was when his troubles began with the authorities. His proposals for reform of religious policy led to his imprisonment in Mallorca in 1808. On his release he rejected the post of minister of the interior under José Bonaparte, fleeing instead to Cádiz as the Asturian representative to the Supreme Central Junta.
11. Pérez Garzón, Juan Sisinio, *Las Cortes de Cádiz*, Madrid: Síntesis, 2007, p. 207
12. It is worth pointing out that the first attempt to abolish the Inquisition

took place in 1808, with José I on the throne. The French monarch banned the so-called Holy Office, transferring its ecclesiastical goods to the Crown. The officially recognised proscription was that decreed in the Constitution of Cádiz. While the Spanish Inquisition is commonly portrayed as a reign of terror, this does not conform to historical realities. For instance, between the late fifteenth and early nineteenth centuries, only 1.2% of those charged with witchcraft or heresy were condemned to death. In Spain's overseas colonies, between the sixteenth and seventeenth centuries, often cited as the Inquisition's most bloodthirsty period, fewer than three people a year faced the death penalty.

13. Ramos Santana, Alberto, *Cádiz en el siglo XIX*, Madrid: Sílex, 1992, p. 183
14. García Serrano, José Luis, 'Tráfico de esclavos en Cádiz', NIUS (Noticias, información, análisis y última hora), 20 June 2020
15. Holmes, Richard, *Wellington*, London: Harper Perennial, 2007, p. 183
16. Carr, *Spain 1808-1975*, p. 137
17. The French victory is commemorated in Paris at the Place du Trocadéro, close to the Bois de Boulogne. The Duke of Angoulême was honoured with the title of Prince of Trocadero.

6. IN THE EYE OF THE STORM

1. Bustos Rodríguez, Manuel, *Recorrido por la ciudad de Cádiz y su historia*, Madrid: Sílex Ediciones, 2012, p. 72
2. Rafael Primo de Rivera was the first in a dynasty of politicians who exercised great power in Spain until the early twentieth century. He was the father of Miguel Primo de Rivera, who ruled as dictator/prime minister from 1923 to 1930. His son, José Antonio Primo de Rivera, was the founder of the Falange Española, who was captured by the Republicans and executed in 1936 during the Spanish Civil War.
3. Fruzado's comments picked up in an historical feature in *Diario de Cádiz*, 11 March 2013.
4. Edwards, Andrew and Suzanne, Andalucía.com. https://www.andalucia.com/history/people/lord-byron. Accessed April 2024.

Fig. 42: Devastation following the 1947 munitions explosion in Cádiz.

Fig. 43: The interior of the Café Royalty restored to its 1912 splendour.

Fig. 44: Street in the barrio de la Viña.

Fig. 45: Mercado Central de Abastos, Cádiz.

Fig. 46: Cruise ship moored in the Puerto Comercial, Cádiz.

Fig. 47: View of the modern port of Cádiz.

Fig. 48: One of the many singing groups in the Cádiz Carnival.

Fig. 49: Holy Week procession, brotherhood of the Virgen de la Palma, Cádiz.

Fig. 50: Café Las Nieves, one of the oldest cafes in Cádiz.

Fig. 51: Flamenco performance at Peña Flamenca la Perla de Cádiz.

Fig. 52: Calle Compañía, Cádiz.

Fig. 53: Ancient streets of Arcos de la Frontera.

Fig. 54: Ubrique, unique leatherworking town in Cádiz province.

Fig. 55: Flamenco dancers outside a bar in Jerez de la Frontera.

Fig. 56: Buying *turrón* at La Dulcería de la Rondeña, Calle Sagasta, Cádiz.

Fig. 57: Chequered courtyard of the Hotel Boutique Convento, Cádiz.

Fig. 58: Punta Candelaria.

Fig. 59: Cádiz seafront at Avenido Campo Sur, looking towards the cathedral.

NOTES

5. Jacob, William, *Travels in the South of Spain in 1809 and 1810*, London: J. Johnson & Co., 1811, p. 14
6. Ford, Richard, *Gatherings From Spain*, London: John Murray, 1851, p. 153
7. Ibid.
8. Burns, Jimmy, *Spain: A Literary Companion*, London: John Murray, 1994, p. 190
9. Borrow, George, *The Bible in Spain*, London: Thomas Nelson & Sons, 1842, p. 99
10. Ibid.
11. Ibid.
12. Ibid.
13. Sultana, Donald, *Benjamin Disraeli in Spain, Malta and Albania*, London: Tamesis Books, 1976, p. 27
14. Ibid.
15. Ibid.
16. Dumas, Alexandre, *From Paris to Cádiz*, London: Peter Owen Ltd., 1958, p. 197
17. Ibid., p. 209
18. Maugham, William Somerset, *The Land of the Blessed Virgin*, London: Heinemann, 1905, pp. 116-18
19. Bustos Rodríguez, Manuel, *Breve historia de Cádiz*, Cádiz: Ediciones Mayi, 2021, p. 159
20. Mudéjar was the name given to a Muslim who remained in Spain after the Christian reconquest of the Iberian Peninsula.
21. The global movement of goods today stands at some six million tonnes, the best figures since reconstruction work began more than a century ago.
22. Bustos Rodríguez, *Breve historia de Cádiz*, p. 163
23. It was a far cry from the unveiling in 2022 of Spain's first tram-train, the Bay of Cádiz tramway known as Trambahia, short for Tranvía Metropolitano de la Bahía de Cádiz. The fifteen-mile tramway currently connects Chiclana, San Fernando and Cádiz, using a train-tram system that allows the units to run on newly constructed tram lines within towns and standard railway tracks between metropolitan

areas. The line still to be opened is the route from Cádiz to El Puerto de Santa María, Jerez de la Frontera and Jerez airport.

7. CÁDIZ AT WAR

1. To maintain morale in the closing months of the First World War, the belligerent countries minimised early reports of the influenza and its high mortality rate. Spain did not take part in the war, hence the country's newspapers became the only source of information on the disease. These stories created a false impression that Spain was the source of the pandemic, hence the nickname, 'Spanish flu.'
2. Lee, Laurie, *As I Walked Out One Midsummer Morning*, London: Penguin Modern Classics, 2014, p. 132
3. Ibid.
4. Carr, Raymond, *Spain 1808-1975*, Oxford: Clarendon Press, 1982, p. 562
5. Carr, *Spain 1808-1975*, p. 625. Prime Minister Manuel Azaña was forced to resign as a result of an ongoing ideological dispute with Prime Minister Niceto Alcalá-Zamora.
6. Moorish *Regulares* were Spanish Army detachments raised in 1911 in Melilla, one of Spain's Moroccan territories, along with Ceuta. The units were made up of Spanish and Moorish infantrymen, much feared for their ruthlessness during the Civil War.
7. Preston, Paul, *Franco*, London: HarperCollins, 1993, p. 152
8. Beevor, Antony, *The Battle for Spain*, London: W&N, 2006, p. 80
9. Reported in *ABC, Radio Sevilla*, Madrid, 23 July 1936, p. 4
10. Honduvilla, Joaquín Gil, *Militares y sublevación: Cádiz y provincia 1936*, Sevilla: Muñoz Moya Editores, 2013, p. 211
11. Chivite, José Luis Millán, *Cádiz Siglo XX*, Madrid: Sílex, 1993, p. 206

8. CÁDIZ IS RISEN

1. Javier Cabeza de Vaca, chairman of the Cádiz Association of Professional Economists, quoted in *Barómetro Económico de Cádiz*, a report published by Loyola University. https://www.uloyola.es/blog/la-universidad/expertos-en-economia-de-la-universidad-loyola-presentan-el-ii-barometro-economico-de-cadiz

2. Manuel de la Varga López, Cádiz Tourism Board, in conversation with the authors.
3. The city of Cádiz award ceremony.
4. Wals, Lola and Arjona, Rafael, *Cádiz*, Madrid: Grupo Anaya, 2016, p. 77
5. Wals & Arjona, *Cádiz*, p. 128
6. Beltrán Domecq in conversation with the authors.

LISTINGS SECTION

1. Maugham, William Somerset, *The Land of the Blessed Virgin, Sketches and Impressions in Andalusia*, London: Heinemann, 1905, p. 19

BIBLIOGRAPHY

ABC, Radio Sevilla, Madrid, 23 July 1936
Barton, Simon, *A History of Spain*, London: Palgrave Macmillan, 2004
Beevor, Antony, *The Battle for Spain*, London: W&N, 2006
Bendala, Manuel, *Tartesios, íberos y celtas*, Madrid: Ediciones Planeta, 2000
Borrow, George, *The Bible in Spain*, London: Thomas Nelson & Sons, 1842
Bueno Serrano, Paloma, 'Un asentamiento en el Cerro del Castillo, Chiclana (Cádiz)', Istituto di Studi Sul Mediterraneo, Antico (Rome), 2014
Burns, Jimmy, *Spain: A Literary Companion*, London: John Murray, 1994
Bustos Rodríguez, Manuel, *Recorrido por la ciudad de Cádiz y su historia*, Madrid: Sílex Ediciones, 2012
——, *Breve historia de Cádiz*, Cádiz: Ediciones Mayi, 2021
Cañas, Jesús A., 'Spanish researchers discover possible location of legendary temple of Hercules Gaditanus', *El País*, 17 December 2021
Carr, Raymond, *Spain 1808-1975*, Oxford: Clarendon Press, 1982
Catlos, Brian A., *Kingdoms of Faith*, London: Hurst Publishers, 2018
Chivite, José Luis Millán, *Cádiz Siglo XX*, Madrid: Sílex, 1993
Cockburn, Lt. Gen. George, *Voyage to Cádiz and Gibraltar*, London: J. Harding, Vol. I, 1815
Comenge, Agustín, *Historia de Cádiz*, Cádiz: Editorial UCA, 2017
Cózar, María del Carmen and Rodrigo, Martín, *Cádiz y el tráfico de esclavos*, Madrid: Sílex, 2018
Curchin, Leonard A., *Roman Spain*, London: BCA, 1991

BIBLIOGRAPHY

Dumas, Alexandre, *From Paris to Cádiz*, London: Peter Owen Ltd., 1958

Eastman, Scott, *The Rise of Constitutional Government in the Iberian Atlantic World*, Tuscaloosa, Alabama: University of Alabama Press, 2015

Edwards, Andrew and Suzanne, Andalucía.com. https://www.andalucia.com/history/people/lord-byron. Accessed April 2024

Fierro Cubiella, Juan Antonio, *Historia de la ciudad de Cádiz*, Cádiz: self-published, 2004

Font, Julio Molina, *La historia pequeña de Cádiz*, Cádiz: Ediciones Mayi, 2009

Ford, Richard, *Gatherings From Spain*, London: John Murray, 1851

Fornell, Javier, *Guía mitológica de Cádiz*, Cádiz: Kaizen Editores, 2023

Fornis, César, *Mito y arqueología en el nacimiento de ciudades antiguas*, Sevilla: Editorial Universidad de Sevilla, 2019

García, Milagros Alzaga, *El patrimonio arqueològico subacuàtico en la evaluaciòn de impacto ambiental*, Boletindel Instituto Andaluz del Patrimonio Històrico, 2000

García Serrano, José Luis, 'Tráfico de esclavos en Cádiz', *NIUS (Noticias, información, análisis y última hora)*, 20 June 2020

García Vargas, Antonio (translator), Rufus Festus Avenius, *Ora Maritima*, Academia.edu, 2017

García y Bellido, Antonio, *Locosae Gades*, Madrid: Maestre, 1951

Guzmán, Eduardo, *Cádiz 1812*, *Tiempo de Historia*, Issue Number 10, Madrid: September 1975

Harrison, Richard J., *Spain at the Dawn of History*, London: Thames and Hudson, 1988

Hemeroteca Municipal de Madrid, *España 1808-1814*, Madrid, 2008

Hennessey, Shawn, *Discovering Cádiz*, London: Decanter, 2022

Herodotus, *The Histories*, London: Penguin Books, 2003

Holmes, Richard, *Wellington*, London: Harper Perennial, 2007

Honduvilla, Joaquín Gil, *Militares y sublevación: Cádiz y provincia 1936*, Sevilla: Muñoz Moya Editores, 2013

Horozco, Agustín, *Historia de Cádiz*, Cádiz: Editorial UCA, 2017

Howson, Gerald, *The Flamencos of Cádiz Bay*, London: Hutchison, 1961

Jacob, William, *Travels in the South of Spain in 1809 and 1810*, London: J. Johnson & Co., 1811

BIBLIOGRAPHY

Josephs, Allen, *White Wall of Spain: The Mysteries of Andalusian Culture*, Florida: University Press of Florida, 1990

Key, S. J., *Roman Spain*, London: British Museum Publications, 1988

Lee, Laurie, *As I Walked Out One Midsummer Morning*, London: Penguin Modern Classics, 2014

Lely, Peter and Mildren, James, *Sir Francis Drake*, Yelverton: National Trust House, 1988

Lenguineche, Manuel and Torbado, Jesús, *The Moles*, London: Secker & Warburg, 1981

Lomas Salmonte, Francisco Javier, *Nueva historia de Cádiz*, Madrid: Sílex, 2011

Longford, Elizabeth, *Wellington*, London: Abacus, 1969

López-Ruiz, Carolina and Celestino, Sebastián, *Tartessos and the Phoenicians in Iberia*, Oxford: Oxford University Press, 2016

Macías, Esther, *La Voz de Cádiz*, 22 January 2010

Márquez Carmona, Lourdes, 'Recuerdos de un timonel' *Trocadero*, No. 20, 2008, 33–34

Mata, Diego Ruiz, *Phoenicians in Spain*, Lisbon: Instituto Oriental, 1993

Maugham, William Somerset, *The Land of the Blessed Virgin, Sketches and Impressions in Andalusia*, London: Heinemann, 1905

Mejías, Jesús, *La Voz de Cádiz*, 5 September 2021

Melville, Herman, *Moby Dick*, Oxford: Oxford University Press, 2022

Mierse, William Edwin, 'The architecture of the lost Temple of Hercules Gaditanus and its Levantine associations' *American Journal of Archaeology*, Volume 108, Number 4, 545–78, 2004

Moscati, Sabatino, *The World of the Phoenicians*, London: Sphere Books, 1973

Ortiz, Pedro Parrilla, *La esclavitud en Cádiz durante el siglo XVIII*, Cádiz: Diputación de Cádiz, 2001

Pérez Garzón, Juan Sisinio, *Las Cortes de Cádiz*, Madrid: Síntesis, 2007

Preston, Paul, *Franco*, London: HarperCollins, 1993

Ramírez Delgado, Juan Ramón, *Los primitivos núcleos de asentamiento en la ciudad de Cádiz*, Cádiz: Ayuntamiento de Cádiz, 1982

Ramos Santana, Alberto, *Cádiz en el siglo XIX*, Madrid: Sílex, 1992

Reid, Michael, *Spain*, London: Yale University Press, 2023

Richardson, John S., *The Romans in Spain*, Oxford: Blackwell Publishers, 1996

BIBLIOGRAPHY

Rodríguez Muñoz, Raquel, *El hábitat fenicio-púnico de Cádiz*, Oxford: Archaeopress, 2008

Russell, P. E. (Ed.), *Spain: A Companion to Spanish Studies*, London: Methuen & Co., 1973

Solís, Ramón, *El Cádiz de Las Cortes*, Madrid: Sílex Ediciones, 2012

Suárez de Salazar, Juan Bautista, *Grandezas, y Antigüedades de la Isla y Ciudad de Cádiz*, Cádiz, 1644

Suárez, Federico, *Las Cortes de Cádiz*, Madrid: Ediciones Rialp, 2023

Sultana, Donald, *Benjamin Disraeli in Spain, Malta and Albania*, London: Tamesis Books, 1976

Thomas, Hugh, *The Spanish Civil War*, London: Eyre & Spottiswoode, 1961

Tremlett, Giles, *España: A Brief History of Spain*, London: Bloomsbury, 2022

Vidal, Emma D. and Piqueras, José Antonio, *Los británicos en el comercio de esclavos de Cuba*, Barcelona: Universitat Jaume I, 2018

Villarías-Robles, J.R. and Rodríguez-Ramírez, Antonio, *Paleo-Geography of the Gulf of Cádiz in SW Iberia During the Second Millennium BCE*, Greece: University of Patras, 2017

Wals, Lola and Arjona, Rafael, *Cádiz*, Madrid: Grupo Anaya, 2016

Webster, Jason, *Violencia*, London: Hachette, 2019

Williams, Mark, *The Story of Spain*, Málaga: Ediciones Santana, 1990

INDEX

Abarbanel, Isaac, 3
Abbasid dynasty, 45
Abolition of the Slave Trade (1787), 110
Abyla, 8
Aegean Sea, 5
Africa, xiii, 6, 8, 51, 112
  slave trade, 109–11
Agenor, xiv
Aguirre y Corveto, Rear-Admiral Miguel de, 121
Ahumada, Galán de, xvi
Alameda Apodaca, 144
Alameda Gardens, 152
Al-Andalus, 44–6, 49–50
  culture, 46–8
Álava province, 148
Alberti, Rafael, 192–3
Alcáçovas, Treaty of, 55
Alcalá-Zamora, Niceto, 152
Alcolea, Battle of, 125, 128
Alcornocales Natural Park, 185–6
Alexander the Great, 13

Alexander VI, Pope, 54
Alfonso VII, 49
Alfonso X the Wise, xvii, 32, 50–1, 53, 58, 186
Alfonso XII, 128–9
Alfonso XIII, 137, 138, 148, 152
Algeciras, 51
Algeria, 135
Alhambra, 54
'allied community' (*civitas foederata*), 22
Almagro, Deputy Mayor Jerónimo, 170
Almería, 50
Almirante Valdés, 157
Almohad Empire, 53
Almohad tribes, 47, 49–50
Al-Murabitun, 49
Alzaga, Milagros, 13
Andalucía, xv, 21–2, 29, 48, 79–80, 98, 107, 134, 136, 172–3
  election, 151–4
  industries, 148–51
  revolutionaries, 154–9

245

INDEX

transport and tourism, 143–5
war, 159–62
Andalusian baroque style, 106
Andalusian coast, 149
Andalusian heartland, 4
Andalusian hilltop town, 17
Anglo-Spanish War, 66–70
    Cádiz, capture of, 70–4
Angoulême, Duke of, 115–16
Ansón, Luis María, 169
Antilles, 56, 110
Antonio, Juan, 17
Antwerp, 59
Apodaca, General Juan Ruiz de, 99
Aragón, 54
Aramburu, Micaela de, 140
Aranjuez, 94
Arapiles, 111
Archelaus (king of Tyre), xiv, xvii
Arco de la Rosa, 52
Arco de los Blanco, 52
Arcos de la Frontera, 50, 124, 174, 187
Aréizaga, General Juan Carlos, 101
Argentina, 83
Argüelles, Agustín, xviii, 103
Arias, José Rodríguez de, 122
Arjona, Rafael, 188
Ark, 2
Armada, 67–8
    Cádiz, capture of, 70–4
Arrian, 9–10
Artes y Letras de Cádiz, 141
Asia, 112, 114
Asset of Cultural Interest, 53

Association for the Investigation and Dissemination of Cádiz Heritage, 33
Association of Leathergoods Craftsmen, 188–9
Assyrians, 2
Astapa, 17
Astarte, Phoenician Temple of, 15
Astillero de Puerto Real, 122, 167
Astilleros de Cádiz, 149–50
Astilleros Españoles (1969), 150
Astorga, 35
Asturian Battalion, 114
Asturians, 43
Asturias, 45, 52, 105, 161
Atauri, Pelayo Quintero, 14
Athens, 26
Atlantic Ocean, 55
Atlantic, xiii–xiv, 5, 7–8, 58
Augusta, 35
Augustulus, Romulus, 38
Augustus, Emperor, 25, 35
Australia, 83
Austria, 78, 137
Avienius, Rufus Festus, 3

Babylonian king, 19
Bacchus, 30
Badajoz, 50
Baetica, 22
Baghdad, 45, 48
Bahamas, 55
Bailén, 99, 100–1
Bailén, battle of, 100–1
Baker & Dawson, 109

INDEX

Balbus, Lucius Cornelius, xvii, 24–6, 31, 34
Ballesteros, General Francisco, 114–15
Ballesteros, Severiano, 175
Banco de Cádiz, 123
Banu Marin, 53
Barbarossa, Hayreddin, 59–60
Barber of Seville (Rossini), 135, 143–4
Barcelona, 94, 114, 123, 144, 145, 149, 157
Barrero, José Romero, 144
Barriada Obrera, 143
barrio de la Viña, 85
Basque Country, 43, 58, 72, 125, 161
Bay of Algeciras, 171
Bay of Cádiz, xiii, 11, 46, 61, 68–9, 97, 99, 100, 119, 162–3, 166, 184
Belizón, Ricardo, 11
Berbers, 44–5, 58
Berenguer, General Dámaso, 151
Biedma, Gil de, xviii
Bilbao, 145
Blake, Admiral Robert, 79–80
Boabdil, 54
Bolivia, 65
Bonaparte, Joseph, 94, 111
Bonaparte, Napoleon, xvii, 86–8, 92–4, 96–7, 111–12
  battles of, Bailén and Ocaña, 100–1
  Napoleonic invasion, 103
Book of Genesis, 2
Borrow, George, 133–4

Bourbon dynasty, 81, 126
Britain, xvii, 3, 86, 150, 175
  Peninsular War, 93–6
Buckingham, Duke of, 76
Bueno Serrano, Paloma, xvi, 16
Burgos, Javier de, 94, 123–4
Burns, Jimmy, 132
Bustamante y Guerra, José de, 83
Bustos Rodríguez, Manuel, 34, 42–3, 49, 51, 53–4, 74, 120, 142
Byron, George Gordon, xviii, 129–31, 134–5, 143, 148
Byron, Lord. *See* Byron, George Gordon
Byzantine Empire, 38, 39

Cabo Trafalgar (Pérez-Reverte), 88
Cádiz Carnival, 176–9
Cádiz CF, 168
Cádiz Club de Fútbol, 145
Cádiz Football Association, 139
Cádiz Nature Park, 185
Cádiz Tourism Board, 174
Cádiz, Bernardo de, 85
Cádiz-Córdoba faction, 14
Cádiz-Sevilla railway, 176
Caesar, Julius, xiv, xvii, 13, 24–5, 37
café cantante (musical café), 183–4
Caleta de Santa Catalina beach, 71
California, 67
Calle Adolfo de Castro, 152
Callejón de los Negros, 109
Callejón del Tinte, xvii
Calvi, Giovanni Battista, 64–5
Calvo, Vicente, 137
Camarón, 184

247

INDEX

Camino de la Plata, 35
Campos, Captain General Arsenio Martínez, 129
Cañadas, Jesús, 139
Canary Islands, 56, 59, 83, 155, 169
Caño de Sancti Petri waterway, 14, 77
Cape Horn, 83
Cape of San Vicente, 86
Cape Trafalgar, 87–8, 95, 99
Cárdenas, Alonso de, 78
Caribbean island, 56, 78, 109, 137–8
    Battle for, 78–81
Carlist Wars, 124–5
Carlos I, 60, 65
Carlos II, 81
Carlos III, 83
Carlos IV, 93
Carlos, Infante, 124
Carnival Radiance, 173–4
carnival, 176–9
    singing groups, 178–9
Carr, Hispanist Raymond, 102, 115, 153–4
Carraca, 143
Carranza Bridge, 179
Carranza, José León de, 167–8
Carranza, Ramón de, 152, 169-70
Cartagena, 16, 157
Cartago Nova, 16, 35
Carthage, 19–20
Casa de Contratación (House of Commerce), 59–60, 65, 121
Casas Viejas, 153–4
Castaños, Francisco Javier, 100
Castelar, Emilio, 120, 130

Castile, 50
Castilian plateau, 91
Castilla y León, 107
Castillo, José, 155
Castillo, Prime Minister Antonio Cánovas del, 137
Castle of San Lorenzo, 72
Castro, Adolfo de, xv, xix
Cataluña, 125, 162
Cecil, Edward, 76–7, 78, 85
Centre for Underwater Archaeology (CAS), 13
Centro de Arte Flamenco, 183
Cepeda, Rosario, 54
Cerro de los Mártires, 14
Cerro del Castillo, xiii, xvi
Cervantes, Miguel de, 75
Ceuta, 57, 103
Cevallos, Pedro, 97
Charles V, Holy Roman Emperor, 65, 92
Charlie Chan Carries On (Fox Film), 150
Château de Valençay, 94–5
Cheyne, Thomas Kelly, 2
Chiclana de la Frontera, xiii–xiv, 11, 15–16, 119, 143
China, 56, 83, 171
chirigotas, 178–9
Chivite, historian José Luis Millán, 164
Church of Nuestra Señora de la Palma, 85
Church of San Felipe Neri, 106
Church of San Francisco, 75
Church of Santa Cruz, 46
Church of Santiago, 187

INDEX

Churruca, 157
Cicero, 31–2
Cine Gades, 150–1
Civil War, 177
Clotald, 75
CNT. *See* National Confederation of Labour (CNT) union
Cockburn, Admiral Sir George, 94–6
cofradias, 180
Columbus, Christopher, xvii, 54–7, 83, 150
Columna Salvochea, 139
Comillas, Marquis of, 122
Compañía Gaditana de Crédito, 123
Compañía General de Negros (General Company of Blacks), 110
comparsas, 178
Condor Legion, 158
Conil, 175
Coningsby (Disraeli), 134
Consejo de Castilla, 96–7
Constantinople, 38
Constitution (1812), 106–8, 145
    battles of, Bailén and Ocaña, 100–1
    Cádiz, Cortes of, 101–6
    May uprising, Second of, 96–7
    Peninsular War, 93–6
    Poza de Santa Isabel, Battle of, 97–9
    slave trade, 109–11
    Trafalgar, Battle of, 86–9
Contract House, 82–3
Cook, Captain, 83

Córdoba, 4, 14, 45, 46, 50, 58, 125, 135, 144
Córdova, Admiral Luis de, 130
Cornelius Scipio, Publius, 21
Cornwall, 3
coros, 179
Corsica, 20
Cortés, Hernán, 65
Count of Monte Cristo, The (Dumas), 135
Covadonga, Battle of, 45–6
Crédito Comercial de Cádiz, 123
Crete, Minoans of, 5
Cromwell, Lord Protector Oliver, 78–9
cruise line industry, 173–4
Cruz, José Monje (Camarón de la Isla), 184
cuartetos, 179
Cuba, 83, 110, 114, 136–8
Cubagua Island, 57
Cubiella, Fierro, 17

d'Estampes, 94
Damascus, 45, 48
Davis, Miles, 180
Decree XXXI, 107
Decrès, Navy Minister Denis, 98
Defence of Cádiz Against the English, The (Zurbarán), 77
del Toro, Mayor Cayetano, 141–2
Devereux, Robert de, 71–2
Dickens, Charles, 190
Diócesis de Asidonia-Jerez, 51
Disraeli, Prime Minister Benjamin, 134–5

249

INDEX

Domecq, Beltrán, 190
Dominica, 56
Don Quixote (Cervantes), 75
Doñana National Park, 185
Doria, Andrea, 60
Drake, Francis, xvii, 67–9
drug trade, 182
Duero, 35
Dumas, Alexandre, 135–6, 148
Dupont, General Pierre, 98–9, 100
Dutch Provinces, 76, 77
Duyvenvoorde, John de, 71
Dyrrhachium, 25

East Indies, 6
Eastern Coptic Orthodoxy, 39
Ebro River, 20, 35
Echevarrieta y Larrinaga shipyard, 149
Echevarrieta, Horacio, 166
El Deseado, 97
El Duende de los Cafés (The Elf of the Cafés), xviii, 112
El Escorial Monastery, 66, 91–2
El Pópulo, 31, 34
El Puerto de Santa María, 167, 189
El Puntal, 77, 82
Elío, General Francisco Javier de, 113
Elizabeth I, 66–8
Emanuele, Vittorio, 128
Empresa Nacional Bazán de Construcciones Navales Militares, 165
Empresa Nacional Elcano, 165
England, 65–6

English-Dutch war, 81–6
  invasion of, 66–70
  slave trade, 109–11
  Trafalgar, Battle of, 86–9
  See also Constitution (1812)
Episodios Nacionales (Galdós), 88
Eratosthenes, 3
Erythia, 8
Erythraea, 5
Erythraean Sea, 5
Escámez, Colonel Francisco García, 156
Eslava, Miguel, 145
Espoz y Mina, General Francisco, 120
Estadio Nuevo Mirandilla, 168
Estadio Ramón de Carranza, 167–8
Esteve, Antonio Sánchez, 150
Estoril, 156
European Economic Community, 193
Eurystheus (king of Tiryns), 8
Exemplary Novels, The (Cervantes), 75
Ezekiel, 2

Factoría Naval Gaditana, 122
Fajardo, Francisco Castillo, 82
Falla, Manuel de, 140
Falmouth, 134
Fascist Party, 155
fatum (sea of Cádiz), xv
Federal Canton, 128
Felipe I, 59
Felipe II, 65–70, 91–2
  Cádiz, capture of, 70–4
Felipe III, 74, 92

INDEX

Felipe IV, 78–9
Felipe V, 60, 82–3, 92
'Felon King', xvii
Ferdinand VII, 91
Fernando III, xvii, 50, 54, 55, 57
Fernando VII, xvii, xviii, 89, 93–5, 97, 106, 111–14, 123
Festus Avienius, Rufus, 38
Fierro Cubiella, Juan Antonio, 67, 72–3
Fiesta de la Vendimia, 190–1
Fiestas Típicas Gaditanas, 177
fishing industry, 171
five-star hotels, 175
flamenco, 180–1, 182, 183–4
Flanders, 81
Flavian Amphitheatre, 32
Flores, Lola, 184
Florinda, 44
Fonda de Europa, 135
Fontainebleau, Treaty of, 88
Ford Motor Company, 149
Ford, Henry, 149
Ford, Richard, 132–4
Fort San Luis, 116
France, 27, 36, 76, 81, 86, 143, 150, 152, 162
Franco, Francisco, 155–9, 160, 162–4, 166–8, 177
Fruzado, Francisco Alba, 127

Gabriel, 88
Gádeira, 10
Gades Nova, 26–7
Gades, 3
    allied community, 22–7
Gadir, 3–4, 19

founding of, 4–7
'Gaditana', 110
Gaditanos, xiii, xvii
Gaditanum, 43
Galdós, Benito Pérez, 88, 130
Galicia, 68, 114, 155, 161
Gaul, 25
Genoa, 58
Genoese, 56
George III, 86
Germany, 78, 168, 175
    See also World War I; World War II
Geryon, 8
Gibraltar, 126
Gijón, 105
Gilabert, Antonia, 183
Gillen de Berja, 52
Girón de Salcedo y Briviesca, Fernando, 77
'Global Emporium', 84
Glorious Revolution (1868), 119, 128
Goded, General Manuel, 151
Godoy, Manuel, 86, 93–4, 103
Gold Medal for Work Achievements, 168
González Hontoria Park, 191
Gordon, Charles, 129
Goya, Francisco de, 96
Gran Balneario Reina Victoria spa, 144
Gran Teatro Falla, 140, 178
Gran Vía, xvi
Granada, 29, 53–4, 184
Grand European Tour, 143
Grant, Cary, 150

251

INDEX

Gravina, Pierre-Charles, 87
Gray, Lord, 130
Grupo Soluciones, 175
Guadalete River, 7, 11
Guadalquivir River, 2, 11, 17, 23, 50–1, 59–60, 65, 125, 132, 135
Guadiana, 11
Guam, 114, 137
Guerrero, Rafael Soto, 160
Guinea, 55
Gulf of Cádiz, 43, 51
Guzmán, Juan Alfonso de, 186

habeas corpus, 106
Habsburg dynasty, 71, 81, 91
Hadrian, emperor, 35
Hakluyt, Richard, 67
Hamburg, 158
Hamilcar, xvii
Hannibal, xvii, 13, 17, 20, 21–2
Harriet, 132
Harrison, Richard J., 9, 12
Hasdrubal, xvii
Havana, 83, 148
Haynes, Thomas, 121
Hebrew prophet, 1
Hebrew, 3, 47
Hepburn, Katharine, 150
Herakles, 12
Hercules, Temple of, 7–9, 10, 14, 50
Herodotus, 9–10, 12
Hispania, 31, 34–9, 41–2
Hispaniola, 55–6, 79
Historical Memory Law, 168–9
HMS *Marlborough*, 95
HMS *Messenger*, 134

HMS *Shannon*, 134
Holy Roman Empire, 59
Holy Week celebrations, 179–81
Homer, 3
Honduvilla, Joaquín Gil, 161–2
Horacio Echevarrieta, 150
Hospital de Mora, xviii, 140
Hotel Atlántico, 148
Howard, Charles, 71, 73, 77
Hoyos, Vice-Admiral Juan de, 80
Huelva, 2, 145

Ibañez, Vicente Blasco, 139
Iberian Peninsula, 2, 41, 51, 84–5
Iberian tribes, 19–21, 26, 35
Iglesia de Santa Cruz, 51
Iglesia del Carmen, 154
Ilipa, Battle of, 17
Indias, 60
indios (Indians), 55
INI. *See* Instituto Nacional de Industria (INI)
Instituto Nacional de Industria (INI), 165
International Maritime Exhibition, 122
Ireland, xvii, 70
Iriarte, General Tomás de, 105
Isabel II, Queen, 117, 119, 123–8, 152
Isabel la Católica, xvii, 54–5, 57
Isaiah, 1–2
Ishmael, 3
Isla de León, 7, 86, 98–9, 101–6
Islam, 45
    culture, 46–8
Islamic Umayyad Caliphate, 41

INDEX

Israel, 1
Italy, 2, 21, 27, 35, 60, 81, 128–9, 143, 166, 168
  See also Mussolini, Benito

Jabal Tariq, 41
Jacob, William, 131–2
Jaén, 99
Jamaica, 79, 110
Jean-Baptiste, Marshal, 111
Jebel Musa, 8
Jeremiah, 1–2
Jerez de la Frontera, 26, 34, 49, 51, 151, 167, 174, 189–94
  airport, 190
  Flamenco Festival, 191
  rail journey, 192
  Vino de la Tierra status, 189
  wines, 189–90
Jerez Horse Fair (*Feria del Caballo*), 192
Jews, 46–7, 134
Joinville, Treaty of, 66
Jonah, 1, 3–4
Jones, Indiana, xvi
Jonson, Ben, 190
José María Pemán Theatre, 169–70
Joseph I, 96–7
Josephs, Allen, 47
Jovellanos, Gaspar Melchor de, xviii, 102, 105
Juan Sebastián Elcano, 149
Julian, Count, 44
Junta del Puerto, 141
Junta, 96–7, 101, 102, 126–7
Juvenal, 29–30

Kindelán, General Alfredo, 157
Kommos, 15

La Barrosa Beach, 175
La Bella Escondida, 64
La Caleta beach, 148
La Caleta, 37, 75, 140
La Carraca Arsenal, 97, 99, 121
la Casa de Iberoamérica cultural centre, 183
La Cebada Square, 116
La Española, 56
La Hoyacana, 145
'La Marseillaise', 152
La Pastora, 154
La Pepa, xviii, 102, 167
La Perla de Cádiz, 181
'La Piñata Gaditana', 177
Labours of Hercules, 11–12
Lacassagne dock, 122
'Lady of Cádiz', 14
lapis Gaditanus, 31
Latorre, Juan Cabrera, 140
Lebanon, xiii, 2, 5, 6
le Page Renouf, Peter, 2
Lee, Laurie, 148–9
León, 50
Lequerica, José María, 105
Lerma, Duke of, 92
Leslie, Hurricane, 32–3
Levant, 5, 8
Levante wind, xiii
Liberal Party, 123–5, 137, 139
Liberal Union party, 125
Linares, 23
Lisbon earthquake, 33, 85–6
Lisbon, 71, 80

INDEX

Livy, 13
Lo que puede un empleo ('What a Job Can Accomplish'), 104
Loire Valley, 94
London, xv, 75, 78, 95, 126, 136
Longford, Elizabeth, 101
López, Antonio, 122
Lorca, Federico García, 159–60
Louis IX, 81
Louis XVIII, 115
Lower Andalucía, 46, 50, 127
Luisa, María, 93
Lusitanians, 35
Lutheranism, 66
luxury resorts, 175

MacDonell, 98
Macías, Francisco, 85
Madrid, xv–xvi, xix, 77, 78, 91–2, 96, 98, 103, 111, 114, 116, 138, 144, 145
  economic stability, 162–5
  revolutionaries, 154–9
  war, 159–62
Madrid: The History (Quevedo), xv
Madrileño, xv
Magellan, Ferdinand, 56–7
Maghreb, 43
Magna Carta (1812), xviii, 104, 106
Mago, 17
Majaceite, battle of, 124
Malaspina expedition (1789-1794), 83
Malaspina, Alessandro, 83–4
Malecón, 148

Malta, 3, 134
Manzanares, xvi
Mapple, Father, 3
Marañón, Gregorio, 169
Marinid tribes, 53
María Cristina, Regent, 117, 123, 137
Marmont, Marshal Auguste de, 111
Marqués de Medina Sidonia, 134
Márquez Carmona, Lourdes, 100–1
Marseilles, 61
Martial, 29
Martínez de la Rosa, Francisco de Paula, xviii, 104–5
Mary Queen of Scots, 66
Massachusetts, Chapel of, 3
Matagorda dry dock, 122
Matagorda Fort, 82
Matagorda y Echevarrieta y Larrinaga, 74, 82, 165
Mateos, María de Aranda, 54
Maugham, William Somerset, 136
Mauretania Tingitana, 39
Mauretania, 43
Medina Sidonia, 46, 50, 164, 186–7
Medina Sidonia, Duke of, 69
Mediterranean, xiii, 5–6, 19, 24, 39, 82
Melilla, 57, 157
Melkart, Temple of, xiv, 10, 12
Melkart-Hercules, xix
Melville, Herman, 3
Mendizábal, Finance Minister Juan Álvarez, 119

INDEX

Meneses y Bracamonte, Governor Bernardino, 79
Meredith, William, 134
Mérida, 35
Mexico, 65
Mierse, William Edward, 10
Middle East, 2
Ministry of Culture, 53
Mirandilla, 183
Mirandilla stadium, 145
Moby Dick (Melville), 3
Model T cars, 149
Mola, General Emilio, 156, 162
Monte Testaccio, 27
Moore, John, 98
Moorish rule, 3
Moorish Spain, 45
Moors. *See* North Africa
Mora, José Moreno de, 140
Moreno, Matías, 50
Morla, 98–9
Morocco, 8, 29, 44–5, 49–50, 57, 61, 152, 171
Mountain of Tariq, 41
Mozambique, 3
Muhammad II, 53
Muñoz-Torrero, Diego, xviii, 103–4
murex sea snail, 9
Murillo, 152
Museum of Cádiz, 13
Muslims, 46–7
Mussolini, Benito, 155

National Confederation of Labour (CNT) union, 139, 153, 161
National Library of Madrid, xvi

Navantia shipyard, 172, 173
Navarre, 125
Nazi Germany, 157–8
Neapolis, 31
Nebuchadnezzar, 19
Necropolis, 13
Nelson, Admiral Horatio, 87–8
The Netherlands, 71
New Cathedral, 87
New Zealand, 83
Nigg, 122
Niña, 55
Nineveh, 1
Noah, 2
North Africa, 7, 20, 43, 49–51, 53, 57, 60, 80, 134, 156
North America, 67, 83
northern Israel, 5
northern Morocco, 53
northern Palestine, 5
northern Sri Lanka, 3
Novo Sancti Petri, 175
Nuestra Señora de la Paz, 187
Nuestra Señora de los Remedios, 52
'Nueva Cádiz', 57
Nueva Gadeira, xiv
Nusayr, Musa ibn, 43

O'Donnell, Leopoldo, 177
Ocaña, battle of, 100–1
oil crisis (1986), 171
Old Testament, 1, 2
Old Town, 174
'Old World', 6
Oratorio San Felipe Neri, 141
Ortega, Daniel, 163

INDEX

Ottoman Empire, 60
Our Lady of La Palma, 85

Pacific Ocean, 67, 83
Palos de la Frontera, 55
Pamplona, xv, 94, 114
Panama, 67
Paseo de Canalejas, 142
Paseo de Recoletos, xvi
Pavía, 125, 138
Pavía y Rodríguez, General Manuel, 125
Pedro de Estopiñán, 57
Pelayo, Don, 45–6
Peninsular War, 88–9, 100–1, 113, 121, 129, 185
Penn, Admiral William, 79
Pérez de Guzmán, Alonso, 55, 69
Pérez-Garzón, Juan Sisinio, 105
Pérez-Reverte, Arturo, 88
Persia, 113
petroleum export, 172
Pharsalus, Battle of, 25
Philippines, 63, 83, 114, 137–8
Philostratus, 23
Phoenicians, 5–6 mythology, 7–9
Phoenix, xiv
Picos de Europa, 46
Piedras, 11
Pinillos Sáenz, Miguel Martínez de, 140
Pinta 55
Pinzón, Vicente, 55
Pizarro, Francisco, 65
Plymouth Sound, 76
Plymouth, 68, 87

Pompey, Roman General, 24–5, 37
Pope Pius V, 66
Port of Cádiz, 135
Portsmouth, 79
Portugal, 35, 55, 71, 78, 86, 88–9, 93–4, 104, 156
Poza de Santa Isabel, Battle of, 97–9, 100
Prado Museum, 77
Prat, Antonio, 106
Preston, Paul, xv, 156–7
Prim, Juan, 125–6
Primo de Rivera, 151
Progressive Party, 125
Pueblos Blancos, 186
Puente de la Constitución, 167
Puente Zuazo, 77
Puertas de Tierra, 34, 141, 158, 159, 160, 166
Puerto de Santa María, 74
Puerto de Santa María, Jerez, 50
Puerto Rico, 83, 109–10, 114, 137
Puerto, Admiral Marcos del, 80
Punic War I (264–241 BCE), 20
Punic War II (218–201 BCE), 13, 20–2
Punta de la Vaca, 13
Punta del Boquerón, 185
Puntal bulwark, 72
Puntales district, 121
Purvis, Admiral John Child, 98
Pyrenees, 35–6, 94, 115–16, 144

Qādis, 3
Queipo de Llano, General Gonzalo, 159–60

INDEX

Quevedo, Francisco de, xv
Quiberon Bay, 95

Radical Democratic Party, 126
al-Rahman, Abd, 45–6
Real Academia Hispano Americana de Ciencias, 141
Real Compañía de Comercio de La Habana (Royal Trading Company of Havana), 110
Real Consulado de Indias (Royal Consulate of the Indies), 92
Reconquista, 51
Redbeard, 60
Regency Council, 96–7
Reina Victoria dock, 141
Reina Victoria spa, 144
Rendón, Milagros, 160, 163
Residents of Cádiz Award, 182
Richard, Henry, 103
Riego, Lieutenant Colonel Rafael del, xviii, 114–16
Rif War (1920-27), 152
Rio de la Plata, 83
Río Tinto, 23
Rivera, General Miguel Primo de, 151
Rivera, Lieutenant General Rafael Primo de, 126
Rock of Gibraltar, 41
Rodrigo, 41, 42, 44
Rodríguez Vázquez, José, 182
Rojas, Cristóbal de, 74
Roman aqueduct, 33
Roman Colosseum, 32
Roman Empire, 3, 20
Romans, 176
Rome, 16
 culture, 46–8
 theatre, 30–2
 'Voluptuous Gades', 27–30
Rooke, George, 81–2
Rosily-Mesros, Admiral François de, 98–9
Rossini, Gioachino, 143–4
Rothschild, Lionel de, 134
Rouen, 61
Royal Palace, 114
Royal Spanish Academy, 105
Rubio, Manuel Mayol, 144
Ruiz, Antonia, 30
Russia, 86
Russian Revolution (1917), 147

saetas, 180–1
Sagasta Práxedes Mateo, 126, 137–8
Sahara, xiv
Saint-Malo, 61
Salamanca, 111
Salic law, 116, 123
Salvandy, Narcisse Achille de, 135
Salvochea, Fermín, 138–9
San Carlos prison, 100
San Diego Convento, 120
San Felipe Neri Oratory, xviii
San Fernando Fine Arts Academy, 105
San Fernando, 11, 33, 77, 83, 105, 165, 172
San Francisco, 154
San Ildefonso, Treaty of, 86
San José Cemetery, 170
San Juan Bautista, 16

INDEX

San Miguel Arcángel Christian School, 140
San Roque, 34
San Sebastián, 37, 75
Sánchez Barcáiztegui, 157
Sancti Petri Castle, xiv, 12
Sancti Petri, 175
Sandoval, Colonel José Jiménez de, 125
Sanjurjo, General José, 155–6
Sanlúcar de Barrameda, 56, 57, 174, 189, 190
Santa Catalina, 37, 158
Santa Catalina Castle, 74–5, 85, 165
Santa Cruz, Cathedral of, 30
Santa María Convent, 75
Santa María district, 31, 34, 37, 55, 150, 154, 158–9, 181–4
Santana, Alberto Ramos, 108
Santísima Trinidad (vessel), 88
Santo Domingo (Hispaniola), 78, 79, 154
Sardinia, 21
Savoia, Amedeo di, 128–9
Scipio Africanus, xvii, 22
Scotland, 70, 122
Scots, 66
Seal, Lord Privy, 103
Semana Santa, 179–81
Serer, Rafael Calvo, 169
Serrano, General Francisco, 125
Serrano, José Luis García, 109
Sertorius, general, 35
Seven Years War, 110
Sevilla, 2, 29, 46, 50, 58, 65, 80–1, 92, 101, 129–30, 135, 155

Shakespeare, William, xviii, 26, 190
sherry industry, 189–90
shipbuilding, 171–2
    decline of, 193
Sicily, 20, 21
Sierra de Grazalema Natural Park, 186, 188
Sierra Morena, 23
'Silver Route', 35
Sketches of Spain (Davis), 180
Sola, Emilio de, 152
soleá, 183–4
Solís, Ramón, xiii
Somme, Battle of the, 88
Sotelo, José Calvo, 155
South America, 57, 60, 83
South Korea, 172
South Sea Company, 110
southern Crete, 15
southern India, 3
Spanish Civil War (1936), 139, 150, 158, 162–5, 170
Spanish Communist party (PCE), 163
Spanish flu, 147
Spanish-American War (1898), 137–8
Spice Islands, 149
St Joseph, 102
Stalingrad Group, 164
Stalingrad, Battle of, 88
Stayner, Vice-Admiral Richard, 79–80
Strabo, 9–10, 26, 31
Strait of Gibraltar, xiv, 8–9, 24, 39, 41, 49, 53, 64, 157, 161

INDEX

Suárez de Salazar, Juan Bautista, 36–7
Supreme Central Junta, 96–7, 101, 102
Sweden, 86
Switzerland, 163–4
Syria, 5

Tagus, 35
Talavera de la Reina, Battle of, xvii
Tales of the Alhambra (Byron), 143
Talleres Vigorito, 30
Talleyrand-Périgord, 94
Tangier, 22
Tarifa, 51
Tariq, 43
'Tarshish', 1–4
Tartessos, 2, 4
Tarxien, 3
Tashfin, Yusuf ibn, 50
Teatro de Andalucía, 37
Teatro de Cádiz, 104
Tempul, 33
Tena, Torcuato Luca de, 169
Tenerife, 169
Thirty Years War (1618-48), 78
Three Musketeers, The (Dumas), 135
Tiberius, emperor, 35
Tinto-Odiel, 11
Tintoretto, 152
Tiras, 2–3
Toledo, 44, 91, 101
Topete, Juan Bautista, 125–6
Torre Tavira, 63
Tourism Information Office, 144

tourism, 173–5, 193
Trafalgar (Galdós), 88
Trafalgar, 95, 99
Trafalgar, Battle of, 86–9, 97, 106, 121, 145
'Tragedy of Annual', 152
Trajan, emperor, xviii–xix, 35
Tres Torres Association, 182
Trocadero Fort, 116, 122
Trocadero islet, 122
Trojan War, 3
Troy, 3
Tunisia, 19–20
Turkey, 5
Twelve Labours of Hercules, 12
Tyre, xiii, 8, 19

Ubrique, 188–9
UGT, 161
Umayyad, 43, 45
unemployment rate, 172–3
UNESCO World Heritage Site, 47
United Kingdom (UK), 110, 162
United States, 137–8, 162
University of Cádiz, 14, 140
University of Salamanca, 104
University of Seville, 11, 14
Uriarte, Miguel, 110

Vaca, Javier Cabeza de, 173
Valcárcel, Carlos María Rodríguez de, 177
Valladolid, 92
Valle de la Piedad, 123
Valverde, Juan, 176–7
Vandals, 42

INDEX

Varela, General José Enrique, 158
Varga López, Manuel de la, 174–5
Vargas, Juana (Juana la Macarrona), 183
Vargas, Mercedes Fernández (Merced la Serneta), 183
Vea-Murguía shipyard, 121–2
Vega, Juan de, 69
Venables, General Robert, 79
Venezuela, 57
Vespasian, emperor, 31
Via Herculea, 35
Villadarias, 2nd Marquis of, 82
Villeneuve, Pierre-Charles, 87
Virgen de la Rosa, 52
Virgen de Los Remedios, 52
Visigoths, 38, 41–2, 44–7
Vista Hermosa, 144
'Voluptuous Gades', 27–30

Wals, Lola, 188
War of Independence, 120
warships shipyards, 172
Wellesley, Arthur, xvii, 100
Wellesley, Richard, xvii
Wellington, Duke of, xvii, 100–1, 111, 113
West Indies Board, 83
West Indies, 63, 66, 79
Western Mediterranean, 9–10, 17, 22, 27
Williams, Mark, 6, 7, 87
wines, 189–90
World War I, 147, 148, 150, 163
World War II, 168

Yahweh, 1
Yamm, 4
Yupanqui, Dionisio Inca, 105
Yusuf, Abu Yaqub, 53

Zahara de la Sierra, 187–8
Zapico, Civil Governor Mariano, 158, 159, 161–2
Zaragoza, 114
Ziyad, Tariq ibn, xvii, 41
Zorrilla, Manuel Ruiz, 126
Zurbarán, Francisco de, 77, 152